Re-Envisioning EFL Education in Asia

*Edited by Theron Muller, John Adamson,
Steven Herder, and Philip Shigeo Brown*

Also by this editorial team:

Innovating EFL Teaching in Asia
Exploring EFL Fluency in Asia

Selection and editorial matter © Theron Muller, John Adamson, Steven Herder, and Philip Shigeo Brown 2023
Individual chapters © Respective authors 2023
All rights reserved. No reproduction, copy or transmission of this publication may be made without written permission. For permissions, contact support@itdi.pro.
No portion of this book may be reproduced in any form without written permission from the publisher or author, except as permitted by U.S. copyright law.

First published 2023 by
International Teacher Development Institute (https://itdi.pro)
Sheridan, Wyoming

ISBN 979-8-9880892-1-6 hardcover
ISBN 979-8-9880892-0-9 paperback
ISBN 979-8-9880892-2-3 ebook

Library of Congress Control Number: 2023906046

Library of Congress Cataloging-in-Publication Data
Names: Muller, Theron, 1977-, editor. | Adamson, John, editor. | Herder, Steven, editor. | Brown, Philip Shigeo, editor.
Title: Re-envisioning EFL education in Asia / edited by Theron Miller, John Adamson, Steven Herder, and Philip Shigeo Brown.
Description: Includes bibliographical references. | Sheridan, WY: International Teacher Development Institute, 2023.
Identifiers: LCCN: 2023906046 | ISBN: 979-8-9880892-1-6 (hardcover) | 979-8-9880892-0-9 (paperback) | 979-8-9880892-2-3 (ebook)
Subjects: LCSH Language and languages--Study and teaching--Asia. | Second language acquisition--Asia.| BISAC EDUCATION / Bilingual Education | LANGUAGE ARTS & DISCIPLINES / Linguistics / Sociolinguistics | LANGUAGE ARTS & DISCIPLINES / Study & Teaching.
Classification: LCC PE1068.A7 .R48 2023 | DDC 428.0071/059--dc23

Print and ebook formatting by Jerry Talandis Jr.
Cover design by International Teacher Development Institute
Cover image by densorokin (Depositphotos)

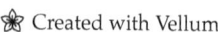 Created with Vellum

CONTENTS

Editor Bios   v

Why Re-Envision Language Teaching and Learning in Asia?   vii
Theron Muller and Philip Shigeo Brown

1. DEVELOPING CRITICAL THINKING SKILLS   1
   A Pedagogical Inquiry into Japanese Learners of English
   Masumi Narita, Natsumi Okuwaki, and Gavan Gray

2. USING THE GENRE-BASED APPROACH TO RAISE UNIVERSITY STUDENT AWARENESS   18
   A Case Study
   Akiko Nagao

3. A CLIL COURSE ON KARATE AND JAPANESE CULTURE   42
   Developing Intercultural Awareness and Language Learning
   Barry Kavanagh

4. PROMOTING PEER COLLABORATION TO DEVELOP LEARNER AUTONOMY   59
   Examples from a Self-Access Center (SAC)
   Dominique Vola Ambinintsoa and Satoko Watkins

5. L2 IDENTITY CONSTRUCTION THROUGH TELETANDEM LEARNING   75
   Kie Yamamoto

6. MULTI-AGENT TEACHING   96
   A Case Study
   Anuja M. Thomas and Philip M. McCarthy

7. STUDENTS FROM ASIA AND TEACHERS IN PARANATIONAL CLASSROOMS   115
   Co-Constructing Identities Amidst Stereotypes
   Mark A. McGuire and Zhenjie Weng

8. RE-ENVISIONING TEACHER RESEARCH BY QUESTIONING ASSUMPTIONS   136
   Gaps and Overlaps
   Theron Muller & Colin Skeates

9. EFFECTS OF EXTENSIVE READING ON JAPANESE LEARNERS' WRITING ABILITY   153
   Kiyomi Yoshizawa, Atsuko Takase & Kyoko Otsuki

10. HUMOR COMPETENCY TRAINING WITH JAPANESE
    LEARNERS OF ENGLISH   173
    John Rucynski and Caleb Prichard

11. EXPLORING EMI IN ETHNIC MULTILINGUAL
    EDUCATION IN CHINA'S IMAR   194
    Disi Ai (Adis)

12. SAUDI FEMALE COLLEGE STUDENTS' L2 ENGLISH
    LEARNING MOTIVATION   215
    Danya Shaalan

13. REVISITING THE NEED FOR FOREIGN ENGLISH
    TEACHERS IN SOUTH KOREA   237
    Laura Taylor

14. EMI BUSINESS PROGRAMS IN A CHINESE UNIVERSITY   250
    Students' Perspectives, Pedagogical Challenges, and Re-Shaped Practices
    Lijie Shao

15. RE-ENVISIONING STUDENT AND TEACHER
    EDUCATIONAL PARTNERING   275
    The Hu-women-ism of Riane Eisler's Work
    Tim Murphey

References   292

Editor Bios

Theron Muller is an Associate Professor at the University of Toyama, Japan. His doctorate, from The Open University, UK, is on research exploring the publication practices of Japan-based language teachers. He has published and presented widely on writing for academic publication, English language teaching and learning, and teacher development including in *Ilha do Desterro, International Journal of Research & Method in Education*, and *Writing and Pedagogy*. He is active with JALT Publications, currently the Publications Board Chair, and a founding member of *English Scholars Beyond Borders*.

- *E-mail*: theron@las.u-toyama.ac.jp
- *ORCID*: https://orcid.org/0000-0001-9690-3738

John Adamson is a Professor at the University of Niigata Prefecture, Japan. Active in editorial work, he received his Ed.D. from the University of Leicester and has pursued research in EAP/ESP provision at the university level, interdisciplinarity, self-access, and developing journal editorial systems. He is a co-editor (with Roger Nunn) of *Accepting Alternative Voices in EFL Journal Articles* (2009) and *Editorial and Authorial Voices in EFL academic publishing* (2012).

- *Email*: adamson@unii.ac.jp
- *ORCID*: https://orcid.org/0000-0003-3492-2583

Steven Herder has been teaching EFL since 1989, from elementary school to the university level, and is currently Professor at Kyoto Notre Dame University in Japan. He prepares students to study abroad and teaches a seminar: *Exploring Leadership*. Since 2010, he has been working with Suken Publishing on the high school textbook series *Big Dipper*, *DUALSCOPE*, and *Blue Marble*. In 2012, he co-founded the *International Teacher Development Institute*, an online teacher training community for teachers by teachers, with over 5000 members and a global reach in over 100 countries.

- *Email*: herder@notredame.ac.jp

Philip Shigeo Brown is the Course Director for the *iTDi TESOL Certificate*. Since 2001, he has taught English in wide-ranging contexts in Japan, Malaysia, and online. In addition to 10 years as a Postgraduate Programmes Tutor for the University of Birmingham, Phil thrives on working with ELT professionals from around the world and shares a variety of teaching and research interests from learner and teacher development to global issues and critical thinking. Since 2020, he has also been working with Suken Publishing on the high school textbook series *Blue Marble*.

- *Email*: philip.shigeo.brown@gmail.com

Why Re-Envision EFL Education in Asia?

Theron Muller & Philip Shigeo Brown

Asia is positioned quite differently compared to when we were working on our first edited book more than a decade ago, *Innovating EFL Teaching in Asia* (Muller, Herder, Adamson, & Brown, 2012). Back then, we were trying to get Asia onto the map as a place for researching and innovating language teaching research, hence the emphasis on English as a foreign language (EFL) teaching and learning. At the time, most theory and thought about language teaching methods originated from Western countries at the center of global knowledge production, such as the UK and the US. In measures of research output, bibliometric research backed this up with the US "far more productive in the top-1% of all [cited] papers" and China (representing Asia) "out of the competition" (Leydesdorff et al., 2014, p. 606). Thus, we were keen to publish work *from Asia about Asia* to showcase how vibrant language teaching and learning in the region is, as well as demonstrate Asia's potential to contribute to larger conversations in the field around issues of contemporary importance. Following that, our second edited book, *Exploring EFL Fluency in Asia* (Muller, Adamson, Brown, & Herder, 2014) took a deep dive into fluency in language education, highlighting its multidimensional nature. We emphasized how EFL students, those in contexts where English tends not to be used in everyday communication, may require more explicit focus on fluency in language education relative to students studying in English-dominant countries. Its chapters explored how educators can approach different aspects of fluency from different directions to meet their classroom needs.

And so here we are with our third book being released into a world transformed after a global pandemic that demonstrated just how interconnected and interdependent we are. Some chapters concern topics and issues relevant to pandemic language education and how it may influence the return to "normal." For example, Yamamoto (Chapter 5) discusses Japanese learners' identity construction through telecollaboration during the pandemic. However, this book offers more than content about the pandemic's influence on language learning and teaching. Each of its 15 chapters present original research into a theme of practical interest, zooming out to a bigger picture to challenge the cliche stereotypes that are still too-often used to characterize language teaching and learning in Asia.

We also re-envision EFL education in Asia, not only as we recognise the increasing diversity of contexts in which English is used as a lingua franca, but also as language teaching and learning transcend physical boundaries. As such, McGuire and Weng (Chapter 7) explicitly deal with what happens when the Asian diaspora leaves Asia to be educated in the US and faces cultural stereotyping due to their region of origin. Within Asia, being Chinese, Korean, Japanese, or Vietnamese are often considered distinct identities, but when people from these countries find themselves outside Asia, their individual identities can be subsumed into a regional identity by the people they interact with. Further, many countries at the center of global knowledge production tend to depict themselves as destination countries for global immigrants, with assumptions that those arriving from elsewhere are planning to stay (Nakamura, 2005). However, many who seek education in, for example, the US, see their futures in their countries of origin, not where they find themselves studying, creating further potential for confusion and incorrect assumptions in interactions. On the flip side, Asian countries such as China, Korea, and Japan continue to heavily recruit "native" speakers of English to teach and work in them, creating additional potential for misunderstanding expectations (Taylor, Chapter 13).

Another easy dichotomy that we challenge is the "second" in *English as a second language* (ESL). In reality, much of the world's population is multilingual, interacting in more than two languages. Language research increasingly recognizes this through, for example, the growing emphasis on "translanguaging" (Garcia, 2007, p. xiii) as more accurately representing how people use language in everyday life. People use multiple languages simultaneously in everyday interactions, or translanguage, as different languages are interconnected at the individual human level. Or, as Canagarajah (2018) describes translanguaging, it "indexes a way of looking at communicative practices as transcending autonomous languages" (p. 31) by "focus[ing] on the need to transcend verbal resources and consider how other semiotic resources and modalities also participate in communication" (p. 31). Bringing such easy dichotomies into critical focus, Ai (Chapter 11) questions assumptions of cultural homogeneity within a given country, showing how multilingual and multiethnic identities require negotiating more than just English as a foreign language. Ai explores how students from ethnic minorities within China negotiate use of their home language, Mongolian, as well as the country's presumed first language, Mandarin, in addition to learning English.

Other cliches that we challenge include the description of Asian students as passive, quiet, and uninterested in learning languages. Kavanagh (Chapter 3) demonstrates how international students predominantly from Europe and Asia were integrated into a content-based English language course in Japan to give students a chance to learn both language and culture simultaneously while developing intercultural understanding. Ambinintsoa and Watkins (Chapter 4) show how Japanese students collaborate, using the languages they are learning, to support one another's language development and learner autonomy. In addition, Rucynski and Prichard (Chapter 10) show that once they know how to use it, Japanese students are more than happy to employ humor in English.

This Book's Organization

While acknowledging that no ordering is perfect, we've generally organized chapters from more classroom teaching-focused to more policy-oriented. We start with classroom pedagogy-based studies that seek to re-envision teaching at a relatively local level. Early on, for instance, Nagao (Chapter 2) explores integrating systemic functional linguistics (SFL) principles into teaching English writing. Later, we move to chapters that question common and well-established assumptions. For example, Muller and Skeates (Chapter 8) discuss re-envisioning classroom research, advocating that teachers question more basic processes in their classrooms, such as how students do group work, rather than assuming they already know how students do this work.

Our hope is that this book speaks to classroom teachers looking, for instance, to connect their classroom practices to postgraduate studies or other professional development endeavors. This stems from our having been in these teachers' shoes when we did our own postgraduate studies. To some extent, we are still in those teachers' shoes, as our main responsibilities tend to be to teach rather than to research, so we try to straddle our time and attention between both. Over the years, we've found that connecting our teaching to our research (and our research to our teaching) helps facilitate this balancing act of being teacher-researchers. However, classrooms are not islands unto themselves, and because policy often impacts what and how teachers teach, later chapters include investigations into how policy impacts students' experiences. To illustrate, Shao (Chapter 14) discusses how institutional language policies can potentially be improved to further improve educational outcomes.

Our Definition of Re-Envisioning

Keeping in mind the various constraints that teachers and researchers operate under, we feel that setting one definition of re-envisioning for all of the chapters in this book to follow is inappropriate. That would have excluded some and preferentially included others. We feel re-envisioning one's circumstances should be open to all, not just the few who happen to agree with a predetermined definition that we established. As such, some chapters re-envision a particular aspect of skills teaching in the classroom, such as critical thinking skills in Narita et al. (Chapter 1). Other chapters re-envision the different actors in the classroom, conceiving technology as another partner in the teaching and learning team in addition to teacher, teaching assistant, and students (Thomas & McCarthy, Chapter 6). This is a particularly timely observation given the booming prevalence of AI chatbots such as *ChatGPT* in the current educational discourse. There is also re-envisioning in terms of how skills learning may be interconnected, with Yoshizawa et al. (Chapter 9) exploring how extensive reading training may help improve students' writing. Further, the limitations of not taking into account the intersections of culture and language learning, and how to address this in terms of Saudi females learning English is discussed in Shaalan (Chapter 12). Finally, Murphey (Chapter 15) suggests turning the teacher as a domineering leader model of classroom management on its head, exploring how collaboration may be a key to unlocking greater student potential in language learning.

1
Developing Critical Thinking Skills: A Pedagogical Inquiry into Japanese Learners of English

Masumi Narita, Natsumi Okuwaki, and Gavan Gray

In 2018, Japan's *Ministry of Education, Culture, Sports, Science, and Technology* (MEXT) announced new curriculum guidelines for foreign language education in Japanese high schools. The aim was to reinforce the balance between acquiring knowledge or language skills and developing the ability to think, judge, and express oneself (MEXT, 2018b). In heightening the focus on thinking and productive abilities, MEXT also established three new elective subjects: *Logic and Expression I, II*, and *III*. It launched the most basic subject, *Logic and Expression I*, in April 2022. These courses aim to foster active English learners who can express their own logically constructed opinions in English. This need to develop logical thinking skills had already been recognized in Japanese English education. Efforts were made prior to these new course of study guidelines, especially in writing courses (Hirose & Harwood, 2019; McKinley, 2013). MEXT's emphasis on "logic" suggests that young Japanese learners, who will build Japan's future, need to develop skills for the 21st century, including those focused on problem solving and cross-cultural communication.

When considering the high school–university connection, English education at the university level should strengthen logical thinking and critical thinking (CT) skills so that students can employ these abilities when entering society as adults (see e.g., Gray, 2020; Oi, 2005, 2018). CT skills have been defined in numerous ways (Anderson & Krathwohl,

2001; Bloom, 1956; Dummett & Hughes, 2019; Kusumi, 2015), but the following consensus statement by the American Philosophical Association's *Delphi Report* (Facione, 1990) has significantly impacted language education:

> We understand critical thinking to be purposeful, self-regulatory judgment which results in interpretation, analysis, evaluation, and inference, as well as explanation of the evidential, conceptual, methodological, criteriological, or contextual considerations upon which that judgment is based. CT is essential as a tool of inquiry. (p. 3)

As such, four essential abilities need to be fostered among university students: to interpret, analyze, evaluate, and infer from multiple points of view. This may require demanding educational practices in the classroom, especially in EFL settings.

The goals of this paper are twofold. The first is to review the discussion on socio-cultural obstacles faced by East Asian English learners and the potential instructional practices have for enhancing CT skills in Asian EFL contexts. The second aim is to share the strengths and challenges of a new CT and content-based English language teaching curriculum for non-English majors that we launched at a Japanese university in 2017. This curriculum was designed to nurture logical, higher-order CT skills in line with our university's diploma policies through four separate skills courses in communication, discussion, reading, and writing, all of which are required courses in the students' first three years of university. A unique element of the curriculum is that the three second-year English courses cover the same themes in order to increase the quality and quantity of students' English while deepening their learning about these themes. To address the second aim of this study, after five years of curriculum implementation, course evaluation questionnaires and focus group interviews were conducted online with course instructors and students in January and February 2022. Survey results are presented, and pedagogical implications for further developing CT skills within academic English instruction are discussed.

Controversies Concerning Socio-Cultural Obstacles Faced by East Asian Learners of English

Kaplan (1966) presented five cultural thought patterns through an analysis of written discourse produced in English by foreign student learners. "Oriental" was one of them, in which Chinese or Korean writers' main claims could be understood only at the end of their writing after circuitous description, which is different from the linear logical progression found in the North American style of academic prose. Also in 1966, Leggett published a paper in Japan describing the logical development and linguistic characteristics prominent in academic papers written by Japanese physicists based on his experiences proofreading English papers during his one-year stay in the country. Puzzled by Japanese researchers' argument structures, he pointed out that "in English the sequence of thought should always be made quite explicit, even when, in Japanese, it would be legitimate to leave the reader to fill in the connection for himself" (Leggett, 1966, pp. 791–792). These two seminal papers made a significant contribution to rethinking English writing pedagogy in East Asia by highlighting how East Asian learners of English produce a culturally-bound rhetorical flow unintelligible to readers from Western cultural backgrounds.

Later research pointed out how the socio-cultural influences of a student's native language in foreign language learning make it difficult for East Asian learners to develop CT skills normalized in Western cultural contexts. For instance, Fox (1994) examined the English writing styles of international students from various cultural backgrounds at a large, established American university. Through conversations and interviews with the students, it was revealed that their writing styles were distinct from U.S. norms. Fox suggested that these students' non-analytical writing styles in English were rooted in "the ways students have learned to see the world, to see social relations and identity and the negotiation of social roles" (p. xix), thus making their way of expressing themselves robust against Western modes of instruction. Following this, Atkinson (1997) focused on CT pedagogies in *Teaching English to Speakers of Other Languages* (TESOL), suggesting that "critical thinking represents a set of social practices" (p. 79) and that language educators should seriously question how well non-native learners of English who are from distinct socio-cultural backgrounds can adapt to CT skills instruction in the classroom.

In the 21st century, the importance of fostering global communication has become more widely recognized, and the development of CT skills has been strongly articulated as a mission of higher education. The learnability of CT skills has been explored through various pedagogical approaches in East Asian EFL contexts. To illustrate the possibility of cultivating CT skills in East Asian English learners through well-designed instructional practices, the remainder of this section overviews three educational efforts at the tertiary level in China, South Korea, and Japan.

Wang and Seepho (2017) explored how Chinese EFL learners, all English-major freshmen at a Chinese university, developed their CT skills during a semester-long English reading course by learning three strategies: group discussion, concept mapping, and analytical questioning. The students were engaged in collaborative student-centered activities of "identifying, analyzing, synthesizing, and evaluating arguments in reading materials" (p. 4). The effectiveness of teaching the strategies was evaluated through questionnaires and semi-structured interviews. Results suggested all three strategies contributed to developing students' CT skills, although the students were raised in Confucian cultural contexts where in the classroom rote learning and group harmony are more important than engaging in debate and expressing one's own opinion (Atkinson, 1997).

DeWaelsche (2015) also employed a student-centered approach in three semester-long topic-based courses for English majors at a Korean university to examine how higher-level questioning and group conversation activities promote students' CT skills. The students were asked to generate and respond to higher-level questions in small group discussions. Three kinds of data were collected for evaluation: a questionnaire, recorded conversations, and a focus group discussion. The questions posed by the students were categorized as *analyze*, *evaluate*, or *create*, based on *Bloom's Revised Taxonomy* (Anderson & Krathwohl, 2001), and their responses were rated by the researcher on a four-point scale (*excellent/insightful, adequate, limited,* or *poor*). DeWaelsche (2015) found: (1) students generally believed the learning activities fostered their CT skills; (2) less proficient students had a hard time responding to the higher-level questions and actively participating in the group discussions; and (3) some students were hesitant to share their ideas with peers because they were used to traditional teacher-centered instructional methods.

In Japanese tertiary educational settings, some researchers have explored fostering CT skills in Japanese EFL learners through academic writing courses (Heffernan, 2015; Oi, 2005; Stapleton, 2001). Using research into Japanese EFL learners' characteristic English writing rhetorical structures, Oi (2018) aimed to foster CT skills through academic English writing instruction for high-intermediate EFL students at a national university, most of whom were in their first year. Over the course of one academic year, paragraph/essay writing basics were first addressed. Instructional practices employed argumentative essay writing using the *Toulmin Model* (Toulmin, 1958), which guided students in constructing a logical structure for their arguments by making them aware of the importance of providing strong supporting evidence for solid argumentation. The process-writing approach, which involved creating multiple essay drafts, providing feedback, and engaging students in self-reflection during revisions, was found to be an effective instructional treatment. The students' progress was evaluated through three sets of data: changes in essay length, changes in self-evaluation questionnaire scores, and changes in students' essay quality. The self-evaluation questionnaire translated "25 questionnaire questions" from Cottrell (2005, p. 13) into Japanese (Oi, 2018). Analysis revealed that both the length and quality of students' essays improved significantly (i.e., they were longer and better), and 11 out of the 25 CT skill self-evaluation questions showed significant improvement (Oi, 2018).

In summary, at least in China, South Korea, and Japan, instructional methods in English education are undergoing a transformation from traditional teacher-centered approaches to more learner-centered ones. Furthermore, educational outcomes are demonstrating the potential of developing CT skills in East Asian EFL contexts despite socio-culturally inhibitory factors that may also be at work. Next, we present an overview and evaluation of the content-based academic English curriculum we developed for non-English majors that focuses on cultivating CT skills. We also discuss the synergistic effects of horizontal collaboration in which multiple courses cover the same subject areas in parallel, a topic which has not seen much exploration in previous studies.

Case Study: Content-based English Curriculum for Non-English Majors

Overview of the Curriculum

In 2017, a private Japanese university established the College of Policy Studies as a new department. Students are required to study academic English, social sciences, and data sciences as foundational subjects to develop CT and problem-solving skills to meet the needs of the modern era. The current English curriculum consists of four compulsory courses aimed at fostering communication, discussion, reading, and writing skills. The curriculum spans students' first three years of enrollment and nurtures higher-order CT skills while accumulating specialized knowledge.

Table 1 illustrates the overall design of our content-based English courses. The language of instruction is English. The average class size is about 17 students. All courses aim to help students build skills year to year. The first-year students use some commercially available textbooks to improve their basic skills. Second and third year students watch videos or read authentic articles from online news sites and journals before discussing their opinions or ideas.

Table 1

Overall Design of Our Content-Based English Courses (as of 2022)

Year (Phase)	Communication/Discussion courses	Reading/Writing courses	Subject areas
1st year (Basic) ↓ 2nd year (Enhanced) ↓ 3rd year (Integrated)	• Develop students' ability to think about issues from multiple points of view and express themselves in conversation, speech, and presentations • Develop the CT skills students need to analyze and talk about a wide variety of subject areas related to their fields of study	• Develop students' ability to comprehend authentic English texts • Develop students' ability to express their ideas clearly and coherently in writing • Carry out text-based research on a wide variety of subject areas and produce problem-solving essays	Demographics Economics Education Gender issues Global issues Law Mass media NGOs & IGOs Politics Work culture

    The curriculum's subject areas, which include content related to students' majors in policy studies, were selected using four criteria: career relevance, societal relevance, personal relevance, and academic relevance. They were chosen so that "what they [our students] study can be shown to have clear practical benefit to both their lives and careers" (Gray, 2020, p. 39). Once the subject areas were fixed, specific in-class activities and assignments were designed, typically as weekly worksheets or short presentations to promote understanding, multi-faceted analysis, or evaluation of key issues within each topic area. Students learned to examine the main arguments in online materials, such as topic-related videos or news stories, and produce their own opinions, together with the rationale behind them, prior to or after each class meeting.

    As Table 1 shows, the four obligatory courses are vertically linked, so students can reinforce their English and CT skills as they progress. Another feature of this curriculum is its thematic linkage between the three second-year courses via discussion, reading, and writing. These courses cover the same subject areas over three academic terms: mass media, gender issues, and global issues. The reading/writing instructors can refer to the *Discussion Course Guide* document to review class content and in-class activities, and use this information to assign tasks such as summarizing what students learned in their discussion course. Thus, these horizontal links expand the depth and breadth of student knowledge and thinking on the target subjects, which helps them quantitatively and qualitatively produce better oral discussions, writing responses, and essays.

As described previously, preparing thought-provoking questions about the content for in-class activities and weekly assignments is a significant part of our instructional process. Students are asked to reflect on how a certain issue fits into their own environment and what measures, if any, need to be taken. Below are examples of questions posed about the materials covered in mass media:

- What are the dangers of biased media sources?
- Do you think there is any truth to the idea that the media can be a negative influence? If so, what should be done about it?
- In the movie, a lawyer said, "It takes a village to raise a child. It takes a village to abuse one." What does this lawyer's comment mean?
- Describe the changes you have seen in recent Japanese TV dramas and movies, in terms of diversity and inclusion.

Evaluating Students' CT Skills Within the Curriculum

Students' CT skills were assessed through a written quiz (15% of their score) and a one-on-one interview (25% of their score). Since the course focused on developing CT as a tool for communication, more objective written tests, such as the *Watson-Glaser Critical Thinking Appraisal* (1991) were considered unsuitable in terms of their level of complexity for English language learners and their focus on reading and textual analysis. Instead, rubrics were created to assess students' written and verbal output. These rubrics were later revised to incorporate ideas from Reynders et al. (2020), who created a robust format for the assessment of CT skills in STEM students as a valid, reliable gauge of CT abilities.

Our curriculum's rubric (Appendix A) outlines five criteria: one for basic English ability and four for evaluating how the language was utilized to demonstrate core CT skills, including analysis, evaluation, inference, and synthesis. Instructors were advised to assess students following a similar standard so that their skill development could be measured from term to term and year to year.

Assessing the Overall Curriculum

Methods

After the last term of the 2021 academic year, both student and instructor surveys (questionnaires and focus group interviews) were conducted online in January and February of 2022 to identify the current curriculum's strengths and weaknesses. Perhaps because the questionnaire was voluntary and only administered after the courses had ended, the student response was only at about 10%. Although the survey results are not generalizable, they are still a useful means of examining students' attitudes regarding the curriculum. 14 respondents, or about half the English instructors in the program, participated in the instructor survey. The focus group interviews were semi-structured, and each session lasted approximately 1.5 hours. Student interviews were conducted separately for each year cohort, with 27 interviewees chosen in advance to avoid any bias towards those with more advanced English proficiency. Some survey question examples are included in Appendix B.

Results of the Student Survey

Despite the small number of respondents, the focus group interviews that were conducted by year cohorts elicited a great deal of candid and constructive feedback. The questionnaire provided some validation for student responses, which were categorized into one of four options: *very much*, *quite a bit*, *a little*, or *not at all* (excluding the free-response option). Positive feedback examples obtained from the student survey are summarized in Appendix C. In general, students reported improved academic motivation, English language skills, multifaceted thinking practices, reasoning skills, and a more critical mindset as a result of the curriculum's learning activities.

The results of the two surveys indicated that: (1) over 70% of the students expressed a high satisfaction with the in-class activities, course content, and level of difficulty, despite the challenges; (2) the integration of the three second-year courses helped students develop a deeper understanding of the subject areas and allowed for diverse opinions and viewpoints to be shared among peers; and (3) most students found the curriculum helpful in clarifying their career goals and improving their practical English skills. Furthermore, interviews revealed that the courses helped students recognize the complexity of issues discussed. This led to a shift in understanding of the subject matter, their perception of its significance for society, and its impact on various aspects of life.

Although the curriculum received an overall positive evaluation, there were some areas identified for improvement. These included maintaining a better balance between individual and group activities in class, as well as expanding the scope of subject areas covered in the English curriculum to include topics such as science and technology. Developing students' background knowledge on subject matter, both in and outside the classroom, was deemed as another significant factor to consider. Students realized that having sufficient background knowledge facilitates the generation of balanced ideas and in-depth discussions.

Results of the Instructor Survey

When reflecting on their courses, the instructors offered candid evaluations and constructive feedback. For example, they appreciated how each course built students' skills and knowledge step-by-step, which positively impacted English and CT skill development. The consensus was that by adhering to a uniform format each term, students were able to organize their studies effectively and track their progress from one term to another and from year to year. By using a common rubric (Appendix A) they noticed growth in CT skills. Moreover, they felt that the subject areas offered ample opportunities to practice English language skills and that their content was relevant not only for students' professional pursuits but also for fostering broader social awareness. In addition, some of the reading/writing instructors noted that thematic links between the English program and the students' fields of study could stimulate their curiosity and lead to self-directed learning.

The instructors felt that the students engaged with the coursework and that their effort ranged between reasonable and good. The most critical issue was differences in English proficiency within each class. For instance, in the case of the discussion courses, higher-level students could easily engage with content in English, whereas lower-level students often had difficulty continuing discussions in English and therefore had to resort to using Japanese. Writing instructors also highlighted that this in-class English proficiency gap made it difficult to establish and conduct effective peer feedback on essay drafts. While the current program offers two advanced classes and five regular ones, the instructors noted that the current system of class placement needs to be reconsidered, perhaps to create more variety among class English levels.

Discussion and Pedagogical Implications

The results of our case study suggest the potential for developing English and CT skills through content-based EFL instruction. Based on *TOEIC Listening and Reading Test* scores, an exam widely administered in Japan, our students' English proficiency improved over their three years of study. After two years of study, the average score increased significantly by over 100 points ($p < .01$).

An analysis of CT skills for the entire student body is still pending. However, a sample group of 32 students from two classes revealed that their average scores for tests and interviews improved steadily over the course of three years, from 10.1 (out of 15) and 16.3 (out of 25) in their first year, to 12.2 and 19.1 in their second year, and finally 12.6 and 21.2 in their third year. For the written tests, this represents a 20% increase between the first and second years and a 27% increase between the first and the third years. For the spoken interviews, the increase was 17 percent between the first and second years and 30% between the first and third years. In short, both assessments demonstrated clear evidence of student improvement. As the revised rubrics were only introduced in 2021, a further analysis of students from that point onwards would provide a more accurate evaluation of which CT skills are developing the most.

While the survey results indicate that the current curriculum has yielded promising outcomes, our evaluation is limited due to both a low response rate to the student questionnaire and the fact that we have not assessed students' CT skills independently of their language skills. Our educational framework aims to integrate the cultivation of CT skills into content-based English language instruction, yet we acknowledge the need to explore the practicality and validity of existing CT skills tests in Japanese educational settings. Furthermore, as suggested by Sato (2022), we plan to explore ways to enhance the current rating criteria for argumentative essay writing, specifically to enable a more precise evaluation of the "relevant and salient CT features of argumentative essays" (p. 5).

To continue improving our pedagogy, we should address two items. Firstly, our case study's instructors suggest that promoting CT skills in content-based English language teaching requires a more thoughtful approach to learners' English language proficiency. In fact, some previous studies have addressed the impact of language proficiency on CT skills development (DeWaelsche, 2015; Lun et al., 2010; Rear, 2017). Among others, Lun et al. (2010, p. 164) has warned of the potential detrimental effects of second language proficiency on CT: "Critical thinking skills such as verbal reasoning and argument analysis demand a certain level of language proficiency. Even the mere act of reading a scenario or understanding a problem presented in a language requires certain levels of verbal abilities." EFL instructors who aim to improve their students' CT skills and second language proficiency should consider incorporating various instructional frameworks and scaffolding interventions proposed by Campbell et al. (2007), Kusumoto (2018), and Wilson (2016) into class assignments and in-class activities.

Furthermore, our students realized the importance of having sufficient subject matter background knowledge. This aligns with research by Stapleton (2001), who found that students' capacity for critical thinking is largely determined by their familiarity with the content, rather than by socio-cultural factors. For example, when reading a passage, students may need to create semantic coherence by making inferences about missing information in the text. To facilitate reading comprehension and meaningful discussion, it is necessary to have a deeper understanding of the topic, which requires more background knowledge to draw accurate inferences. Because background knowledge is essential for effective CT instruction, instructors can enhance their teaching by providing supplementary materials that spark student curiosity and motivate further research. Additionally, they can use *concept mapping* techniques, such as those discussed in Wang and Seepho (2017), to identify knowledge gaps and link related concepts.

Conclusion

Developing CT skills in EFL instruction presents a challenge since it requires simultaneous attention to second language development and the cultivation of logical, objective, and rational thinking abilities. While acknowledging its lack of generalizability, our case study's results suggest that encouraging horizontal and vertical connections between English skills courses that embed CT-oriented teaching can yield pedagogically promising outcomes in instructional methodology and curriculum design. By sharing and accumulating different CT instruction methodologies and their results, educators can offer students opportunities to develop their CT skills and prepare for the challenges that arise in our global society, both now and in the future.

Acknowledgements

This work was supported by Grants-in-Aid for Scientific Research (JSPS KAKENHI) Grant Number 18K00840 and Tsuda University's Funds to Support Faculty Development for the 2021 academic year. We would like to express our deepest gratitude to Professor Emerita Hiroko Tajika of Tsuda University, for her continued support for the English program at the College of Policy Studies, Tsuda University.

Author Bios

Masumi Narita is a Professor in the College of Policy Studies at Tsuda University, Japan. She received her PhD from Nagoya University, Japan. Since her research interests include learner corpus-based studies, she has been exploring linguistic features that characterize academic writing produced by second language learners. Any comments or questions regarding this chapter can be addressed to her at narita@tsuda.ac.jp

Natsumi Okuwaki is a Professor in the College of Policy Studies at Tsuda University, Japan. She received her PhD in applied linguistics from the University of Essex, England. Her research interests encompass the use of formulaic language by second language learners, second language acquisition of tense and aspect, and vocabulary learning and teaching.

Gavan Gray is a Professor in the College of Policy Studies at Tsuda University, Japan. He holds a PhD in Politics and International Relations from the University of Leicester in the United Kingdom. His research interests include the application of critical thinking skills in language acquisition, responses to gender-based violence, and political communication.

Developing Critical Thinking Skills | 15

Appendix A
Rubric for Evaluating CT Skills

Critical Thinking Evaluation Rubric for Interviews and Tests						
Category	Scores					
Interview (25)	0	1	2	3	4	5
Test (15)	0	1		2		3
General English Ability		**Hesitant** speech and clear problems regarding **grammar** and use of suitable **vocabulary**.		**Comfortable** delivery with **minor errors** and some problems finding the right words.		**Smooth** delivery with effective use of stress and tone. Appropriate use of **higher level** vocabulary.
Analysis		**Failure to identify** distinct elements of the topic.		Able to identify **key elements** of the topic.		Able to highlight both **major and** important but **minor** elements of the topic.
Evaluation		**Failure to identify** either the positive or the negative aspects of the topic.		Able to identify **either** the positive aspects of the topic **or** the negative aspects.		Able to identify **both** the positive **and** negative aspects of the topic.
Inference		**Failure to predict** possible impacts and effects of the topic.		Able to predict **at least one** possible impact of effect of the issue on society.		Able to predict **more than one** possible effect of the issue and **extrapolate** their impact.
Synthesis		**Unable to suggest** new policy ideas.		**Able to suggest** how new policies might respond to the issue.		Able to **suggest new policy** responses and **identify barriers** to their introduction.
Comments						

Appendix B
Sample Survey Questions

For Students:

- Have these courses helped you develop your understanding of social issues?
- Have these courses helped you examine and analyze issues in a critical manner?
- Have these courses helped you develop confidence in expressing your own views and opinions?
- Have these courses helped you develop clearer career goals?
- What are the best characteristics of these courses?
- Are there any other topics that should be included in future courses?

For Instructors:

- Do you feel that these courses are improving students' ability to understand and analyze social issues?
- Do you feel that these courses are improving students' English proficiency?
- In general, do you think that students make a strong effort in their classes?
- Do you think that our course materials are appropriate for students, in terms of difficulty level?
- What are the best characteristics of these courses and teaching methods?
- What specific skills did you find the most difficult for students to master?

Appendix C
Summary of Positive Feedback from Students

Communication/Discussion courses	Reading/Writing courses
• These courses gave me many opportunities to think about my future and how to interact with others, which was really fun and helpful.	• I think I have improved my ability to read lengthy academic texts and online news stories on various social issues in a logical and thoughtful manner.
• These courses helped me to express my views on issues I have been studying in policy studies in a way that is often not possible in Japanese classes.	• These courses helped me to examine the authors' opinions critically.
• The good atmosphere of the class motivated me to participate. Almost all students and instructors were willing to listen to the others' different opinions.	• By examining other materials relevant to the topic in question on my own, I was able to have different thoughts from the author and/or my peers, together with supporting reasons.
• I was able to learn about social issues in these courses that I had not known well before.	• I can now make better transitions between sentences and paragraphs (i.e., better logical development).

- Based on the knowledge I gained in discussion and reading courses, I became able to construct my own opinions and express them through the writing class.
- I was able to learn about the topic in more depth through the materials and articles covered in the second-year discussion, reading, and writing courses.
- I was able to maintain a consistent awareness of the issues, both inside and outside of class. Also, the linkage of themes between three of the second-year courses deepened my interest in and understanding of these themes.

2
Using the Genre-Based Approach to Raise University Student Awareness: A Case Study

Akiko Nagao

Several factors have limited EFL writing instruction in Japanese universities. First, EFL learners need significant writing practice (Bhowmik, 2021) that includes teacher feedback (Ferris, 2011; Hyland & Hyland, 2019) as well as time for editing and revisions (Joyce & Feez, 2012) to conceptually understand English essay writing. However, many teachers in Japan are unfamiliar with explicit L2 writing teaching approaches, and few teacher-training hours are devoted to teaching writing. Thus, in their lessons, teachers in Japan tend to allocate limited time for writing tasks, giving more emphasis to communication-based English speaking and listening practice (Benesse kyōiku sōgōkenkyūsho, 2022). A characteristic of student L2 essays is that some learners struggle with grasping the appropriate level of formality required, often resulting in their work being structured more like narratives (Nagao, 2018, 2020). One way to counteract this is through genre-based L2 writing, an important element of this study. Studies of genre-based L2 writing in Japanese EFL have been conducted in the fields of second language acquisition, literacy pedagogy, TESOL, and applied linguistics (de Oliveira et al., 2020; Nagao, 2018; Pessoa et al., 2018; Yasuda, 2015). These studies focused on changes in learners' understanding and awareness of genre structure and their target-genre essays' lexicogrammatical features. However, few studies have longitudinally tracked changes in learners' writing proficiency based on generic structures and linguistic features using the *systemic functional linguistics* (SFL) framework of meta-functional features for assessments.

Writing in English, particularly academic writing, has been considered a peripheral leaning activity in high schools and universities in Japan (Komiyama, 2017, 2018). EFL learners may need additional writing instruction to learn how to compose multi-paragraph texts and write using different genres. This instruction could include understanding the phases of planning, writing, and revising written texts as necessary, learning opportunities that teachers need to provide (Lawrence, 1972). Understanding the difference between directly writing down one's thoughts and the purpose of academic writing is also important for EFL learners (Pham & Bui, 2022). Thus, this study introduced a teaching approach for writing in English across the curriculum to enhance Japanese EFL learners' writing skills, especially for composing multi-sentence paragraphs in different genres. This small-scale research reports on previously unpublished data using a teaching and research framework further elaborated in Nagao (2018, 2019, 2020).

LITERATURE REVIEW

The Sydney School GBA Program and SFL

This study uses the *Sydney School genre-based literacy programme* for its core pedagogical approach (Halliday, 1994; Hyon, 1996; Johns, 2002; Martin, 2000; Martin & Rose, 2008; Rose, 2013). This programme is rooted in *genre-based approach* (GBA) theory (Martin & Rose, 2008), SFL (Halliday, 1994), and sociocultural theory (Vygotsky, 1978). GBA refers to "a multi-staged, goal-oriented, and social process" (Martin & Rose, 2008, p. 13), while SFL theory addresses the fundamental functions of language (Halliday, 1975, 1994). The latter's three meta-functions are ideational, interpersonal, and textual, which are reflected in speaking and writing (Halliday, 1994). The ideational meta-function provides grammatical resources for describing events, participants, circumstances (such as when, what, who, where, and how), as well as situational and background information (Droga & Humphrey, 2002; Halliday, 1994).

According to Oliveira (2015), interpersonal meanings pertain to the relationship between the reader and writer (e.g., subjective/objective). Textual meanings, as defined by Halliday and Martin (1981), refer to the organization and structure of linguistic information within a clause to produce a cohesive and coherent text. In SFL, writers and speakers choose lexicogrammatical features to make meaning depending on cultural and situational contexts.

The ZPD, or *zone of proximal development* (Vygotsky, 1978) encompasses the *teaching and learning cycle* (TLC) of GBA L2 writing lessons (Kuiper et al., 2017). According to Vygotsky's ZPD (1978), individuals can acquire abilities to perform tasks beyond their independent capabilities through collaboration and scaffolded support. In other words, there is a continuum of tasks that learners can perform without support to tasks that they can perform with scaffolding. The learning stages of the TLC (Nagao, 2020, p. 147; see also Feez & Joyce, 1998) are:

1. building a context,
2. modelling and deconstructing the model text(s),
3. joint construction of new and target genre texts,
4. independent construction, and
5. linking related other genre texts.

The GBA for teaching writing used in this research includes a TLC (Feez & Joyce, 1998) that along with the ZPD can provide a principled pedagogical approach to support learning.

SFL GBA

GBA teaching and pedagogy have been applied to various educational contexts, such as primary and secondary schools along with immigrant populations in Australia (Norton & Christie, 1999; Zhang, 2012). Due to the limited number of GBA classroom practitioners, it is difficult to study this approach in Japan. Individual teachers may apply the SFL GBA to writing and reading lessons in their classrooms, but it is not recognized at the national- or university-level as a form of literacy education. Despite the high demand for English writing practice in Japanese universities, EFL learners in Japan do not receive sufficient opportunities due to inadequate English pedagogy, curriculum, and system (Morita, 2017).

In Japanese high school English lessons, the most frequently introduced task is learning grammar, followed by reading popular English texts, while writing tasks are limited as learning activities. Specifically, writing lessons focus on tasks such as memorizing sentence patterns and fixed phrases, as well as translating Japanese into English (Miyata, 2002). This limited writing input and output could influence writing ability, as Japanese EFL learners tend not to experience teaching methods that help them enhance their writing. The SFL GBA for teaching writing can help, thus this research aimed to develop and apply this teaching method, curriculum, materials, and lesson plans to the Japanese classroom context.

Cornelius and Cotsworth (2015) explained SFL GBA's potential in classroom learning settings: Novice writers, particularly lower proficiency English learners in Japanese universities, may encounter difficulties grasping the conventions of EFL academic writing. To address this, the *Sydney School Genre approach*, namely the *Teaching and Learning Cycle* (TLC), holistically facilitates learners' text composition comprehension (Cornelius & Cotsworth, 2015). Language learners must acquaint themselves with the purpose, structure, and linguistic characteristics of a text by undertaking activities that scrutinize exemplar genre texts (Martin & Rose, 2008). The GBA method helps novice Japanese EFL learners by ensuring they can accomplish these tasks (Cornelius & Cotsworth, 2015).

Previous SFL GBA research has uncovered explicit scaffolding and learner support regarding a text's form-meaning connections (e.g., Gibbons, 2006; Nagao, 2020; Yasuda, 2015). The research offers rich descriptions of how students learn about genres in school and expectations for genres with a focus on accurate language (Schleppegrell et al., 2014). Moreover, SFL GBA studies have identified that changes occur in learners' understanding of target genre texts and writing composition skills along with what elements of writing proficiency improve using SFL framework assessments.

Methods

The current study introduces an instructional framework based on a genre-based syllabus design, examining its effects. The aim of the study was to determine if explicit writing instruction focusing on generic structure and lexicogrammatical features would improve EFL university students' academic writing proficiency. The research question was: How are the three meta-functional features of SFL reflected in GBA discussion essays written by EFL learners?

Participants

31 first-year university students in Japan enrolled in two English for Academic Purposes reading and writing classes were selected based on their proficiency levels, as assessed by pre-class essays. These students were taught writing using a combined SFL GBA. 15 students were placed in the (relatively) higher English proficiency group (average TOEFL iBT: 84–85 in week 15). Eleven of these students had some previous experience with SFL GBA writing lessons. The other 16 were in the lower English proficiency group (average TOEFL iBT: 68 in week 15). Only four of these students had prior SFL GBA instruction.

The study's objective and rationale were explained to all participants before obtaining their informed consent, with the same information reiterated each time the participants submitted material for analysis. The participants granted informed written and verbal consent, understood the research objectives, and were aware that their identities would be kept anonymous.

A questionnaire, based on Sakai et al. (2015), was administered in week 15, at the end of the semester, to assess students' backgrounds. Most participants (n = 29) had graduated from a high school in Japan, the majority had practised translating English to Japanese and vice versa, and some had written short opinion essays. A smaller number indicated that they had also been taught to understand topic sentences and supporting evidence and had practised writing one paragraph and an essay containing three or more paragraphs in English. In sum, while most learners had experience writing English sentences, their exposure to writing longer pieces such as paragraphs or essays was limited. This was particularly true of the lower proficiency group, as they had a limited understanding of generic structures and lexicogrammatical choices in their target genre. However, in week one, most understood the concepts of paragraphs, topic sentences, and supporting evidence.

Procedures

Student essays were collected prior to classroom intervention (week one, n = 31) and again at the end of the course (week 15, n = 31). This section describes the classroom intervention, followed by a description of essay data collection and scoring.

Classroom Intervention

In the SFL model, the curriculum and teaching plans provide explicit guidance for each task dimension (Hammond, 2001; Kongpetch, 2006; Martin & Rose, 2008; Rose, 2015). The TLC was used three times during the 15-week course (Feez & Joyce, 1998). Completion of one TLC took three or four weeks, and data were collected from the third cycle (weeks 12 to 15). The original five-stage TLC was supplemented with additional scaffolding tasks. In this SFL GBA cycle, learners were first shown PowerPoint instructions on the discussion-genre essay. Second, a model text was analysed for 12 generic and lexicogrammatical features that were explained using diagrams and graphs. Third, after discussing the writing sample, learners read four relevant journal articles and wrote content summaries. Next, they wrote a discussion-genre essay. Finally, they analysed their essay using the SFL GBA rubric.

Data Collection: Pre- and Post-Class Essays

Data collection for the pre-class essay was conducted in week one, before the classroom SFL GBA intervention. During class, the participants were assigned a timed writing task (60 minutes) in which they wrote a discussion essay on the pros and cons of Japanese university students studying abroad. Before they started, the instructor provided background information on the topic using PowerPoint slides and video materials. The learners were asked to take notes while listening and watching. No explicit rule-driven writing instruction was provided, but the participants were briefly introduced to the generic structure of a discussion essay (Issue > Argument for and against, or in more complex forms, with Discussions > Statement of differing points of view > Conclusion), language features, and the purpose of a discussion-genre text. Students were encouraged to find relevant reading materials and use that information in their pre-class essays. Students were asked to address the following prompt:

> Some people believe that participating in higher education study programs abroad has advantages. Others think that the experience of studying abroad has disadvantages. Discuss the arguments for and against participating in these programs, using both supporting and opposing views. Then, give your own opinion. When providing supporting evidence, avoid making arguments based solely on personal experience and instead, utilize information from your readings as evidence. Please write between 300 and 500 words.

The post-essay was collected in week 13, following the in-class SFL GBA writing lesson (the intervention). In class, students wrote for 60 minutes on the topic of World Englishes, addressing the following prompt:

> We have learned about the concept of World Englishes, including researchers' supporting and opposing arguments. While some people believe that only standard English, such as American English, should be used in the workplace, others support and accept the use of different forms of English with its varying accents and intonations. Discuss both supporting and opposing views regarding the use of World Englishes in working environments. Then, offer your own opinion. When seeking supporting evidence, it is important to refrain from relying on personal

experience and instead draw upon the information presented in your readings. Please write between 300 and 500 words.

The students were not allowed to use the model genre text introduced in week 11. They were again encouraged to find relevant reading materials and use the information they read in their post-essay writing.

Essay Genre and Scoring Rubric

The study employed the discussion essay genre, which includes an introduction stating the topic and issues, two paragraphs presenting arguments for and against the major issue, and a concluding paragraph explaining personal opinions on the issue (Nagao, 2018; New South Wales [NSW] Department of School Education, 1989). Thus, in coherent and cohesive essays, learners presented a set of arguments and provided supporting evidence. The genre's lexicogrammatical features (New South Wales [NSW] Department of School Education, 1989) are:

1. ideational meaning, including human and non-human participants, citations, and understanding information related to the essay topic;
2. interpersonal meaning (e.g., use of auxiliary verbs and adverbial modals) to convey the probability of an event or indicate its level of certainty; and
3. textual meaning, such as the use of conjunctions, *zig-zag techniques*, topic sentences, and supporting evidence

An SFL GBA rubric was used to score each discussion-genre essay. The three meta-functions (ideational, interpersonal, and textual meanings) were subdivided into four categories (topic knowledge, lexicogrammatical features, generic structure, and sentence-level grammatical structure). These were matched to 12 scoring criteria. Excellent essays received scores between 91–120, demonstrated complete control of language features and structures typical of the discussion genre, and contained few grammatical mistakes (text comprehension not affected). Essays with good scores (ranging from 61 to 90) or moderately good scores (ranging from 31 to 60) exhibited mastery of the generic structure and moderate proficiency in language features. However, they contained a high frequency of grammatical errors. Conversely, essays that scored less than satisfactory (0-30) evinced minimal command of both generic structure and language features and featured a wide spectrum of grammatical inaccuracies that significantly impeded text comprehension. This rubric's purpose was not to identify the writers' grammatical mistakes. Rather, the focus was their use of lexicogrammatical features.

Analysis: Three Phases

The first step in the study's data analysis compared group level changes (lower and higher English proficiency groups) in the pre- and post-class essays for the three SFL meta-functions. The second analysis considered individual changes in essay scores as a function of the classroom interventions for five learners with the lowest and five learners with the highest pre-class essay scores. These learners' pre- and post-class essays were analysed to identify changes in lexicogrammatical resources in the three meta-functional categories. The third phase was qualitative, designed to understand participants' insights into the SFL GBA process. For this purpose, semi-structured interviews were conducted with a subset of participants for 50 minutes after the 15-week lesson.

Results and Discussion

Phase 1: Lower and Higher English Proficiency Groups

In Figure 1, the mean scores of the three SFL GBA meta-functions for the pre- and post-class essays of the lower and higher English proficiency groups are presented.

Figure 1

Mean Scores on Pre- vs Post- Discussion Essays

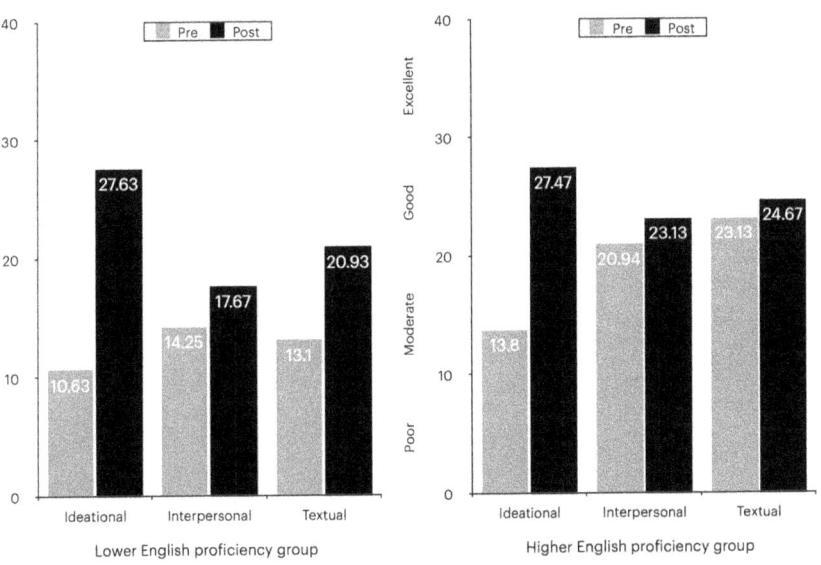

In general, the average scores for both groups exhibited enhancement following the intervention period. The lower English proficiency group demonstrated the greatest improvement in ideational meaning (post/pre score difference = 17.0), while the higher English proficiency group showed a similar improvement (post/pre score difference = 13.67). The meta-functional mean scores of the post-class essays were good for the higher English proficiency group, ranging between 20 and

40 points. Conversely, the lower English proficiency group scored below 21 points.

Tables 1A—1C show the results of the mean group scores for ideational meaning on the pre- and post-class essays. The "understanding information related to the essay topic" scores visibly improved among the lower English proficiency group (pre = 3.56, post = 7.19), as their increased understanding of how to use accurate, relevant knowledge found in the text(s) they read improved their essays.

Table 1A

Scores for Ideational Meaning on Pre- and Post-Class Essays: Criteria 1-4

Assessment criteria	Lower proficiency class				Higher proficiency class			
	Pre-		Post-		Pre-		Post-	
	Total	Mean	Total	Mean	Total	Mean	Total	Mean
1. Understanding topics/knowledge (1)	57	3.56	115	7.19	77	5.13	113	7.53
2. Lexico-grammatical features	0	0	93	5.81	3	0.20	77	5.13
3. Understanding topics/knowledge (2)	58	3.63	110	6.88	80	5.33	109	7.27
4. Generic structure	55	3.44	124	7.75	47	3.13	113	7.53
Total	170	10.63	442	27.63	207	13.79	412	27.46

Table 1B

Scores for Ideational Meaning on Pre- and Post-Class Essays: Criteria 5-8

Assessment criteria	Lower proficiency class				Higher proficiency class			
	Pre-		Post-		Pre-		Post-	
	Total	Mean	Total	Mean	Total	Mean	Total	Mean
5. Lexico-grammatical features	46	2.88	72	4.8	72	4.5	76	5.07
6. Sentence-level grammar structures	78	4.88	93	6.2	106	6.63	115	7.67
7. Lexico-grammatical features	26	1.63	55	3.67	44	2.75	63	4.2
8. Lexico-grammatical features	78	4.88	45	3	113	7.06	93	6.2
Total	228	14.27	265	17.67	335	20.94	347	23.13

Table 1C

Scores for Ideational Meaning on Pre- and Post-Class Essays: Criteria 9-12

Assessment criteria	Lower proficiency class				Higher proficiency class			
	Pre-		Post-		Pre-		Post-	
	Total	Mean	Total	Mean	Total	Mean	Total	Mean
9. Lexico-grammatical features	42	2.63	61	4.07	75	4.69	59	3.93
10. Generic structure	56	3.5	79	5.27	102	6.38	106	7.07
11. Generic structure	55	3.44	89	5.93	95	5.94	101	6.73
12. Generic structure	56	3.5	85	5.67	98	6.13	104	6.93
Total	209	13.1	314	20.94	370	23.14	370	24.66

The overall scores for items 5, 6, and 7 clearly improved, especially among the lower English proficiency group. However, their understanding of the final paragraph and the use of personal pronouns decreased. That is, some learners in this group used only the personal pronoun "I" when describing their opinions rather than alternative genre-appropriate strategies. Conversely, among the higher English proficiency group, understanding each interpersonal meaning element somewhat improved.

For the lower English proficiency group, the generic structure of discussion essays shows that Issue > Argument for (or against) > Argument against (or for) > Conclusion improved more than other meaning features (post–pre difference = 2.49). For the higher English proficiency group, understanding topic sentences and supporting evidence use improved the most (post–pre difference = 0.8). On the other hand, their use of conjunctions (e.g., by contrast, conversely, in contrast, on the contrary) when introducing an opposing topic decreased (post–pre difference = - 0.76).

Phase 2: Individual Change

To better understand individual changes in SFL meta-functions over the TLCs, data from the learners with the five highest and five lowest pre-class essay scores were analysed. Due to space constraints, Figure 2 shows the change patterns only for the top and bottom three. The learners with the lowest scores showed improvements from the pre- to the post-class essay on each of the three meta-functions, especially ideational meaning. These changes were more varied among the learners who had higher pre-class essay scores. Although their post-class essay scores improved in at least one meta-function, they were stable for one or more meta-functions. Improvements in ideational meaning were again the most evident. In the highest scoring pre-class essays, textual meaning seemed less likely to benefit from the intervention.

Figure 2

Pre- and Post-Class Essay Scores on Three Meta-Functions

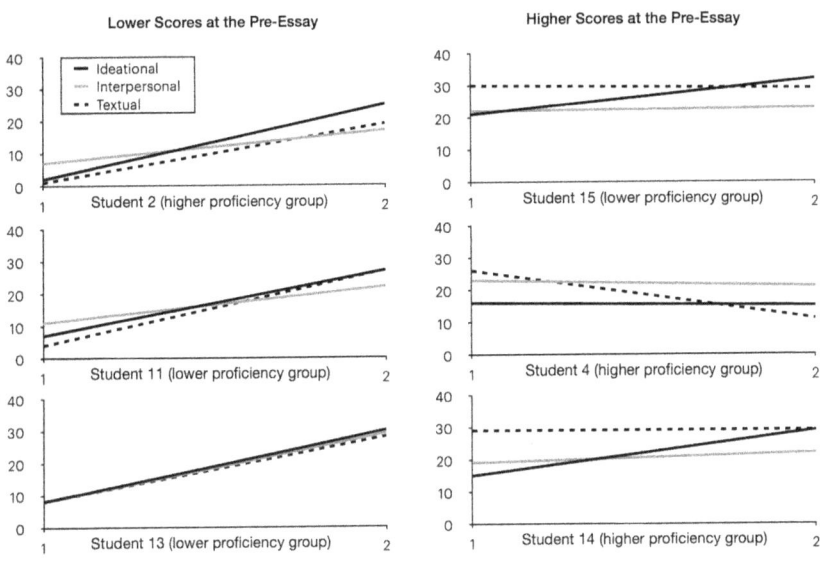

One possible reason is that learners might not have participated in enough grammatical tasks during stages 2 and 3 of the TLC. This result suggests that teachers should incorporate more tasks to raise learners' awareness and use of target lexicogrammatical features.

Phase 3: Interviews

Student 2

Figure 3 is an example of Student 2's pre-class essay (score 10/120 points, higher English proficiency group with a lower score in the pre-essay). This student had no previous SFL GBA writing instruction. Short sentences were simply placed next to one another and were mostly incomplete. In the first paragraph (the issue paragraph), the student included minimal topic-related information. In the body section, the topic sentences were introduced with no supporting evidence or citations. The student's opinion was written in the last sentence, which served as the final paragraph. Thus, overall, the student seemed to understand the function of each paragraph in a discussion essay. As for lexicogrammatical features, in this pre-class essay, no auxiliary verbs, mental verbs, adverbs with -ly, signposts, or conjunctions were used. In the final sentence, this student introduced their opinion with "I think."

Figure 3

Student 2's Pre-Class Essay Example

The advantage and disadvantage to study abroad	Title
More and more students are choosing to study at colleges and universities in a foreign country. This trend has both good and bad points.	Issue
(TS 1?) we can make many friends.	Argument for ?
(TS 2?) it is very difficult to learn foreign language.	Argument against ?
I think it is better to go study abroad because we can make many friends.	Conclusion ?

Student 2 elaborated on their grasp of the discussion topic when writing the pre-class essay:

> I had no understanding of the topic. Moreover, I did not know how to write about it even though the teacher explained the essay structure briefly. I did not understand the use of adverbs with -ly in this essay. Also, I was told to write my own opinion in the last paragraph, so I expressed my feelings by using "I think." I only know how to use this way of writing to express my opinion.

On the other hand, the same student's post-intervention essay

(Figure 4) showed moderate improvements in generic structures, three meta-functions, and improved lexicogrammatical features.

Figure 4

Student 2's Post-Class Essay Example

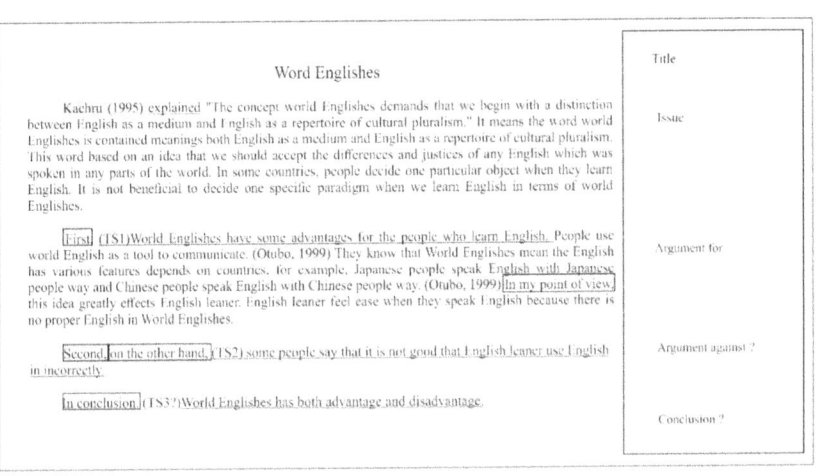

Paragraphs 1 and 2 were clearly written. Even though there was not enough supporting evidence in subsequent paragraphs, the student tried to compose four paragraphs. One highlight of the student's understanding of the essay structure was the first topic sentence in the second paragraph, which introduced the supporting argument's main point. Both the second and third sentences in this paragraph were supported with citations. Then, the student reflected on or paraphrased the context of previous sentences by using the words "In my point of view." During the interview, Student 2 reflected:

> I know I am a slow writer, and I could not finish it. I clearly understood what I needed to write in the first paragraph, and I wrote the definition of world Englishes. It was relatively easy for me to write this first paragraph, because the teacher gave me some information about the topic and I read the journal materials. However, I had some difficulty writing

the second and third paragraphs, because the context of both needed to be coherent. I mean, I knew it was important to write the argument's point A in the second and the third paragraphs, and I needed to write relevant evidence and points to rebut the content of the second paragraph. That is why I could not complete the third and fourth paragraphs.

Student 2 clearly described the focus topic in this essay by citing accurate and relevant knowledge. Moreover, a few reporting verbs were found (ideational meaning). As for interpersonal meaning, there were no adverbs with -ly or auxiliary verbs. In SFL theory, writers express attitudes through modal verbs, such as may, can, could, will, and the use of adverbs, such as probably, absolutely, and possibly. These vocabulary items (interpersonal lexicogrammar) are categorised under interpersonal meaning and function. They provide more options to negotiate relationships between the writer and readers (Halliday, 1984). When asked about the limited used of lexicogrammatical features of ideational meaning in their post-class essay, Student 2 answered:

> I am still unsure how to use the adverbs with -ly within the sentence, but I know their function. So, if I were to use it now (during the interview), I would put it in the last paragraph, especially in the sentence expressing my opinion.

Finally, with regards to textual meaning, Student 2 was able to use conjunctions and signposts.

Student 8

Figure 5 shows a sample from Student 8's pre-class essay (score 12/120, lower English proficiency group). Student 8 had no prior experience with SFL GBA. Most of the sentences were short and placed next to one another. The fourth paragraph was missing. Hence, this text did not exhibit the structure of a discussion-genre essay. Student 8 explained in the interview:

I did not have enough time to finish this essay. Before I started to write it, I was thinking of the structure…I needed to write the introduction, the body, and the conclusion…and I tried to think of the contexts for what I could write. I could not write irrelevant information in each paragraph. So, I was thinking how I could make these paragraphs cohesive. I was thinking about this in Japanese. This process of thinking in Japanese about essay structure took a lot of time. That is why I could not complete this essay.

Figure 5

Student 8's Pre-Class Essay Example

Gggggggg	Tittle (??)
Recently, there are many students who study at foreign country. There is an advantage and an disadvantage on this trend.	Issue^
First, (TS1) advantage is English skill improve. Today, globalization is spreading all over the world. English skill is necessary for everyone to communicate with foreigner in this age.	Argument for^
Second, (TS2) the disadvantage is decline of culture of home country. Language commonality cause	Argument against^ Conclusion is missing.

Figure 6 shows a sample of Student 8's post-intervention discussion essay. Most of the generic structures, three meta-functions, and lexicogrammatical features were used with moderate success. Although the post-intervention essay's generic structure was incomplete, the student still wrote four paragraphs, explaining, "I managed to think about the structure in English this time. For this essay, I did not think of the content in Japanese, so I managed to write a few paragraphs." Clearly, Student 8 applied the strategies introduced in the intervention to their post-class essay writing.

Figure 6

Student 8's Post-Class Essay Example

<table>
<tr><td align="center">World Englishes and Our World</td><td>Title</td></tr>
<tr><td>Today's world is more globalized than ever before. It enables people easier communication and transportation. This innovative age led to increased mutual cultural influences across national and regional boundaries, so cultural diversity is expended. Thus, English become 'World Englishes' and it spreads more widely. It also drive other languages to extinction (Mufwne, 2010).Kachru(1995) mentioned about World Englishes, which is used for all over the world. There are two means, one is English as a medium and the other is English as a repertoire of cultural pluralism. The most spoken language is Chinese and it is spoken by 12 million on the other hand people who speak English as a first language is third place in the world. However, why English are used as official language in the world? It because the number of people who use English as second language or leaning it is about 830 million in the world (Ling,2015).</td><td>Issue</td></tr>
<tr><td>(TS1)There are some good points to accept World Englishes, First, according to Kachru (1995), when we say English as a global medium, we can communicate with other community's people more easily. Through using English, people can do interlocutions with each other. In addition, Otsubo (1999) mentioned that World Englishes implies that each country has it own English pronunciation, so it accept us that is of course.</td><td>Argument for</td></tr>
<tr><td>On the other hand, (TS2) some people disagree with World Englishes, becausethey say that it caused language domination, cultural domination , and sprit domination.</td><td>Argument against</td></tr>
<tr><td>As a result, using English as one way of the communication tole, we need to know about the character of English.</td><td>Conclusion ?</td></tr>
</table>

This essay exhibited complete control of generic structures and language features. Although the conclusion is limited, readers can readily comprehend the essay's topic since the student provided sufficient information pertaining to the when, where, what, and who in the first paragraph. This information is rooted in precise and pertinent knowledge derived from source texts, thereby representing ideational meaning. In this post-class essay, there were some reporting verbs and enough citations to support topic sentences (ideational meaning). Though limited, some auxiliary verbs were included (interpersonal meaning). However, -ly adverbs related to the writer's opinions and showing degrees of topic support or opposition were not included (interpersonal meaning). According to the student:

> I understood the function of auxiliary verbs and used them in this writing, but I was not aware of how to use them when I wrote the pre-class

essay. Plus, it was very helpful to have the model text. Whilst writing the post-class essay, I could go back to the model text to check what my essay was missing when I was confused.

As for the text's language features giving ideational and interpersonal meanings, the student tried to incorporate their prior knowledge of the topic in the pre-class essay, but they used limited supporting evidence. Regarding interpersonal meaning, most verbs were existence types, such as **is** and **are**, and there were no mental state verbs. For textual meaning, some signposts, such as **first** and **second**, were included, but there were no contract conjunctions. In terms of sentence-level grammar, the final sentence was incomplete, and there were several grammatical mistakes.

Summary

"How are the three meta-functional features of SFL reflected in GBA discussion essays written by EFL learners?" I answered this research question by exploring how EFL university learners in Japan reflect the three meta-functional features in their discussion essays before and after instruction (SFL GBA cycles). The changes in understanding were related to interpersonal meanings, indicating that comprehension of the three features did not improve dramatically, even when ideational and textual meanings improved. The features of interpersonal meaning in the discussion essay were: (a) using auxiliary verbs to convey an event's degree of probability or certainty (e.g., can, should, need to, must, could) at a sentence level; (b) using lexicogrammatical features (i.e., -ly adverbs) related to the writer's views to show the latter's degree of support or opposition; and (c) avoiding the use of lexicogrammatical resources related to personal pronouns, especially **I** in the final paragraph and replacing these with other words or phrases to indicate subjectivity.

The results of the micro analysis showed individual-level changes. Ten learners were chosen from the top (n = 5) and bottom (n = 5) of the pre-class essay scores. When learners had lower pre-intervention essay scores (bottom 5), all three meta-functions (ideational, interpersonal, and textual meaning) improved, with interpersonal meaning showing the most improvement. The function of interpersonal meaning helps maintain social relations, which can be expressed by the lexicogrammatical features of mood and modality. However, Student 4 had a high score on the pre-class essay and lower meta-function scores on the post-intervention essay. This may indicate that understanding lexicogrammatical features related to interpersonal meaning in the discussion genre was challenging for these EFL learners. A finding from learners who had initially higher scores regards their understanding of textual meaning (i.e., cohesive and coherent writing), as these showed less improvement.

During the TLC, to enhance students' understanding of textual meaning, a variety of tasks could be used to identify theme and rheme, as well as to develop themes further. *Coherence* and *cohesion* refer to the texture and structure of a text (Halliday & Hasan, 1976; Eggins, 2004). When a text is coherent and cohesive, it gives readers some idea about what to expect from the text. Thus, the writer's ability to organise relations within the text is a critical factor in creating a cohesive discourse (Piriyasilpa, 2010). In other words, writing skill refers to the ability to mark coherent words in an essay, while text cohesion and coherence are necessary to write successfully. To improve the cohesion and coherence of the target genres, it is essential to understand the theme and rheme. Skilful writers can organise the theme and rheme in each clause to construct a coherent message (Choung & Oh, 2017). The enhancement of EFL learners' theme-rheme proficiency yields a discernible improvement in their written compositions (Guan, 2015; Rustipa, 2010).

Even though the pre- and post-class essay scores were not high for the students included in the low micro-analysis group, during the interviews they demonstrated improved awareness and understanding of English modalities following the SFL GBA writing intervention. Thus, this study furthers pedagogical understanding regarding institutional and cultural contextual features, particularly EFL language learning in Japanese classrooms. This includes the extent to which a genre-based pedagogy is feasible for EFL teachers in a Japanese university, and whether such an approach could be introduced more broadly to improve and standardise L2 writing curriculum and teaching methods to refine literacy education in the target university and similar contexts.

Another contribution involves better understanding whether a GBA to teaching EFL writing to undergraduate students in Japan can lead to improvements in EFL learners' understanding of L2 writing and their ability to write academic texts in English. This addresses whether an explicit, text-based, Vygotskian (1978) pedagogical approach is effective for learners in Japanese tertiary EFL contexts. The findings shared here give a clearer picture of the implementation of this pedagogical approach in this university context, and in others with similar curricular, institutional, and cultural factors. Overall, there were substantial gains in learners' understanding of ideational meaning, which concerns the essay content and its function in using language to express experience. That is, these EFL learners' understanding and knowledge improved in relation to the essay topic. It may be that some tasks, during the third stage of the TLC, can influence essay topic understanding (Rose & Martin, 2012).

Cornelius and Cotsworth (2015) described the Sydney School of Genre approach as a viable alternative for EFL learners to comprehend text composition holistically. Some of the research results from this study support their idea. However, it is necessary to explore appropriate learning tasks whose focuses are different depending on students' English proficiencies. Stage 3 student tasks included listening to lectures about the essay topic, reading journal articles related to the topic, and writing summaries. However, the reason students' understanding of textual meaning did not similarly improve may relate to the nature of the TLC's stage 3 tasks: grammar and vocabulary training. Other tasks focusing on lexicogrammatical features, such as conjunctions, could be introduced, and grammar and vocabulary training tasks can also be included in the first two stages.

Conclusion: Limitations and Future Work

One potential limitation of this study is the possibility that other variables, such as prior English language learning experience or exposure to other instructional approaches in secondary school, may have influenced the development of learners' writing skills. As there was no control group available for comparison, this study's conclusions regarding the comparative effectiveness of teaching methods are limited. Further research should introduce additional writing tasks and include experimental and control groups to establish the effectiveness of teaching methods of SFL GBA L2 writing lessons. Moreover, the timing of the interviews may have affected the responses. As such, future studies should conduct interviews immediately after essay completion.

Notwithstanding the limitations, the findings support implementing explicit teaching approaches in L2 writing, with particular emphasis on generic structures and lexicogrammatical resources. This serves to mitigate the discrepancies among learners with varying degrees of English proficiency. Additionally, this study underscores the significance of instructing writing skills at the post-secondary level. Consequently, the present investigation exposed the subjects to diverse textual genres, requisite for fulfilling the academic writing prerequisites of Japanese tertiary level institutions. An evaluation rubric based on the SFL approach was created to incorporate SFL methodology into language learning environments. It is recommended that it be tested across diverse reading and writing contexts. By aligning learners' self-evaluations of their grasp of linguistic resources with their writing proficiency, the application of SFL-GBA to writing instruction in EFL classrooms can support future English language learners to comprehend textual structures, make effective lexicogrammatical choices, and express their ideas in their academic essays in more sophisticated ways.

Author Bio

Akiko Nagao (Ph.D.) is a lecturer at Ryukoku University in Japan who is interested in investigating the genre-based approach (GBA) within a systemic functional linguistics (SFL) framework to assess the development of English learners' understanding of target-genre essays. She is also interested in how novice EFL learners in Japan become experienced learners/EFL writers through SFL-GBA writing lessons.

Acknowledgements

I would like to thank the editors and reviewers for their valuable comments and suggestions. Furthermore, I acknowledge the contribution of Dr Cassi Liardét (Macquarie University), Dr Peter Mickan (The University of Adelaide), and the teachers at Adelaide Education Group, whose thoughtful comments and feedback significantly improved the research framework and teaching methods used in this study.

Postscript

This work was supported by a Grant-in-Aid for Young Scientists (B) Grant [Number 19K13278] from the Japan Society for the Promotion of Science and the Ryukoku University researchers' fund (2021-2022 Academic Year). No potential competing interest was reported by the author. The data that support the findings of this study are available on request from the corresponding author. The data are not publicly available because they contain information that could compromise the privacy of the research participants.

3

A CLIL Course on Karate and Japanese Culture: Developing Intercultural Awareness and Language Learning

Barry Kavanagh

This paper examines how a content and language integrated learning (CLIL) course called *Karate and Japanese Culture* promoted intercultural awareness and language learning. The course was taught at Tohoku University, Japan, and enrols foreign exchange students and Japanese English language students. CLIL facilitates improving learners' *intercultural communicative competence* (ICC) and their ability to use language in different cultural and linguistic environments. As Carrió-Pastor (2009) points out, intercultural understanding and sensitivity are fundamental to realizing CLIL. Further, Japan's *Ministry of Education, Culture, Sport, Science and Technology* (MEXT) has been working to reform English language education to better reflect the need for English proficiency among its citizens due to the demands of its globalized economy. Notably, one of MEXT's stated aims is for students to develop an understanding of languages and cultures through various experiences (MEXT, 2020). MEXT (2018a) cites CLIL as a teaching approach compatible with its English language education aims. However, how to develop ICC or intercultural understanding through CLIL is still not very well understood, particularly in Japanese or Asian contexts. To address this, this chapter briefly overviews the literature and describes this course's content, syllabus, and assessment. This is followed by an outline of the methodology, results, and discussion of findings in relation to how this

CLIL course develops both intercultural understanding and aids in the development of L2.

The Pedagogical Framework: CLIL and ICC

CLIL emphasizes learning a subject through a foreign language so students learn the taught subject and the foreign language simultaneously. Coyle et al. (2010) have suggested that this approach starts with content (the subject being taught) and focuses on the correlation between the content, communication (language), cognition (critical thinking), and culture (awareness of self and *otherness*) to build on the synergies of integrating learning (content and cognition) and language learning (communication and cultures).

A CLIL class does not always just use the language of instruction; sometimes students' L1s are used to help negotiate meaning. This translanguaging role in a typical CLIL class refers to the "multiple discursive practices in which bilinguals engage in order to make sense of their bilingual worlds" (García, 2009, p. 45). Lin and He (2017) found that, despite the mainstream discourse throughout Asia that insists on only using the target language within the classroom, translanguaging, or the use of L1(s) and target language naturally, flows from classroom interactions and activities in a bilingual or multilingual classroom. Méndez García & Pavón Vázquez (2012) suggest that CLIL can benefit from the use of both L1(s) and target language, leading to a deeper understanding of language(s) and the concepts taught.

Byram's (1997) model of ICC describes intercultural awareness as recognizing and understanding other cultures and customs as well as appreciating differences and similarities. This can lead to interpreting one's own culture in relation to others and to implement this understanding when communicating with people from different cultures. Byram (1997) describes ICC as "the ability to interact with people from another country and culture in a foreign language" (p. 71).

In an era of globalization, the need to integrate *interculturality* and ICC into the language curriculum has become stronger. Interculturality refers to the relations that exist through the interaction of culturally diverse people within a given society (Hahl & Löfström, 2016). This can expand a student's world vision (Kramsch, 2001) and help them in real-life situations as cultural contact is inevitable in a globalized, interconnected society (Cusick, 2015). ICC essentially means that students can effectively and appropriately interact in intercultural situations and diverse cultural contexts, which CLIL can help students realize through its theoretical principles, which are based on the notion that learners should be prepared for a more culturally and linguistically diverse society (Rozas, 2009).

Although the application of CLIL from the 4Cs perspective of *content, communication, culture,* and *cognition* has been examined (Yamano, 2013), empirical research on how CLIL can benefit students' ICC while also focusing on the "C" for culture within the core dimensions of the 4Cs conceptual framework is still very much underrepresented (Méndez García, 2013).

Some studies, however, have illustrated the potential of focusing on the C for culture in CLIL classes. For example, Maruki (2020) reported how her Japanese language and literature students at an American university immersed themselves with a "foreign viewpoint" through authentic texts aimed at developing cultural understanding. Similarly, Karatsu (2016) observed that the integration of film in a CLIL class paved the way for critical intercultural awareness and understanding of the notions of culture. Expanding on these ideas, Sudhoff (2010) suggests that the integrative nature of CLIL classes can provide an opportunity for taking not only a dual-focused but a triple-focused approach, simultaneously combining foreign language learning, content subject learning, and intercultural learning. Sudhoff also describes how CLIL classes can offer students a sense of interculturality by providing a variety of viewpoints on intercultural issues. However, these kinds of studies and discussions are limited, with little research exploring the role of culture within CLIL (Lochtman, 2021).

A model for acquiring intercultural competence in bilingual education that is compatible with CLIL was developed by Hallet (1998). This model is based on the following three concepts: (1) aspects of students' own culture; (2) aspects of the target language culture; and (3) intercultural aspects, which cover global phenomena (Hallet, 1998).

Utilizing the CLIL 4Cs concept, Sudhoff's (2010) triple-focused frameworks for CLIL, and Hallet's (1998) bilingual triangle, this paper illustrates how a CLIL class incorporating foreign and Japanese students within a multicultural and multilingual classroom environment can help students improve their ICC.

THE KARATE AND JAPANESE CULTURE CLIL COURSE

The Karate and Japanese Culture course brought together two different groups of students. The first group were Japanese students of English who signed up for an elective *Practical English Skills* (PES) course. The second group were foreign exchange students taking courses within the *International Program in Liberal Arts* (IPLA). Classes were 90 minutes long, and no textbook was used. The IPLA program provides an opportunity for students at Tohoku University's partner institutions to study Liberal Arts classes in English at Tohoku University, including economics, management, education, law, history, and literature. IPLA students are from around the world but are predominately from European and Asian countries. They all have a high level of English proficiency and are interested in Japanese culture and language. Some are majoring in Japanese culture and language in their home countries. For this course, a PES class with IPLA students were combined into one group in order to learn about Karate and Japanese culture. The data discussed in this chapter is from the first iteration of the course. In both groups, students were in their first and second years of undergraduate study. Eleven PES Japanese students with advanced English proficiency (three had TOEFL iBT scores of over 500) were enrolled. Thirteen foreign proficient English speaking IPLA students were enrolled from the following countries: Austria (2), France (7), Germany (1), Russia (2), and Sweden (1).

The Karate and Japanese Culture CLIL Syllabus

The syllabi for the PES and IPLA students were different. For the PES students, the class was offered as an advanced CLIL English class on Karate and Japanese culture combined with IPLA students. Evaluation was focused on English proficiency learning goals. For these students, the course aimed to improve language skills through international collaboration, discussion, presentations, writing reports, and engaging in "natural conversational settings" using real-world English. The focus, therefore, was on a language-driven "soft" CLIL approach, where content was used to learn English and language learning the priority (Ohmori, 2014).

In contrast, the IPLA students were offered this course as an opportunity to study Karate and Japanese culture with Japanese PES students. The course aimed to expose the foreign exchange students to Japanese culture through the class themes and to have them collaborate with Japanese PES students, who could explain the cultural concepts covered. Thus, the IPLA students experienced a more content-driven "hard CLIL" approach, where the students were assessed on their understanding of the course materials rather than on their English abilities.

Assessment

The course was not designed as an English class for the IPLA students because their English was already proficient. As a result, they were assessed on solely the course content. The Japanese PES students, however, were evaluated on both their understanding of the course content and their English abilities. For example, written reports by the PES students were evaluated for grammatical errors, structure, and content understanding. For IPLA students, reports were assessed on the content, understanding, opinion, argument, and flow of ideas. Both groups were also given review quizzes based on class content.

For the final assessments, students collaborated on presentations about karate in Japan and abroad. In the ninth class of the course, students were placed into presentation groups and provided with criteria in terms of content and length. They had 30-40 minutes of lesson time in classes 12 and 13 to coordinate their presentations. The groups worked outside of class time to prepare.

Each group consisted of one IPLA student and two PES students, except in one case where two IPLA students and one PES student were grouped together. The presentations were 30 minutes long, including audience Q&A. Most students spoke five to seven minutes each, leaving about ten minutes for questions. The presentations were evaluated on content understanding, delivery, organization, and research. 60% of the PES students' assessment rubric was also used for evaluating their English use in their presentations.

A Typical Karate and Japanese Culture CLIL Class

The course made use of a *flipped learning* approach, where the students prepared a presentation or research task outside of class for the following lesson, such as answering a series of questions. Where applicable, a bilingual glossary of vocabulary was given to students for each lesson theme along with teacher-generated handouts.

In a typical lesson, students were introduced to the theme, such as *karate history*, to check their prior knowledge of the topic. This was followed by content teaching that utilized integrated quizzes and discussion. Cultural concepts and *kanji* were also often part of the class. This allowed PES students to discuss the meaning of various characters and cultural concepts with IPLA students, who were keen to learn.

After teacher input, quizzes, discussion, and feedback, students were given homework. One example exercise was to watch a series of film clips of Japanese and American karate movies. Students were introduced to the concept of *Orientalism* and how Asian characters are often portrayed in American martial arts films, along with a set of questions and suggestions to help them analyze the film clips. These exercises provided examples of how cultural perspectives can differ. For example, the IPLA students found examples of *whitewashing* or *yellowface* abhorrent, whilst the Japanese PES students largely found these instances unproblematic. In addition, the use of stereotypical Japanese accents, such as the one the Mr. Miyagi character exhibits in *The Karate Kid*, was not considered overly demeaning or racist by the PES students, with some finding it amusing and unoffensive. The concept of *othering* an ethnic minority in film split opinion between the Japanese and foreign students and became an illustration of the differing attitudes students held towards contemporary cultural issues and concepts. Through these discussions, the students were able to notice different perspectives and come to understand why classmates felt the way they did. This resulted in students becoming more interculturally aware of each other's opinions and stances.

Methodology

Students were given a pre-course and a post-course survey with the same 5-point Likert scale questions (see Appendix), except that the post-course questions were prefixed with, "Now that you have finished the course." Some of the questions were targeted either for the PES or IPLA students.

The survey questions were based on the CLIL 4Cs and examined the progress students felt they had made in understanding content as well as improving their communication skills, ICC, and critical thinking skills (cognition). The pre-course and post-course data was compared to give a picture of which student learning outcomes were achieved.

Regarding knowledge of course content, students rated themselves from (1) *Not knowledgeable at all* to (5) *Very knowledgeable*. They also rated their confidence from (1) *Not confident at all* to (5) *Very confident* for each question in both surveys, with their pre-course and post-course responses compared. Options to give reasons for their ratings were also provided. Finally, the post-course survey also included an open-ended question meant only for the PES students.

The pre-course survey was administered during the first class, and the post-course survey was given during the final lesson. To investigate potential statistical differences between the pre- and post-course surveys, a *Wilcoxon signed-rank test* with an alpha level of .05 was used for the non-parametric data because such tests do not require data to follow a normal distribution, such as a conventional bell shape.

Results

The results have been divided into the 4C categories of content, communication, culture, and cognition. Where applicable, it is stated when questions were only asked to one group. The results from the Likert scale questions are presented first via a comparison of the pre- and post-survey results, followed by a summary of the open-ended question for PES students.

Questions Based on the C for Content

For the question "How would you rate your knowledge of karate?", the PES students rated their knowledge as being higher after the course, with a shift from *slightly knowledgeable* to *knowledgeable*. The Wilcoxon signed rank test revealed that the post-survey results were significantly higher (Md = 4.00, n = 11) compared to the pre-course survey results (Md = 3.00, z = -3.071, p = .002). Similar results were found with the IPLA students, where the post-course survey scores (Md = 2.00, n = 7) were statistically significantly higher than the pre-course survey scores (Md = 4.00, z = -2.428, p = .015).

When giving reasons for their ratings in the pre-course survey, PES students commented that they knew someone who did karate, but that was their only knowledge of it, or that they had done some form of karate in elementary school but could not remember the style they had practiced. None of the Japanese students had any notion of how karate is perceived or practiced abroad. However, in the post-course survey, PES students stated that their knowledge of karate in the context of Japan and abroad had improved through viewing films, documentaries, and interviews. One student commented, "Watching the different videos about karate and how professionals viewed karate was refreshing, it allowed me to understand the philosophy behind karate better."

In the pre-course survey, most of the IPLA students mentioned that they had little knowledge of what Japanese karate is like and that their image of the sport was mainly developed through media and Hollywood films. Students mentioned that they had seen movies such as *The Karate Kid* and the spin-off TV series *Cobra Kai*, with their perception of karate largely driven by Western media. In the post-course survey, IPLA students mentioned that they had deepened their understanding of Japanese culture and how it influences martial arts. This was related to various concepts covered in class, such as how hierarchal structures like *kohai* (junior) and *senpai* (senior) relationships are reflected within the dojo, bowing towards the *kamidana* (miniature altar), and links to the Shinto religion. In this way, students also learned about the importance of respect and humility in Japanese culture and how it may differ from the West.

Some students commented, "I realized that not all Japanese know about karate." This was evident in discussions in class when the teacher had to intervene and help students explain or answer some of the IPLA students' questions. This was perhaps to be expected, as karate is not as popular in Japan as other martial arts such as judo or sports like baseball.

Questions Based on the C for Communication (Collaboration) and Culture

The PES students were asked two C for communication (collaboration) and culture questions. When reflecting on "How confident are you discussing Japanese culture in English (including how different it is to other cultures) with the foreign exchange students?", some students commented that they had no experience of discussing Japanese culture in English. Further, if they had previously talked about manga or anime with foreign students, they used Japanese. There was a significant difference in their post-course survey levels of confidence ($Md = 3.00, n = 11, z = -2.460, p = .014$) compared to their pre-course survey responses ($Md = 2.00$). For "How confident are you in using your English to collaborate with foreigners in a multicultural classroom/environment?", many of the PES students stated that this was their first time learning and using

English in a multicultural classroom with foreign exchange students. As the emphasis of the course was on active learning and communication, some students had to be reassured of their ability to keep up and participate in the class. Other more confident students felt the course was good practice for their study abroad program and would help them discuss Japanese culture while living abroad. This was reflected in their questionnaire responses, which revealed a doubling of their confidence between the pre-course (Md = 2.00, n = 11) and post-course questionnaires (Md = 4.00, n = 11, z = -3.017, p = .003).

The IPLA students were asked "How confident are you in communicating and collaborating with your Japanese classmates (about Japanese culture) in this class?" There was no significant difference between the pre-course results (Md = 4.00, n = 7) and the post-survey levels of confidence (Md = 4.00, z = -1.342, p = .014), perhaps because for the IPLA students, communicating with classmates from different nationalities and cultures was nothing new as they experienced this at their respective universities.

The IPLA students commented that the class was conducted in a "nice atmosphere" and that they "Enjoyed working with Japanese students and learning from them." From a cultural perspective, they "learned how Japanese students interact with each other." The IPLA students commented that they liked the fact that they worked a lot in groups, and that it was interesting to hear the opinions and thoughts of the Japanese students. One student mentioned that "Being in the class with Japanese students helped broaden my perspective on Japanese culture, and I also learned how self-discipline is important to Japanese people."

Questions Based on the C for Cognition

The C for cognition question was "How confident are you in using critical thinking skills (For example: discussing, analyzing, debating, explaining, and evaluating class content in class) when learning about themes related to karate and Japanese culture?" Both PES and IPLA students rated their level of confidence for this question significantly higher in the post-course survey data ($z = -3.071$, $Md = 3.00$, $n = 11$, $p = .003$) and ($z = -2.121$, $Md = 3.00$, $n = 7$, $p = .034$) respectively when compared with the pre-course data (PES: $Md = 2.00$; IPLA: $Md = 3.00$). The IPLA students commented that in their home country universities, their seminar class professors expect them to demonstrate critical thinking skills through discussion and problem-solving. One student from Austria noted that "if students remain silent, they would be criticized and may not even get credit." This would perhaps explain why, before the course, all of the IPLA students were slightly more confident than the Japanese students in using higher-order thinking skills.

English Communication Skills Through Course Content

A final open-ended question in the post-course survey for the PES students asked "Did you improve your English communication skills through the course content and by working and collaborating with IPLA students in this class?" This question sought to understand how students felt their English communication skills had improved through the content (class and homework activities) and collaboration opportunities (group work and group presentations). Some PES students stated that their vocabulary, listening, and ability to communicate in a natural setting improved considerably. One student mentioned:

> This class was a good environment to improve my communication skills. In the dojo, we Japanese were taught kata by Barry sensei and an IPLA student and practiced it with classmates, so they were a lot of chances to talk with them both in the dojo and in class.

However, a few students conceded that some classes were difficult because the "IPLA students were like native speakers, so difficult to keep up at times but they were kind and understanding." Another student wrote that they realized "that by working with international students I have to study hard to improve, especially to fulfill the goal of going abroad." Such comments reflect the modesty of some students as they addressed their shortcomings and plans to further improve their English.

One potential issue pointed out by a PES student was that on occasion "Japanese students and Japanese-speaking students can end up using Japanese during discussions." The Japanese level of the IPLA students ranged from elementary to pre-intermediate, and they were keen to learn more as they were taking Japanese classes. Therefore, there were some instances when the IPLA students asked about Japanese vocabulary or how to use specific expressions as they came up in the context of conversations. This was only observed intermittently in the context of discussing class themes. As such, Japanese use was allowed in class to explain concepts, especially when students were asked to explain cultural concepts and the meaning of certain kanji. This use of translanguaging (using both Japanese and English to negotiate meaning), or the use of dictionaries when required, was a natural way to pursue dialogue in this multinational and multilingual environment and was not detrimental to the PES students learning English. Notably, one PES student commented:

> Because every non-Japanese student is a very active speaker, it is hard for me to talk with them. However, thanks to them, I think I become able to speak English a little better than ever. The last presentation is a good practice and chance to improve my English with my foreign classmates.

DISCUSSION AND CONCLUSION

This chapter has illustrated how a joint CLIL class on Karate and Japanese culture conducted in English with foreign and Japanese students supported language learning and ICC development. Conceptually, the discussion here utilized the CLIL 4Cs concept together with Sudhoff's (2010) triple focused CLIL approach and Hallet's (1998) bilingual triangle frameworks. Using Byram (1997)'s definition of ICC, both groups of students were able to interact, collaborate, and discuss issues with students from different cultural backgrounds. Many of the Japanese

PES students had not previously studied or collaborated with foreign exchange students. In pre-course survey findings, their confidence in working with the IPLA students in a multicultural environment was relatively low. However, their confidence was significantly higher in the post-course survey. Further, the Japanese PES students stated that their English ability and motivation for learning had improved. Some students commented that they had to work harder on their English after comparing their English level to their English-proficient IPLA classmates.

These results illustrate how this CLIL approach can fulfill the role of simultaneously combining foreign language learning, content subject learning, ICC, and intercultural learning. The students demonstrated an ability to interact and collaborate with students from different cultures in a multicultural and multilingual environment. Translanguaging was also present, enabling students to negotiate meaning and leading to both groups learning about aspects of their own cultures in relation to other cultures.

However, this study does have some limitations. For example, the results are based on student perceptions and confidence levels taken from pre- and post-course surveys. Objective measures of ability would be needed to better understand whether their changes in perception are reflected in changes in their ability. Further, the class size and data sample are relatively small, and the number of questions within the survey is limited. It would be interesting to see if similar results could be replicated consistently with other students who took the same course. Nevertheless, the findings discussed here help to demonstrate the potential of a dual-CLIL approach like this one for bringing different groups of students together to pursue different but compatible learning goals.

Understanding and explaining one's cultural perspective relative to different cultural viewpoints is essential for the development of ICC. Within rich CLIL environments, this can lead to an exploration of different cultural outlooks that can establish a relationship between students from various backgrounds, evident here through class content that produced diverse opinions. The CLIL pedagogical approach described here, based on the framework of the 4Cs of content, communication, cognition, and culture, can therefore help students critically evaluate and analyze class content cross-culturally from different perspectives. This relativizing of one's cultural perspective in addition to understanding foreign cultural perceptions is essential to intercultural education and developing intercultural competence.

Author Bio

Barry Kavanagh is an associate professor at Tohoku University, Japan where he also received his PhD. His research interests include CLIL, intercultural communication, bilingualism, and computer mediated communication. He is the Vice President of the J-CLIL pedagogy association and chair of the J-CLIL Tohoku chapter.

Appendix
Pre-Course and Post-Course Survey

The surveys were separated into PES and IPLA surveys. For the sake of brevity, the questions have been combined. PES students answered every question except #5, which was solely directed at the IPLA students. IPLA students answered questions 1, 4, and 5.

When the same Likert scale questions were given again in the post-course survey, each question was prefixed with, "Now that you have finished this course how would you rate…?" or "Now that you have finished this course how confident are you…?"

Q1. How would you rate your knowledge of karate?

1. Not knowledgeable at all
2. Slightly knowledgeable
3. Moderately knowledgeable
4. Knowledgeable
5. Very knowledgeable

Q2. How confident are you in explaining Japanese culture in English (including how different it is to other cultures) with the foreign exchange students?

1. Not confident at all
2. Slightly confident
3. Moderately confident
4. Confident
5. Very confident

Please give reasons for your choice

Q3. How confident are you in using your English to collaborate with foreigners in a multicultural classroom / environment?

1. Not confident at all
2. Slightly confident
3. Moderately confident
4. Confident
5. Very confident

Please give reasons for your choice

Q4. How confident are you in communicating and collaborating with your Japanese classmates in this class?

1. Not confident at all
2. Slightly confident
3. Moderately confident
4. Confident
5. Very confident

Please give reasons for your choice

Q5. How confident are you in discussing, analyzing, debating, explaining, and evaluating themes related to karate and Japanese culture?

1. Not confident at all
2. Slightly confident
3. Moderately confident
4. Confident
5. Very confident

Please give reasons for your choice

Open-ended question
(Given with the post-course survey for PES students only)

Q6. Did you improve your English / communication skills through the course content and by working and collaborating with IPLA students in this class?

4
Promoting Peer Collaboration to Develop Learner Autonomy: Examples from a Self-Access Center (SAC)

Dominique Vola Ambinintsoa and Satoko Watkins

In this chapter, we, two learning advisors (LAs) working at a Self-Access Center (SAC) at a university in Japan, share how we promote peer collaboration among our students through advising and nurturing learning communities. First, we introduce our context, including the SAC and its aims. Second, we discuss literature concerning the importance of promoting peer collaboration in language learning and in developing learner autonomy, including advising and the significance of collaborative learning. Third, we provide practical examples of literature and research-supported student-led peer collaborations, including student-to-student peer advising. Our context is a SAC, an environment outside the classroom. Therefore, the examples we share are easily adapted to other SACs. We also offer practical ideas and activities that can be implemented in English classrooms at the end of the chapter.

The Context

The SAC that this chapter focuses on is part of a private Japanese university of around 4,000 students. The university specializes in teaching foreign languages, other subjects related to languages (e.g., linguistics and international communication), and global studies. Our SAC provides students with a learning environment that accommodates their individual differences in terms of learning experiences, motivations, beliefs, and ideas (Mynard, 2012). It also enables them to develop and co-construct their knowledge within a community comprised of learners, teachers, and learning advisors (Mynard, 2012). It is a nurturing environment that helps students develop their learner autonomy and fosters their well-being (Kanda University of International Studies Self-Access Learning Center [KUIS SALC], 2020). To do this, our SAC offers advising services, including spoken and written advising, as well as opportunities for students to thrive in collaboration with others through learning communities.

WHY PROMOTE PEER COLLABORATION

Peer collaboration is necessary in language learning because it maximizes opportunities for language practice and interaction (Benson, 2011; Neumann & McDonough, 2015; Oxford, 2003; Palfreyman, 2018). Another reason not specific to language learning is the social nature of human beings; as Seligman (2011, p. 145) puts it, "Human beings [...] are ineluctably social, and it is our sociality that is our secret weapon." In the context of language learning, Seligman's statement can be related to peer collaboration in that such collaboration can increase learning motivation as it enforces relatedness and a sense of belonging, a basic human psychological need (Ryan & Deci, 2017). Feelings of being supported by peers are likely to influence learners' willingness to try (Dörnyei & Ushioda, 2021). Further, as highlighted by a study on Japanese students' beliefs about peer interaction and peer corrective feedback, "a collaborative classroom environment and positive social relationships between learners" are conducive to successful learning (Sato 2013, p. 61). The influence of peers on learners' mindsets and motivation is also explained by Murphey's (1998) *Near Peer Role Model* (NPRM). The model suggests that seeing and learning with peers who are "near" (e.g., in age, gender, social, or professional status), using English successfully can "change students' beliefs about risk-taking, making mistakes, and the importance of enjoying what they are studying" (Murphey, 1998, p. 201). Peer collaboration is thus a rich resource for practicing the language itself as well as for motivational and socio-cultural reasons. According to Mercer et al. (2018), the goal of language education is to foster linguistic and socio-cultural competence in students. The latter competence requires self-awareness, openness, and tolerance, which can be developed through peer collaboration and authentic communication. Peer collaboration plays an important role in the development of learner autonomy. The definition of learner autonomy by Dam et al. (1990, p. 102) as "the capacity and willingness to act independently and in cooperation with others, as a socially responsible person" as well as the recognition by learner autonomy researchers (e.g., Little et al., 2017; Murray, 2014; O'Leary, 2014; Palfreyman, 2018) that it has a social dimension, all indicate the significance of social competence in the development of learner autonomy. As Little (2007, p. 14) explains, the concept of learner autonomy has shifted from "a matter of learners doing things on their own" (a view from the early 1980s) to "a matter of learners doing things not necessary on their own but for themselves." Collaborating with others, seeking help, and providing assistance are crucial skills for individuals living in a society. Peer collaboration can aid learners in their personal and collective development, as suggested by Little et al. (2017).

ADVISING

Advising is a one-to-one interaction between a learner and an LA. The objective is to guide learners in reflecting on their learning processes. Through effective dialogue, learners can enhance their awareness of their goals, strategies, and available resources, as well as monitor their emotional states and evaluate their progress (Carson & Mynard, 2012; Kato & Mynard, 2016; Mozzon-McPherson & Tassinari, 2020). Advising, therefore, supports learners in developing their learner autonomy collaboratively through dialogue. In our case, we use *Intentional Reflective Dialogue* (IRD), which involves deliberate active listening as well as advising skills and strategies from counseling and life coaching, together with strategies developed for advising in language learning (Kato & Mynard, 2016). In IRD, the LA leads learners to better understand themselves and their learning situation, such as their strengths and weaknesses, what strategies work for them (or not), what their priority is, what the root of a given problem is, and what steps they can take to reach their goals. As Little (1999) explains:

> Learner autonomy cannot be externally imposed as a form of behavior modification; it must grow, quasi-organically, out of the ongoing encounter between the critical goals of the educational enterprise and the particularities of cultural context. (p. 16)

As LAs, we do not impose learner autonomy. Rather, we provide learners with a nurturing, reflective context to support them to take charge of their learning. In the end, however, despite LAs' implicit and explicit mediation, it is up to the learners to make decisions on what actions to take and when to deliver on those actions (Watkins, 2015).

In our SAC, we offer one-to-one spoken advising sessions that all students at the university can access. Students can book a 30-minute session with the LA of their choice or consult with one for up to 90 minutes at a drop-in desk, without the need for a reservation. There are no restrictions on the number of visits, and students may schedule appointments at their convenience. We also offer written feedback advising to students optionally enrolled in the SAC's self-directed learning courses. During these 15-week courses, students engage in reflection exercises concerning their language experiences, language goals, and learning skills, including motivation, time management, and energy management. They subsequently select resources and strategies that are relevant to their goals and individual learning needs. Next, they create and implement a learning plan. They are supported by an LA who gives weekly feedback that includes reflective questions and encouragement. Although the courses focus on the individuality of each student, they also include promoting peer interaction and collaboration through *Google Classroom* (Peeters & Mynard, 2019). Here students can ask each other questions, offer encouragement, as well as share goals, activities, strategies, and anything else related to the courses and their learning experiences. Such interactions remind students that though they may have different goals and work individually, they can support one another in their learning communities, both face-to-face and online.

One issue that our self-directed learners have is the tendency to "study" English without "using" what they have studied, often due to their teacher-directed educational backgrounds (Kushida, 2020) and lack of confidence speaking English (Curry, 2014; Watkins, 2015). Not using what they have studied negatively influences the effectiveness of their learning and their motivation. Through advising, our students often realize their need for social learning opportunities. Therefore, when advising, LAs also encourage students to join such opportunities when they are organized in the SAC. Moreover, LAs help students reflect on how peer collaboration has been beneficial to their learning and build their confidence to use English with others. Our belief, supported by seven years of experience in promoting peer advising and learning communities, is that peer collaboration facilitates the creation of diverse student communities and fosters a more accessible learning environment for all.

EXAMPLES OF PEER COLLABORATION

Here we introduce some literature and research-based practical examples of student-led peer collaboration: interest-based learning communities, tandem learning, and peer advising.

Interest-Based Learning Communities

Student learning communities promote student-centered learning while bringing coherence and connectedness to curricula. Institutions have formed communities (e.g., linked courses, project groups within a class, or students in the same dormitory) that positively impact student retention, deepen learning, increase respect for different cultures, and lead to greater civic contributions (Cox & Richlin, 2004; Lenning et al., 2013). Community-based learning has proven effective in EFL settings, enabling learners to use English in social contexts outside the classroom despite contextual constraints. Examples include an English learners' café and its virtual space in mainland China (Gao, 2007), peer-led conversation sessions at a SAC (Acuña González et al., 2015), and interest-based activities or communities at another SAC (Magno e Silva, 2019). Learner-led language learning communities have been observed to provide numerous benefits, such as fostering profound social relationships where students learn from each other in a judgment-free environment (Gao, 2007; Watkins, 2022), encouraging the belief that learning can take place outside the classroom while having fun, and promoting greater awareness of learners' purposes for learning English, such as communicating with people from other countries.

In our interest-based learning communities, students who have similar interests or goals meet regularly to learn with and from each other to practice autonomous language learning. Students organize about ten learning communities with three to 30 members each semester. Some are content-based (e.g., social issues, pop culture), some skill-based (e.g., digital arts, IELTS test-taking skills), while others focus on languages (e.g., casual English conversation, French conversation), but all use a language other than Japanese as a communication and learning tool. One remarkable feature of these communities is that the members, who are often assumed to have teacher-led learning histories (Egitim, 2021; Kushida, 2020; Sakata & Fukuda, 2018), autonomously participate and learn without a formal teacher and without receiving course credit for their work. According to *Self-Determination Theory* proposed by Ryan & Deci (2017), people's intrinsic motivation and well-being depend on the support of three psychological needs: autonomy, relatedness, and competence. Watkins (2022) analyzed the narratives of core members in these communities and found that they create a supportive environment that promotes learners' sense of autonomy, relatedness, and competence. Specifically, learners have the freedom to choose topics and content they are interested in, and decide how much time they devote to the community, fostering a sense of autonomy. Connections are made with students of various ages, majors, and English proficiency, promoting relatedness. In addition, learners improve their language skills and content knowledge, while contributing to the community and others' learning, developing a sense of competence. Notably, Hooper (2020) emphasizes the desire of community members to join imagined communities of English users that are accessible to students with different proficiency levels and encourage legitimate peripheral participation. These communities promote equal and reciprocal learner relationships, which provide a sense of relatedness among learners and create an accessible learning environment. This contrasts with traditional Japanese *senpai-kohai* (senior-junior) hierarchical-based relationships.

One of the approaches for creating communities that are more sustainable, accessible, and prosocial is to assist them to become *Communities of Practice* (CoP). Wenger et al. (2002) describe CoP as a social learning process for people who share strong motivational aspects (e.g., a common purpose, interests, and/or concerns) where the members exercise collaborative control over their learning and the organization of the community. This does not mean that CoPs only appreciate shared and collective knowledge; they also acknowledge each individual and their unique contributions. To promote individuality, Wenger et al. (2002) suggest leaders design communities that allow various levels of participation and fluid movement between the levels. According to Watkins (2022), leaders play an important role in these learner-led communities in enhancing the satisfaction of members' psychological need for autonomy, relatedness, and competence as well as promoting cohesion to enhance the quality of learning experiences (Gao, 2007). Watkins (2022) recommends the use of IRD to support community leaders in developing insights and promoting autonomy among members, rather than relying on a controlling leadership style. In addition, Watkins offers a course for leaders that teaches autonomy-supportive skills, such as advising techniques for creating more prosocial learning environments (Reeve, 2016). Like other self-directed learning courses offered by our SAC, the leaders work one-to-one with an LA and reflect on their leadership experiences while implementing newly learned theories and skills in their communities. See Watkins (2021) and Watkins & Hooper (2023) for the course details.

Tandem Learning

Tandem language learning offers two learners who may have different language and cultural backgrounds an opportunity to learn with and from each other. Little and Brammerts (1996) suggest two principles for successful tandem partnership: reciprocity (both learners giving equal support) and autonomy (learners taking responsibility for their own and their partner's learning). When learners develop an effective learning partnership, they gain various benefits. For example, learners can: (a) choose topics and content to suit their interests and needs, deciding when and how to learn (Little & Ushioda, 1998; Ushioda, 2000); (b) increase awareness of their own and their target languages (Appel, 1999); (c) build confidence in communicative skills through practicing in a comfortable, private environment (Pomino & Gil-Salom, 2016; Wakisaka, 2013); and (d) develop communicative competence, cross-cultural awareness, and learner autonomy (Lewis & Walker, 2003).

Our SAC offers two types of tandem learning support. The first consists of reservation-based sessions with international students enrolled at our university, which can be scheduled through our website. These international students volunteer time in the SAC for language and cultural exchange and to make new friends. The reservation can be a one-off 30-minute session (15 minutes in each of the pairs' proficient languages, usually English and Japanese), but we often see our students booking the same international students repeatedly for meetings in the SAC as their learning partnerships develop. The second is through introducing self-directed learners to English-speaking partners learning Japanese at universities overseas our school has connections with. In this case, the pairs schedule weekly meetings online over a semester. Our students are offered a self-directed learning course that integrates tandem learning into their individual learning plans.

While most research on tandem learning has examined classroom collaborations, our students who engaged in self-directed tandem learning reported experiencing the same benefits as documented in the previously reviewed literature. Further, some students have identified "learning how to learn" (e.g., learning to evaluate one's own speaking skills) as an additional benefit (Watkins, 2019). Moreover, as reflection is key to promoting the tandem learning principles of learner autonomy and reciprocity (Ushioda, 2000), encouraging IRD through advising and offering self-directed learning support (via a learning journaling along with LA feedback) is important to learners engaging in learning, promoting their reflection of the learning process, and sustaining the partnership over time (Watkins, 2019).

Peer Advising

Peer mentoring involves matching two learners of similar age and social position to provide each other with psychological and social support, in contrast to hierarchical mentoring, which pairs individuals with different social positions, such as learning advisor-student or teacher-student (Collier, 2017). In other words, peer mentors can be NPRM (Murphey, 1998) who can positively influence their mentees' learning beliefs, attitudes, and eventually learning achievement (Murphey et al., 2022). College learners often rely more on peers than on family as a source of social influence, as peers can provide role models and a sense of belonging, and can also help bridge formal learning in the classroom with informal learning outside of it (Newton & Ender, 2000).

The literature on peer mentoring suggests that successful peer mentor (more experienced learners) and mentee (less experienced learners) interactions benefit both parties. The mentorship helps the mentees adjust to campus, become more involved in school activities, and reduce dropout rates (Colvin & Ashman, 2010). Mentors find the experience rewarding and improve their own learning through reapplying concepts they have already learned (Colvin & Ashman, 2010). In the field of language education, Kuwabara et al. (2020) explain that their peer mentors used their personal experiences as a basis in mentoring sessions and recommend learning activities they had practiced, such as joining a language lab, to their mentees. When the peer mentors feel their personal experiences are not sufficient, they try new activities or strategies to see whether they can recommend them to their mentees (Kuwabara et al., 2020). Additionally, through reciprocal interactions, mentors and mentees can develop learner autonomy through enhanced responsibilities, increasing confidence and motivation, and improving their self-directed learning skills (Kao, 2012).

In our SAC, through a program we call *peer advising*, our advisees/mentees make appointments with peer advisors/mentors for a 30-minute meeting to receive emotional and learning support. Although we have full-time learning advisors working in our SAC, the value of hiring and training students as peer advisors because of the reciprocal learner benefits described previously is undeniable. Given that our peer advisors work in the SAC, their active engagement and promotion of its services are crucial. Therefore, two qualities that we look for in peer advisors are (a) being active users of the SAC and (b) having completed at least one of our self-directed learning courses. We also have them try various SAC resources during their training to expand their experiences and basis for their advising (see Curry & Watkins, 2016 for details on peer advisor qualities and training contents). Additionally, we encourage peer advisors to plan events in the SAC, and they are also invited to assist in workshops and class visits led by LAs. Peer advisors are more approachable than teachers or professional advisors for students who lack confidence in their learning, as noted by Kao (2012). Peer advisor-led activities enable us to reach students who might not otherwise be engaged, while also promoting student ownership of the SAC. Although peer advisors do not replace LAs, they play an invaluable complementary role.

Summary of Peer Collaboration Examples

Table 1 summarizes examples of peer collaboration, including key features, key facilitators and roles, and how they promote learner autonomy.

Table 1

Summary of Peer Collaboration Examples

	Advising	Peer collaboration		
		Internet-based learning communities	Tandem learning	Peer advising
Key facilitators/ roles	Learning advisors	Student leaders	International students	Peer advisors/ mentors
Key features	• Professional • One to one • IRD • Learning support • Affective support	• NPRM • CoP • Shared interests and goals • Can use language outside the classroom	• NPRM • CoP • Language & cultural exchange • Can use language outside the classroom	• NPRM • One to one • IRD • Learning support • Affective support
Promoting learner autonomy by...	• Promoting reflection • Introducing self-directed learning skills	• Student-led social learning with other learners • Empowerment though using language for their own goals	• Reciprocal learning relationship • Empowerment though using language for their own goals	• Reciprocal learning relationship • Promoting reflection • Introducing self-directed learning skills

AFFORDANCES FOR DEVELOPING LEARNING COMMUNITIES BEYOND THE CLASSROOM

We previously shared examples of student-led peer collaboration that are promoted in our SAC. However, it is not always easy for learners to initiate something new. Fostering peer collaboration opportunities often takes time and requires affordances. To create social language learning opportunities outside the classroom, Murray and Fujishima (2013) suggest seven affordances for developing communities of learners: (a) classes, (b) social networking, (c) intercultural exchange, (d) information, (e) learning support, (f) talking about learning, and (g) personal freedom.

In our SAC, peer advisors and learning communities occasionally offer workshops and events that function as classes and social networking opportunities. Moreover, our students state that the benefits of participating in peer collaboration activities include four of the affordances: social networking, intercultural exchange, receiving (and offering) learning support from other learners, and sharing concerns about their learning experiences (Watkins, 2019; 2022). These are further enhanced through advising intervention, such as assisting learning leaders to be autonomy-supportive.

Personal freedom is key to peer collaborations in our SAC, as it allows learners to decide when and how much to participate in activities, for both participants and organizers alike. We respect leaders' autonomy and promote their sense of ownership; they create the communities and decide how they should be organized and how much time and energy they devote to them (Hooper & Watkins, 2023).

Despite the formation of communities in the SAC, many learners may not participate due to busy schedules and a lack of motivation for extracurricular activities. Additionally, Kushida (2020) notes that learners may be deterred from entering the SAC and participating in its activities due to a lack of awareness about the importance of practicing language skills outside of class (LeBane et al., 2016) and anxiety about their language proficiency (Fujimoto, 2016). Thus, LAs support community leaders by sharing information about the communities to other students and faculty. We help with promotion through email, posters, the SAC website, SNS, and verbal invitations in our advising sessions, courses, or informal meetings with students. When we find students interested in student-led activities, we introduce them to leaders so the leaders can personally invite them. We promote our SAC by emphasizing that all students are welcome to join, regardless of their language proficiency. We also reassure students that our learning community leaders understand and accommodate students with different levels of proficiency. For instance, the French learning community offers monthly sessions for beginners, where leaders introduce basic vocabulary to ensure inclusion for all levels of students.

Implications for Educators

This chapter has focused on examples of peer collaboration and learning communities at our SAC. We hope these descriptions are helpful to educators working in SACs to promote learner autonomy through interdependence. Recognizing that not all schools have SACs and that not all SACs have staff to organize peer advising or support students in creating learning communities, we aim to offer guidance to all educators on how to facilitate peer collaboration in the classroom, whether you are an English teacher, class tutor, or lecturer.

Building effective learning communities in the classroom often begins by learners learning about who their classmates are and their interests. This develops an inclusive classroom that promotes understanding and respect as well as establishes their identities (Sanger & Gleason, 2020). In an inclusive classroom, learners are encouraged to have open conversations and recognize their commonalities and differences (Marks & DeWitt, 2020). For instance, the *Personal Identity Wheel* activity (Pabdoo, n.d.) has students identify and share their shared skills and hobbies and list adjectives to describe themselves. Through it, they can find common ground with peers and build communities. Also, it is common in English classrooms at the beginning of the academic year to ask learners about their interests as an ice-breaking activity. Our suggestion is to follow up on those activities by giving learners opportunities to meet others who share similar interests, building in-class communities. Some practical examples of activities they can do are to (a) talk about topics of interest among in-class communities (e.g., news, updates, activities related to their interests) to practice speaking; (b) report about news, updates, or activities to other communities through presentations or informal talks; (c) report about interests collaboratively in writing; (d) choose their own topics for a class project; and/or (e) teach others about their interests (which can include language skills, such as vocabulary). The existence of communities inside the classroom enables students to maintain motivation through feelings of ownership of the class and a sense of belonging (Murphy, 2014). Learner autonomy is likely to develop as they can control what they learn. Also, dealing with student interests is likely to motivate them to learn (McLoughlin, 2020; Mynard & McLoughlin, 2020; Renninger & Hidi, 2016). Moreover, learners will feel that they can contribute to the class and have knowledge to share with others. Little et al. (2017) argue that every learner has areas of expertise and areas of novice regardless of their age and language proficiency. Learner expertise in the language classroom can benefit everyone by improving language learning, motivation, and autonomy. Even beginner language learners and young children can benefit from this approach (Little et al., 2017).

Although we do not present classroom-based studies showing the effectiveness of these suggestions, in advising sessions and our self-directed learning courses, we always ask about learners' interests, guide them to elaborate and connect these with their learning, and encourage them to work with peers who have similar interests. We also encourage them to continue working together outside the classroom. This has resulted in some new learning communities, such as one built around IELTS practice.

In addition, we promote IRD amongst peers in class, such as by having learners reflectively discuss their learning. For example, some LAs and English teachers collaboratively conduct two or three in-class reflective sessions per semester. Working in small groups, students reflect on their language learning struggles and successes, such as improvements in their motivation. They are encouraged to listen to one another, ask further questions to prompt deeper reflection, and discuss how to overcome their struggles. This exemplifies the principle of tandem learning partnerships, where students are responsible for their partners' learning as well as their own. To assist them, they are given example expressions such as those provided in Ambinintsoa & MacDonald (forthcoming):

- Tell me more about your struggles.
- Why do you think … is difficult for you?
- Well done on…
- Why is this success important for you?
- How did you overcome…?

- What do you think you can do to…?

Apart from reflecting on struggles and successes once or twice each semester, students are also encouraged to share their previous learning experiences, what learning strategies they use (e.g., "What do you do to learn new words?" or "What do you do when you don't understand a text?"), and what they found most useful from what they learned (e.g., new vocabulary, new learning strategies, and/or advice from peers, teachers, or others). By engaging in group reflective sessions, students not only gain a deeper understanding of themselves as learners but also practice active listening skills, offer advice, and learn from one another. Following each session, students individually reflect on what they learned, emphasizing the most salient points. These post-session reflections not only enhance students' awareness of the importance of reflective learning but also foster prosocial behaviors that contribute to others' learning.

Such prosocial behaviors and peer reflection can be enhanced through tools such as learning journals. For instance, using *Action Logs*, students rate class activities as useful, interesting, and difficult using a Likert scale and then evaluate themselves as an ideal classmate for others based on the question of, "What could your classmates do to help you learn better and enjoy your classes better?" (Murphey, 2021b, p. 44). The teacher responds weekly to acknowledge their feelings and promote learner agency (Murphey, 2021b). Such written dialogue exchange can enhance learner reflections on how they learn, what they learn, and who they learn with. In addition to Action Logs, some samples of learning journals used for the self-directed courses in our institution are accessible at *thesalc.weebly.com* (KUIS SALC Modules, n.d.). The website also includes tools that enable student reflection on motivation, confidence, anxiety, and time management. These materials can be adapted to students' proficiency levels and learning contexts.

Conclusion

In this chapter, we highlighted the importance of peer collaboration in language learning, giving examples of student-led peer collaboration in our SAC and how we support such collaboration. We also offered ideas to help students build learning communities in classroom contexts. We believe that, in re-envisioning language teaching and learning, our role as educators is to provide students with opportunities and affordances for peer collaboration and to reflect on their collaborative experiences. Students should be the owners of the learning communities they create.

Author Bios

Dominique Vola Ambinintsoa is a learning advisor, lecturer, and graduate school instructor at Kanda University of International Studies in Chiba, Japan. She holds a PhD in applied linguistics from Victoria University of Wellington and a Master of Education in TESOL from the State University of New York at Buffalo. She is a co-managing editor of the *Research Institute for Learner Autonomy Education's Relay Journal*. Her research interests include learner autonomy, advising in language learning, and positive psychology in education.

Satoko Watkins is a Principal Learning Advisor and Associate Professor in the *Self-Access Learning Centre* at Kanda University of International Studies, Japan. Her research focuses on learner autonomy, advising, self-directed language learning, learning communities, and inclusive practice. In her center, she has developed several student-led prosocial learning communities and programs.

5
L2 Identity Construction Through Teletandem Learning

Kie Yamamoto

Over the last few decades, there has been a growing interest worldwide in implementing *telecollaboration*, a form of internet-mediated intercultural foreign language education (Belz & Thorne, 2006) to develop learners' foreign language skills and intercultural competences via online interactions. Since early 2020, due to the COVID-19 pandemic, institutions of higher education have attempted to tackle problems with the absence of international student mobility by promoting online peer learning programmes (O'Dowd, 2021). The learning outcomes of telecollaboration include attainment of linguistic improvement, intercultural awareness, critical thinking, and digital competences (O'Dowd & Dooley, 2020). Of the various forms of telecollaboration, *teletandem* is specifically aimed at nurturing social aspects of language learning through reciprocal and autonomous learning.

The main body of research on teletandem has investigated L2 learners' linguistic and intercultural competences, following the major research on other forms of telecollaboration. However, participants' selves, specifically their identity construction in relation to others in the virtual context, have yet to be broadly discussed in teletandem research. This study draws on the narrative accounts of two Japanese female first-year university students' teletandem experiences with learners of Japanese in the United States. This qualitative research expands the concepts of teletandem learning from a socially informed approach, shedding light on changes in the focal students' L2 identities and their participation in their new community. Results from this study may also contribute to the adoption of teletandem as an opportunity to build foreign language learners' positive L2 selves, which can potentially contribute to accelerating their growing self-confidence and fostering engagement in learning the target language. The findings also contribute to a better understanding of teletandem learning as an opportunity for participants to invest in new selves and engage in a virtual community of practice, where they can negotiate and reconstruct their identities.

THEORETICAL BACKGROUND OF TELETANDEM LEARNING

For the last decade, telecollaboration, which is also known as online intercultural exchange (Lewis & O'Dowd, 2016), has become a popular pedagogical activity that enhances intercultural communication and online collaborative language learning. It has been implemented in various forms worldwide, including virtual exchange, *collaborative online intercultural learning* (COIL), *e-tandem*, or teletandem. Virtual exchange is widely acknowledged among institutions of higher education in EU countries, while COIL is more commonly used in the United States (Lewis & O'Dowd, 2016). Those two forms of online learning have a greater emphasis on the development of cultural awareness and intercultural communicative competence (O'Dowd, 2016) through collaborative exercises that allow participants to stay in their home countries. On the other hand, teletandem is a form of foreign language learning in which pairs of learners with different mother tongues work together to mutually learn their target languages using video-conferencing systems.

Teletandem, which originates from tandem learning, draws on two interrelated principles: reciprocity and learner autonomy. Reciprocity involves learners dedicating themselves to learning their target language while also supporting their partner's language learning process. Little and Brammerts (1996) highlight the importance of socially structured partnerships in language learning, where learners take an interest in their partner's success and are considerate of their comprehension of the target language. Since both participants in a pair play expert and novice roles, tandem learning allows them to commit themselves to the learning process with "a greater sensitivity, patience, and understanding" (Little & Brammerts, 1996, p. 14). The second principle, learner autonomy, refers to the participants' responsibilities and willingness to take charge of their own learning. The prominence of learner autonomy has been discussed (e.g., Benson, 2001; Kato & Mynard, 2016; Little, 2001; Ushioda, 2011) as a crucial factor in successful foreign language learning. By increasing their self-awareness of motives, setting goals and needs in the target language, and developing learning strategies, language learners become more reflective and autonomous in pursuing their language learning goals.

In addition, separation of language use during the teletandem session, originally suggested by Brammerts (1996), has also been advocated to ensure the effectiveness of tandem learning. While the principle of tandem learning traditionally involves two native speakers of different languages learning each other's first languages, recent studies (Leone, 2014; Leone & Telles, 2016; Tardieu & Horgues, 2020; Woodin, 2020) emphasize the importance of considering the plurilingual dimensions of language learning and critique the traditional notion of linguistic nativeness. The definition of mother tongue or native language, as Wei (2018, p. 15) explains, derives from "artificial and ideological divides"; hence, the stress on the separation of language in teletandem might limit learners' language choice and use. In response to the plurilingual movement, a growing number of (tele)tandem programmes have begun to adopt more socially informed linguistic policies, including using English as a lingua franca and translanguaging in their pedagogical approaches (e.g., Benoit & Lomicka, 2020; McAllister & Narcy-Combes, 2020). Although each principle in the initial definition of tandem learning is still prominent in current teletandem programmes worldwide, their policies and practices have been evolving to situate sociocultural as well as linguistic diversity among language learners in the centre of the learning process.

Social-Constructivist Perspective on Language Learner Identities in Online Contexts

This study draws on a social-constructivist perspective, which informs the inquiry into Japanese English learners' identity construction through a teletandem learning experience. The social-constructivist view conceives learning as constructed through interaction with others; thus, it is seen as a socially ongoing process (e.g., Bandura, 1975; Lave & Wenger, 1991; Lantolf, 2000; Wenger, 1998; Wenger-Trayner et al., 2014) rather than the static result of cognitive processing. Lave and Wenger (1991) and Wenger's (1998) theoretical framework of *community of practice* is a widely acknowledged theoretical framework that offers a comprehensive view of learning as participation in a socially-formed community. The social-constructivist view also defines identity as a situated and subjective construct, taking account of the social, cultural, and temporal context. The construction of identity is a dynamic and discursive process that entails continuous changes in how individuals relate themselves to the physical and mental communities and groups they belong to. Furthermore, the social-constructivist view suggests that this relation, or *positioning* (Davies & Harré, 1990), informs the way an individual constructs their self-identity. Thus, the social-constructivist view provides a comprehensive scope for analysing and interpreting the complexity of L2 learner identities in the arena of applied linguistics (Barkhuizen, 2013, 2017; DePalma, 2008; Gu, 2013; Miyahara, 2015; Morita, 2002; Norton, 2001, Pavlenko, 2002, 2007; Yamamoto, 2019; Yang & Yi, 2017).

In recent years, a growing number of studies have revealed the complexity of L2 learner identity construction and its impact on the language acquisition process in online contexts. Thorne and Black (2011) posit that online communication often captures L2 learners' fluid identities, as the virtual space allows them to negotiate and present their imagined selves, which may not exist in their offline lives, for example through choosing their preferred pseudonym, gender, social status, or avatar. Lewis and O'Dowd (2016) also argue that those who often participate in online language learning may feel a stronger affiliation to their virtual communities than they do to offline ones. Yang and Yi (2017) conducted an illustrative study on the construction of L2 learner identity in an online context. The study focused on pairs of adult Korean and Korean-American learners who participated in teletandem experiences using various mediational tools, such as online chats and blogging. The researchers analyzed how the learners negotiated their identities during these experiences. Their study suggests that dual roles as novice and expert in their tandem learning enabled the participants to embrace L2 learning struggles and engage in a community of teletandem learners. It also encouraged further investment in their target language learning, which also led to confident L2 learner identities.

While multimodality in online communication between language learners allows for a broad range of self-representation, *video-mediated environment* (VME) is often seen as a mere replication of face-to-face communication as it allows learners to present their physical selves virtually. However, recent studies (e.g., Tudini & Liddicoat, 2017; Rusk & Pörn, 2019) highlight L2 learners' challenges in VME meaning-making, including the delay in response time or lack of eye gaze potentially causing disruptions or misunderstanding among participants. According to Debras (2020), VME can make people more self-conscious because they see themselves on the screen while they interact. This is different from face-to-face communication, where people do not see themselves in real time. Debras calls this effect *polyfocality*, meaning that people may be more focused on their self-image than on the conversation itself. This can be distracting and take away from the quality of the communication. From these perspectives, it is arguable that VMEs, including teletandem, offer uniquely complex social practice for identity construction compared to face-to-face communication.

As discussed, online communication plays a crucial role in L2 learning as it provides a platform for learners to negotiate and construct multiple identities. This process not only draws on their social dimensions but also on the unique nature of technology-mediated interactions. This study focuses on L2 learners' participation in a new community of practice in teletandem learning, which may present a more complex environment, especially when virtual representations in video-conferencing systems are involved. The study aims to investigate the learners' identity shifts resulting from their involvement in this community, taking into account the various constructs involved.

Research Questions & Context

The central purpose of this study is to understand how female Japanese university students negotiate and structure their L2 identities through online interactions in teletandem learning. Based on this, this study addresses the following research questions:

1. What has led the research participants to invest in teletandem learning?
2. How do the research participants' identities shift throughout the teletandem sessions?
3. To what extent does their participation in teletandem learning influence their L2 self-perceptions?

Despite the growing popularity of teletandem and telecollaborative learning, few qualitative studies have explored the narrative accounts of Japanese university students regarding their experiences with these approaches. As such, this study aims to shed light on the specific challenges faced by these learners and their motivations for investing in teletandem learning, thus providing a more comprehensive understanding of the topic.

A Teletandem Programme Between Two Universities

The teletandem programme was established in October 2020 between Sakura University located in Chiba prefecture, Japan and ABC University (both pseudonyms) in Illinois, the United States. Due to the COVID-19 pandemic, both institutions were seeking opportunities to provide their students with foreign language learning opportunities using the video-conferencing software *Zoom*. In this study, the first and second periods of the programme between October 2020 and March

2021 were selected for data collection. While the students at ABC University participated in the teletandem programme as part of their curriculum, the students at Sakura University joined it as an extracurricular activity. A total of 15 students from ABC University and 14 from Sakura University participated in the first period of the programme. In the second period, the study included the participation of 15 and 16 students, respectively. The participants from Sakura University had estimated CEFR English proficiency levels ranging from A1 to B1. Meanwhile, the participants from ABC University were enrolled in a Japanese language class. Among the Sakura University participants, ten were second-year students, while the rest were first-year students.

Each period of the teletandem programme consisted of three sessions over the course of six to seven weeks. Each session offered the participants 20 minutes each of target language use. All of the students joined a single Zoom meeting at the beginning of the session, were allocated into pairs randomly, then moved into breakout rooms. They were reminded repeatedly of the separation of language and the time to switch the target language before each session began. After each session, the Sakura University students were asked to write a reflection on their learning experience using *Google Forms*.

METHODOLOGY

Narrative Inquiry

A narrative inquiry approach was employed as it allows researchers to "capture the nature and meaning of experiences that are difficult to observe directly and are best understood from the perspective of those who experience them" (Barkhuizen et al., 2014, p. 8). Previous narrative research studies in applied linguistics (e.g., Barkhuizen, 2017; Early & Norton, 2013; Miyahara, 2015; Rugen, 2013; Yamamoto, 2019) investigated L2 learning or teaching experiences to unfold the intricate process of how L2 learners make sense of themselves while using the target language in relation to a particular sociocultural and temporal context. Narrative inquiry is a valuable tool for investigating the imagination of narrators, including their desires for change. This approach involves cognitive activities that preserve memories, prompt reflections, connect past and present experiences, and assist narrators in envisioning their future (Kramp, 2004). In this study, the research participants share similarities in their socioeducational backgrounds to a certain extent, given that they were born, raised, and educated in the Japanese education system. This study aims to unpack the participants' prior language learning experiences and their views on teletandem as an opportunity for investing in online interactions. The temporal context of this study is also unique due to COVID-19, which suspended most face-to-face interactions in higher education in Japan from 2020. Hence, the narrative of each participant signifies her meaning-making of online interactions with a geographically distanced learner of Japanese during the worldwide pandemic.

Researcher Positionality

In narrative research, researcher positionality plays a major role in the meaning-making process of narratives. A narrative must be understood while considering "the relationship between the storyteller and the interlocutor" (Pavlenko, 2002, p. 214). Hence, the complexity of how the narrative is constructed needs to be thoroughly discussed. Simultaneously, narrative inquiry rests on the researchers' interpretive work (Atkinson, 2005; McKinley, 2015; Miyahara, 2015; Morita, 2002); hence, my own positionality significantly impacts this study. In this research context, I played multiple roles. First, I was the teacher of an English class in which the two research participants were enrolled. In addition, I was also the teletandem programme facilitator at Sakura University. Although the teletandem programme itself was an extracurricular activity, the participants recognised me as a *sensei* (teacher) rather than a facilitator. Simultaneously, I tried to position myself as an "insider" to my research participants, as I share a similar socioeducational background and English learning experience with them. Managing those multiple roles was challenging, especially in my effort to reduce researcher-researchee proximity and lessen the "rigid hierarchical power structure"

(Morita, 2002, p. 71) between the teacher-student relationship in an institutional context.

Research Participants

This teletandem study draws on a larger qualitative investigation of Japanese female university students selected from the group of Sakura University students. For the current study, two of those who shared contrastive learning experiences, Tomo and Hana (pseudonyms), are presented. They enrolled as English Communication majors at Sakura University in April 2020. Due to the COVID-19 pandemic, they had primarily been taking courses online since graduating from high school. Sakura offered most of its courses asynchronously for the first semester in 2020; thus, students, including the research participants, had limited access to social interaction in their education during that period. They all voluntarily signed up for the teletandem programme and participated for three consecutive periods.

Data Collection

This study used narrative interviews as its primary data. While narrative interviewing often takes place in an unstructured form, I took Mueller's (2019) episodic narrative interview approach, which is designed to be experience-centered by formulating a set of questions related to specific episodes that a researcher intends to investigate. As this study focuses on "particular phenomena" (Mueller, 2019, p. 2), the research participants' experiences in teletandem learning, this approach was helpful to guide their storytelling during the interviews while allowing them to go back to different spatiotemporal settings in their lives. Along with the narrative interviews, the reflections written by each participant after each teletandem session were also used as supplementary data. The written items were especially helpful when asking the participants to retrospectively reflect during the interviews. Each interview mainly consisted of three questions about English learning experiences prior to university, decision making in joining the teletandem programme, and perceived changes after joining. All of the interviews were conducted via Zoom following the research context's institutional policy regarding conducting research under the COVID-19 pandemic. Japanese was used as the main language of communication; hence, once transcription was complete, I translated it into English. The transcription also included nonverbal materials from each interview such as chuckles or long pauses, as suggested by Seidman (2006).

Data Analysis

As narrative researchers suggest, narrative data analysis should be iterative, recursive, and emergent (Barkhuizen et al., 2014; Gu, 2013; Miyahara, 2015). In this study, the process of data analysis consisted of three stages and followed Seidman's (2006) inductive qualitative data analysis approach. First, I transcribed each interview and then reread the transcripts multiple times, adding my preliminary comments in areas that seemed significant to the participants' past language learning, their teletandem session experiences, and their personal development. I paid special attention to their emotional commentaries, as these are often generated through social interaction (Prior, 2015). By analyzing emotions such as disappointment, frustration, and excitement, I gained insights into how each participant positioned themselves in relation to others. As Seidman (2006, p. 119) suggests, I opted to avoid labelling or categorising at this stage in order to read transcripts with "an open attitude, seeking what emerges as important and of interest from the text." Also, I adapted Seidman's (2006) means of creating profiles to reduce each interview text. These profiles allow researchers to:

> find and display coherence in the constitutive events of a participant's experience, to share the coherence the participant has expressed, and to link the individual's experience to the social and organisational context within which he or she operates. (p. 122)

The profile, in this sense, is not necessarily comprised of the objective facts, as it rests on the storytelling conveyed by a narrator. It can be understood as narrative truths, which are "evidence for personal meaning, not for the actual occurrence of the events reported in the stories" (Polkinghorne, 2007, p. 479), and thus do not necessarily reflect what exactly happened in the actual interactions. After the first rereading process was complete, I selected the parts that highlighted each participant's emotional dynamics and followed the same step again with "a more demanding eye" (Polkinghorne, 2007, p. 123). When necessary, I went back to the original recording and checked the tone of their voices, the length of pauses, and the interlocutor's (my) responses to their stories. Once each participant profile was generated, I tried rereading and highlighting the positioning of each narrator in relation to others in the narrative. This approach was adapted from Bamberg's (1997) narrative positioning analysis, which allows researchers to uncover: (a) sameness/difference, (b) agentive/recipient, and (c) constancy/change expressed in identity construction. The positioning analysis enabled me to make sense of each participant's interchangeable perception of herself as well as others. In the next section, a selected story for positioning analysis is presented in each participant's case. Drawing on the data retrieved in this stage, I built several interpretive thematic categories, including the impact of their experience on their selves, developing confident selves in teletandem learning, gaining membership in the teletandem community, and identity negotiations.

Findings

To provide readers with a better understanding of Japanese female students' identity construction and their learning experiences in a teletandem context, I present two illustrative cases of female Japanese learners: Tomo and Hana. Each analysis begins with a profile, which was compiled from the interview transcription. Next, selected excerpts from each interview are presented. Specific Japanese expressions that they emotionally emphasised are included in brackets to preserve their nuance in Japanese.

Tomo

Prior to university, Tomo devoted herself to the school's brass band club, which was pretty much "everything [*subete*]" in her high school life. Even though she has graduated, she still visited her high school and got involved with supporting current brass band members. English lessons in her high school were "boring and less communicative," (Tomo, interview) as the lessons primarily forced her to learn grammar and vocabulary to pass the university entrance exams. Although she did not enjoy such exam-focused English learning, Tomo was attracted by English music shared by her teacher at the beginning of each lesson. These encounters with authentic English music encouraged her to pursue an English communication degree at university. However, the results of the university entrance exams were devastating. Despite her desire to focus on learning English, she failed to be accepted into any of the programmes she had applied to other than Sakura University. It was an emotionally "tough [*tsurai*]" experience for Tomo, yet her parents encouraged her to do her best at a place where she would get a chance to focus on learning English.

When Tomo saw an ad for the teletandem programme, she immediately signed up for it, hoping to turn the opportunity into "a chance to overcome my lack of confidence even a little." She also pushed herself towards the chance as "everything else (she was interested in) disappeared [*zenbu nakunatta*] because of Covid-19."

One of the significant stories in Tomo's interview was about how she strategically built successful interaction with her partners online. She described the first teletandem session as "catastrophic [*zen-zen dame*]" since the entire conversation ended up being dull due to her lack of vocabulary and conversation topics. However, she also later came up with her own strategies to build smooth communication with her teletandem partner:

Tomo Excerpt 1

> I started making a list of questions and topics on a sticky note and put it next to me whenever I joined the session, so that I could be mentally prepared and more supportive to my partner. When my partner looks nervous, I can create a non-threatening atmosphere and I can encourage them to speak up. That's something I like about myself now [*chuckle*].

Tomo also explained how she actively supported her partner while constructing her ideal self. In this excerpt, she illustrated the tactical use of written communication and delayed responses, taking advantage of the affordances of online interactions.

Tomo Excerpt 2

> Neither of us were very good at our target languages. My partner asked me questions in English, and I looked up the related words in the dictionary, or if I came up with the answer, I responded to her in English while writing my response in the chat box to make them clearer. So rather than being harsh and direct, I showed the atmosphere in which we were also trying to find those answers together.

Toward the end of the interview, a significant positioning appeared in her narrative. She used the pronoun "we" to describe the participants of the teletandem programme, including herself as part of them, and explained what they share as members of the community:

Tomo Excerpt 3

> By doing so (showing a supportive atmosphere), I can send the message "I am not perfect either. Let's learn together!" The best part of teletandem is that *we* [*minna*] are all learners. There is no need to be afraid of making mistakes and asking questions.

In this story, Tomo was mainly describing how she negotiated her identity as a supportive teletandem partner and how the experience enabled her to imagine herself as a legitimate member in the teletandem community. After the first "catastrophic" conversation, she strategically took advantage of the affordances of online interaction by, for example, putting a sticky note next to her where her partner wouldn't see it to be more confident. Additionally, she highlighted the experience of supporting her partner in a "non-threatening" atmosphere, describing the detailed online communicative tactics, such as using a chat box for responses and taking time to respond when helping her partner. The positioning of her teletandem partner in her story, which was narrated in first-person plural, also evinces that she started seeing her partner as a fellow foreign language learner rather than an English language expert. This can also be interpreted as an indicator that reciprocity helped her imagine the tandem community as a safe social space, where mutual support is necessary.

Hana

Hana's previous learning experience was mostly associated with excitement for learning English. During her high school years, she participated in a school programme that gave her the opportunity to spend a week in Canada. This experience ignited a strong desire to master the English language. Despite her short stay, she found communicating with her host family in English both challenging and exciting. Since then, Hana saw herself as a person who is "really into foreign cultures" [*gaikoku kabure*]. Learning about other cultures, listening to foreign music, and watching foreign TV dramas made her feel as if she had been in a different country. Besides her dedication to learning foreign cultures, she believed she could be more active and felt confident when she spoke English as opposed to her Japanese-speaking self, who was "shy and not talkative at all."

Hana was determined to major in English communication since she was a second-year student in high school. Thus, she chose Sakura University as her first choice, using the non-exam *suisen nyushi* admission system, which is an examination for selected candidates recommended by their high school principals. Although she wanted to make friends and learn English on campus, remote learning was not a challenge for her. In fact, aside from her schoolwork, she actively joined various online meetups organised by international groups to seek opportunities to speak English during the pandemic. Her desire to join the teletandem programme was derived from her willingness to "communicate with native English speakers and make English-speaking friends." In her written reflections during the first period of the teletandem programme, she described in detail how she learned new phrases and words from her partners, which signaled her satisfaction with the learning experience.

Despite Hana's positive past experiences as well as her ongoing English learning, during the interview, when the topic moved onto the second teletandem period, her tone of voice clearly changed. She started storytelling the emotional challenges she experienced while speaking with the highly proficient Japanese learners, who appeared as the central characters in the story. This excerpt clearly presents how the positioning of herself against her teletandem partners changed after the second period began:

Hana Excerpt 1

> Umm… [*long pause*] I paired up with higher-level students this period I feel. They made no Japanese mistakes, while I kept saying, "sorry?" or "Could you say that again?" The students I talked with in the first period weren't perfect so *we* [*otagai ni*] were both learning so I didn't really care about my mistakes. This time [in the second period], I was really disappointed with my own English skill. I thought I would be getting better at communicating in English, but… [*long pause*] I lost my confidence. I asked them to repeat too much because I really couldn't understand what they were saying.

Hana's disappointment was also expressed in her written reflections during the second period. To encourage further reflection, I asked for more details about the situation after referring to her comments. Specifically, when I asked if she had requested that they slow down, she replied:

Hana Excerpt 2

> I did, and I think they did, but I still didn't fully understand what they said. Then I felt I was embarrassing myself by asking [for clarification] too much. They were kind, but I was just... devastated [*dame*]. I am really disappointed with myself right now. I just feel lost...maybe my English has become worse. I am not even sure if I should continue teletandem.

When I asked Hana how she felt about her progress in learning English since the start of the academic year and whether she felt like she was regressing, she responded:

Hana Excerpt 3

> Hmm...[*long pause*] I think I'm definitely better at English compared to the beginning of April [2020] but I am frustrated. I am frustrated at myself... I want to understand what my partners say without asking questions. What should I do?

The self-reflections in these excerpts show how negative emotions such as anxiety and embarrassment impacted Hana's self-perception. From her description "we were both learning" in the first excerpt, it can be inferred that she appreciated the reciprocal dimension of the teletandem learning by positioning her partners as peers. On the other hand, those who she worked with during the second period appeared intimidating given their highly proficient Japanese. This experience forced her to position herself as a novice as opposed to expert Japanese learners. At the same time, when asked about her growth as an English learner, she shared her frustration of not reaching her imagined self rather than blaming her partners for the unsuccessful sessions. Looking back at Hana's profile, it's worth noting that she had a clear vision of herself as a proficient English speaker. She believed that speaking

English would empower her to be more confident and express her ideas. In contrast to Tomo, Hana's storytelling focused on her struggle to reconcile her ideal self with reality, which made her feel like she was on the margins of the teletandem learner community. She felt that other learners were better than her at acquiring the language.

Discussion

Based on the research findings, I will now explicitly address my three main research questions and highlight the recurrent themes that emerged from the analysis of the individual narratives. The first research question was: "What has led the research participants to invest in teletandem learning?" Considering the temporal context, as both participants indicated, teletandem was an attractive opportunity as it allowed them to expand their social networks and friendships beyond Japan at a time when physical social distancing was strongly encouraged. Since asynchronous classrooms were mainly adopted in their institution, telecollaboration itself can be seen as a motivational factor. Moreover, the detailed narrative analysis of each participant case reveals teletandem learning was more than just for language acquisition. Rather, the transformation into confident selves seemed a potent driving force for investing in the new learning opportunity. Prior to university education, most Japanese high school students, including Tomo, are exposed to a high-stakes exam system for university entrance. In Japan, the entrance exam [*juken*] system forces students and their parents to financially and mentally invest in this once-in-a-lifetime opportunity to gain social capital. It is also notoriously known as an "examination hell" (Okada, 2012; McVeigh, 2002) and has been criticised as undermining students' mental wellbeing, self-efficacy, and desire to learn (Okada, 2012). Considering the social context she was situated in prior to university, it is possible that Hana legitimised teletandem learning as an opportunity to reconstruct her sense of self and gain linguistic skills for improved future prospects. Hana's story presents another intriguing insight in terms of investment into her English self. Her description of different personalities when using different languages recalls previous studies focusing on female Japanese learners of English (e.g., Block, 2007; Piller & Takahashi, 2006; Skarin, 2001) who sought to learn English to expand life opportunities (Yashima, 2013). In her case, Hana believed that English would enable her to act confidently and actively whereas Japanese, her mother tongue, would not allow her to. From this perspective, she considered teletandem learning an opportunity to demonstrate her imagined L2 identity by expressing her opinions with confidence rather than simply improving her English skills.

The second research question was: "How do the research participants' identities shift throughout the teletandem sessions?" The findings in this study reveal that teletandem learning generated multiple shifts in learners' positionings through negotiating their L2 identities in the online interactions. In this study, Tomo specifically described her success in providing support for her partner, which gave her a sense of achievement. Moreover, she attempted to negotiate her L2 identities by showing her personality, which was usually challenging to perform in English due to limited linguistic competence. Given that she had perceived herself as a novice English speaker prior to the teletandem programme, the fact that she was acknowledged as a supportive peer by her teletandem partner should be highlighted as a crucial factor in building a positive L2 identity. As Yang and Yi (2017) argue, teletandem learning allows participants to play the dual roles of expert and novice, which can lessen the hierarchical relationship between pairs and create supportive atmospheres in their interactions. However, Hana's story suggests that she felt marginalized as a novice learner because she believed that she lacked sufficient English proficiency to communicate effectively with her partners. Despite this, she remained an active participant in the first session and maintained a central position in the exchange.

What seems clear from these contrasting results is that the negotiation of L2 identities in teletandem learning rests on how learners perceive their partners and themselves within their imagined community of practice. The perception also seems rather fluid depending on the partnership created by two individuals. It is also important to note that the shifting positioning in the teletandem learning can also be attributed to the nature of telecollaboration. Both participants believed teletandem would allow them to strategically act with confidence and be efficient partners (e.g., keeping prepared notes next to them, using the written chat function when utterances were not understood). Physically non-shared spaces as well as the delay in online communication were also perceived as advantages to ease their anxiety.

The final research question was: "To what extent does their participation in teletandem learning influence their L2 self-perceptions?" Participating in the teletandem community had a significant impact on the learners' development, but this impact was shaped by their prior language learning experiences in a complex manner. Tomo's case, on one hand, depicts gradual movement from peripheral to central positions in the teletandem community. While she lacked self-confidence within herself, the reciprocal learning opportunities reshaped her beliefs, which empowered her to build a positive and confident self. On the other hand, Hana's story demonstrates that active participation is not always a conflict-free process and can result in complicated outcomes in teletandem learning. In her case, the discrepancy between her ideal English self and her experience of being a novice was a frustrating factor that prevented her from actively receiving support from her partners and embracing reciprocity in the learning process.

CONCLUSIONS AND IMPLICATIONS FOR PRACTICE

This study explores how Japanese female first-year university students construct their identities through teletandem learning by examining their past experiences, current perceptions, and future aspirations. Although the students share similar socioeducational backgrounds, their L2 identities depicted in the narratives appear uniquely distinct. Through the narrative analysis, it became evident that teletandem learning can be conceptualised as more than just linguistic practice. As witnessed in each participant's story, L2 learners may invest in the learning opportunities to construct confident selves that may not have been attainable in the immediate communities to which they belonged. Although participation in teletandem exchanges can have positive outcomes, the nature of the online context and learners' positioning relative to their partners can also influence the negotiation of their L2 identities and language learning experiences.

Building upon the findings, several practical implications can be offered for implementing teletandem in institutional settings in a similar sociocultural context to that in this study. First, teletandem can offer an engaging learning experience not only for those who can communicate in their target languages but also for those who identify themselves as novices. As this study points out, reciprocal learning experiences in teletandem were an opportunity to redefine learners' L2 selves and (re)gain self-confidence. While teletandem learning is often simply viewed as a form of linguistic training, this study also illuminates the opportunities to embrace linguistic diversity and envision a bigger community of practice beyond the boundary of native/non-nativeness. Additionally, as the participants in this study mentioned, online interactions might be less intimidating for those who have not been exposed to L2 communication with the time lag and the absence of physically shared space. In this sense, teletandem learning is a suitable pedagogical practice to encourage students to pursue ideal L2 selves. Second, incorporating reflective practice not only at an individual but also at a group level promotes transformational learning and in-depth student engagement. Drawing on this study's findings, emotional experiences can powerfully impact participants' self-perceptions. Thus, allowing participants from both institutions to share their reflections on ongoing teletandem sessions in groups may help them support each other linguistically and emotionally. Also, building a shared platform via blogs or an online social networking system (e.g., a *Facebook* group, *LINE* chat, or *Padlet*) might allow them to share their reflections in writing, which would give them sufficient time to express their thoughts in their L2. Moreover, incorporating storytelling may promote further in-depth reflection. During the interviews, I was reminded of the importance of narrative as a means of reflecting upon one's life (Early & Norton, 2013) and expressing oneself to others. Although the interviews were set up for research purposes, they also functioned as places for storytelling, where each participant strived for "an affective response" (Early & Norton,

2013, p. 140). The storytelling is certainly useful for teachers or facilitators who support teletandem learners to better understand where their investment in the learning derives from and what accelerates or hinders their participation.

It is important to note that despite the possibilities for language learning and identity construction that this study provides, it was situated within a specially designed context with a small number of participants; hence its findings are limited in several ways. First, data used in this study primarily consisted of learners' retrospective reflections. Thus, to deepen understanding of their experiences, analysis of actual interaction between pairs in teletandem, as found in other studies (e.g., Helm, 2018; Rusk & Pörn, 2019; Yang & Yi, 2017), would be helpful in future research. Additionally, analysing participant identity shifts from a longitudinal perspective would be preferable. This study suggests that individuals' self-perceptions can vary significantly depending on their teletandem partners. However, because the study only examined six teletandem sessions, it is possible that a longitudinal study with a larger sample size could reveal more nuanced patterns of identity negotiations. Such a study could provide greater insight into the complexity and unpredictability of these interactions.

Given the continued popularity and demand for telecollaboration, it's important to investigate teletandem learning from multiple perspectives. This study has revealed the social nature of participants within a specific socioeducational context. I hope it encourages educators to engage in further discussions about how online L2 learner communities can thrive.

Author Bio

Kie Yamamoto is Assistant Professor in the Department of English Communication, Faculty of Global Studies at Wayo Women's University in Japan. Her research interests lie mainly in teletandem learning, student engagement and learner agency. She is an Ed.D candidate at the University of Bath, UK.

6
Multi-Agent Teaching: A Case Study
Anuja M. Thomas & Philip M. McCarthy

Team-teaching is a pedagogical strategy in which more than one instructor complementarily engages in lesson planning, lesson delivery, and student assessment (Miller & Trump, 1973; Wenzlaff et al., 2002). Team-teaching originated as a means for maximizing educational achievements of students with special needs, particularly those integrated into mainstream classrooms (Bawens & Hourcade, 1995; Cook & Friend, 1995; Platt et al., 2001; Vaughn et al., 1997). Such was the success of team-teaching that it became more commonplace across other educational contexts. For example, subject experts saw the benefits of team teaching in interdisciplinary fields such as technical writing, agrophysics, and biomedical sciences (Chen, 2020; Jacob, 2015; Klein, 2006; Lee & Gaard, 2015; Letterman & Dugan, 2004; Sandholtz, 2000).

Perhaps most relevant to the current study, team teaching has also become a commonplace way to train pre-service teachers (Bacharach et al., 2012; Badiali & Titus, 2010; Baeten & Simmons, 2014; Dang, 2013; Tsybulski, 2019). Indeed, research shows that scaffolding pre-service teachers by allowing them the agency to take on the role of an instructor under the guidance of an experienced mentor teacher leads to increased professional development. This professional development occurs through increased critical reflection on teaching practices and preferences, gaining field experience, and developing self-confidence through increased support (Baeten & Simmons, 2014; Dang, 2013; Gardiner, 2010).

It should be noted that the mentor teacher has as much to gain from team teaching as the trainee. For example, receiving assistance from preservice teachers can contribute to more efficient classroom management, largely the result of a sizeable decrease in the student-to-teacher ratio (Sandholtz, 2000). Effectively, this provides mentor teachers with a lighter immediate workload (Dee, 2012), which allows them to focus greater attention on the highest priority concerns.

Unsurprisingly, these benefits of team teaching contribute to the most important result of all: improved student performance. For example, Schmulian and Coetzee (2019) report that a class of undergraduate students found that co-taught classes provided more opportunities for individual support. Similarly, co-teaching has been shown to improve student perceptions of teaching efficiency and efficacy as well as their enjoyment of the class, leading to higher satisfaction levels (Chanmugam & Gerlach, 2013; Gillespie & Israetel, 2008). Meanwhile, Bacharach et al. (2012) found that students in kindergarten to grade 6 enrolled in co-taught classes showed significant gains in reading and mathematics skills when compared to those enrolled in classes taught by a single instructor.

The strategy of team-teaching is clearly beneficial; however, we argue here that "the team" does not have to be limited to human agents. That is, the modern classroom and today's instructors are well served by viewing technology as part of the instructional team. After all, technology is not about replacing teachers, it is about assisting teaching. This assistance is at its best when it facilitates and develops existing instructor-student structures (McNeely, 2005). To be sure, studies such as McCarthy et al. (2021b) acknowledge that the "galaxy of gadgetry" (p. 338) for the modern classroom can seem daunting. However, they conclude by noting:

> We cannot know if…[everyone] will share our enthusiasm for all that technology has to offer, but shared or not, technology has long since ceased being an option: technology is simply upon us, and it is a willing friend to all those who choose to embrace it. (p. 338)

Viewed this way, technology can be seen as a member of the team, playing a role in all possible aspects of the educational experience (Heick, 2015).

As the current study falls within the field of rhetoric and composition, our focus here is on *Automated Writing Evaluation* (AWE) tools. These tools provide important feedback not just for students, but also for instructors. Similarly, under the right conditions, the students and instructors can provide useful feedback that facilitates the development of the automated tools.

Research suggests that student use of AWE greatly benefits their academic performance and writing development. For example, it allows students access to error analyses and assessments of their writing at any time (Chen & Cheng, 2008; McCarthy et al., 2021a). Such unrestricted access to comprehensive reviews of their work allows students to modify their papers prior to final submission. Furthermore, more recent AWE tools, such as *Auto-Peer* (McCarthy et al., 2021a), are primarily designed to provide feedback rather than correction. Therefore, the use of such systems improves learner autonomy by encouraging students to redraft their papers by addressing issues flagged by the system (Benali, 2021; Chen & Cheng, 2008). Finally, As McCarthy et al. (2021a) point out, when students use AWE within the writing process, instructors can focus on content related issues rather than mechanical and stylistic errors. This change in focus allows instructors to provide faster and richer feedback to students, thus increasing the likelihood that on subsequent drafts students will have the information needed for further improvements and the time necessary to make such changes.

While team teaching and AWE tools have been researched extensively as discrete approaches to enhancing teaching, there is a lack of research that combines these two instructional strategies. To address this gap in the research, collaboration between AWE tools, pre-service teachers, and instructors is essential to optimize student outcomes. As such, this chapter assesses the benefits of developing a *multi-agent* teaching approach. Accordingly, we present a case study of such an approach and discuss ways to enhance multi-agent teaching.

THE STUDY

This study was set in the American University of Sharjah (AUS). AUS is home to a diverse student body, with students representing 89 nationalities (American University of Sharjah, 2021). The university adheres to the American college curriculum, in which all students are required to enroll in a variety of general education classes ranging from Arabic heritage to mathematics.

Our study was conducted across two classes and featured 41 students between the ages of 18 and 20 who were enrolled in a course called *Advanced Academic Writing*. The students stemmed from a wide range of disciplines and had all taken at least two basic academic writing courses. Students in the course were required to write a 10 to 12-page argumentative research paper addressing a specific research question.

The students in our classes were taught by three instructional agents: the lead teacher, a co-teacher who was a pre-service teacher, and Auto-Peer, an AWE tool. Each agent interacted in a complementary fashion and performed specialized and collaborative functions within the team.

The Agents

The lead teacher in this study was a professor who teaches linguistics and writing at both the graduate and undergraduate levels. He has also taught in American grade schools and international English language schools. Cumulatively, he has 30 years of experience in teaching English to students of a variety of age groups and proficiency levels. The co-teacher was a graduate student in the MA TESOL program. The co-teacher's research interests focused on paragraph structure and writing pedagogy. Her previous teaching experience included assisting with an ESP course and as a tutor at the university's writing center.

The AWE tool in this study was the freely available system, Auto-Peer (McCarthy et al., 2021a). Auto-Peer was designed to facilitate student writing development and to provide instructors with insight as to students' perceptions about possible writing issues. Unlike typical

AWE tools, Auto-Peer does not attempt to correct text, nor does it claim to be an automated teacher. Instead, Auto-Peer's role is akin to that of a peer-reviewer: a diligent, enthusiastic, and helpful peer reviewer, but still a peer rather than an authority.

Auto-Peer operates in the following way: First, the student enters the entire paper. Then, the student clicks *Process the Text*. Next, Auto-Peer analyzes the text for 25 common writing issues, such as lengthy paragraphs, wandering sentences, and cohesion issues. Finally, Auto-Peer displays the identified issues for students to consider. At this point, students have the choice to modify the text (an *Explanation of Issues* function is available) or, if they choose, to explain why the text does not need modification. Thus, Auto-Peer reinforces instruction while offering students the opportunity to develop critical thinking skills regarding writing and reviewing strategies. Once students are satisfied with their revisions, a final Auto-Peer report is submitted along with the student's final paper.

Agent Responsibilities

The lead teacher has a wide variety of responsibilities, including providing all the initial course material and lesson plans. They are also ultimately responsible for classroom management, grading, and ensuring that lessons reflect the goals of the course. Above all, the lead teacher is responsible for delivering lessons that meet the needs and requirements of all students.

In a multi-agent classroom, the lead teacher must gradually integrate the entire team into these duties. Thus, while the co-teacher will certainly conduct a great many "observations," it is ultimately actual "teaching" that will be of most benefit to all involved. As such, the lead teacher worked closely with the co-teacher to mutually decide where, how, and to what extent the roles of co-teacher and lead teacher could become indistinguishable.

This integration process also included the available technology. That is, the modern classroom makes use of technology because it helps achieve course goals. Thus, the lead teacher needs to be as knowledgeable, respectful, and appreciative of the technology as they are of their human counterparts. Such a courtesy may seem unnecessary, but students are more likely to use technology effectively if their lead teacher shows understanding and respect for it.

Like the lead teacher, the co-teacher also has a wide variety of roles and responsibilities. In this study, in terms of logistical responsibilities, the co-teacher tracked student absences and communicated with regular absentees. The co-teacher also tracked student participation and encouraged relatively quiet students to engage in discussions. In terms of classroom responsibilities, the co-teacher took the lead in supporting students during group work and in-class assignments. Finally, the co-teacher was available by appointment for conferences with students for personalized assistance. During these conferences, the co-teacher provided students feedback on their drafts, gave them advice on tackling specific issues (e.g., finding credible sources), and sometimes (as all teachers know) she offered emotional support and encouragement. The co-teacher was gradually introduced to further responsibilities, including lesson planning, materials development, and lesson delivery. Therefore, the co-teacher received scaffolded experience in all teaching domains.

In a multi-agent teaching environment, the technology also has responsibilities. Just as the co-teacher is not a casual observer, so too the technology must have clearly defined duties. Requiring students to learn technology is time consuming for all concerned, so the benefits, usage, and requirements must be fully articulated. By the same token, the technology must deliver on its promises. That said, teachers are not perfect, and technology should not be held to a higher standard; however, where and how automated systems can be improved, technology designers have to listen and respond appropriately. Like most systems, Auto-Peer actively encourages students and instructors to identify issues with existing functions and make suggestions for future developments. Thus, like the co-teacher, Auto-Peer is learning as much as it is directing.

Online Teaching Platform

Because of the COVID pandemic, the classes in this study were taught exclusively on an online learning management system (LMS), *Blackboard Learn*. One facilitative feature of this platform is the *breakout groups* function, which allows instructors to randomly divide students into smaller groups. Within each group, students can interact orally and type in a chat box. The relative privacy of smaller groups encouraged students to participate more actively. The difference in participation was especially marked for students willing to speak rather than simply type. The co-teacher and the lead teacher could move between groups as they liked. In this way, the instructional team were able to cover more ground and provide personalized feedback to more students. Over time, the co-teacher gradually took on the role of primary instructor within the breakout groups, using the opportunity to develop pedagogical skills to encourage in-class feedback and participation.

Another advantage of the platform is that it allows moderators to conduct polls to enhance and monitor student participation. The polls included a statement/question with two clickable response buttons. While each individual student's response is hidden from their classmates, the total number of students who chose each response is displayed on the poll. Moreover, instructors can see each student's actual responses as well as which students failed to respond. As such, the instructors were able to see which students did not grasp the concepts discussed in class and which students were not engaged.

Enhancing Multi-Agent Teaching

Throughout the semester, the lead and co-teacher kept extensive notes, engaged in numerous discussions, repeatedly evaluated student interaction with Auto-Peer, and consistently sought formal and informal feedback from students. Accordingly, the team were able to note the strategies that enhanced the teaching experience and kept students engaged and accountable. These strategies are discussed next.

Rapport Development

One important strategy for optimizing student outcomes was the cultivation of positive working relationships between all members of the instructional team, including the lead teacher, co-teacher, and Auto-Peer, as well as between the instructional team and students. Each of these dyads is unique and equally important to the overall advancement of the teaching goals.

Between Mentor and Pre-Service Teacher

There are many ways in which developing a good working relationship helped the human agents optimize student outcomes and satisfaction. First, consistent communication allowed each to complement the contributions of the other. Second, modelling a relationship based on mutual respect encouraged students to trust the co-teacher as a knowledgeable authority figure. Third, the maintenance of strong rapport among the lead teacher and the co-teacher helped create a positive environment within the classroom.

One of the ways the lead teacher and co-teacher developed rapport was through regular meetings. During these meetings, they provided one another feedback to improve future lessons. These meetings also served as an opportunity to renegotiate roles and responsibilities.

In addition to regular meetings, choices made by the lead teacher during classes also improved rapport between them. For example, the lead teacher conferred credibility to the co-teacher by consistently asking for her opinion during class and encouraging her to respond to student questions. Some explicit ways in which the lead teacher did this were through statements such as:

- "Hmm, that's a good question, Anuja. What do you think?"
- "I don't remember, Anuja. Do you know?"
- "I'm not sure about that. Let me ask Anuja what she thinks."

By inviting the co-teacher into the discussion, the lead teacher conferred trust in her. To further demonstrate this trust, the lead teacher often demonstrated agreement with the co-teacher's responses when she took the lead. Moreover, if the co-teacher had more to add or had a contrasting opinion, then the lead and co-teacher would model constructive, cooperative, and respectful principles of negotiating. The lead teacher would sometimes even play the role of stooge and happily acknowledge his errors. Such demonstrations encouraged students to find their own voice and engage in collaborative critical thinking.

Between Lead Teacher and Students

The relationship between the lead teacher and students is a key to developing classroom rapport. As the person with the most apparent authority, it fell upon the lead teacher to engage students and model the classroom environment he wanted to develop: one of *shared friendship* rather than hierarchy. To be clear, "friendship" does not mean abandoning responsibility; on the contrary, friends often need to tell hard truths. However, this relationship is reciprocal; after all, students also have responsibilities, requirements, and personal goals. As such, the instructor's approach was to build bridges based on mutual respect.

How bridges of shared friendship are built is very much an individual matter for instructors, mentees, and students. As an initial step, the lead teacher encouraged students to use his first name instead of "Professor" or "Doctor." As the lead teacher explained, "The best way to show me respect is to fully engage in the course goals." To be clear, that all instructors take this approach is not being recommended; instructors, like students, should be addressed as they choose.

Perhaps at a more important level of building shared friendships, the lead teacher modelled the role of a friend. This modelling was achieved through several actions. For example, he acknowledged his mistakes. Friends make mistakes, and they should not be hidden by apparent authority. A second example was the lead teacher's willingness to acknowledge what he did not know. That is, he was always willing to offer his "best guess" but acknowledged when he was not sure of his response. He would then inform students that he would find out the best answer by the next class, which he invariably did. Finally, the lead teacher consistently asked students how he could improve their learning experience. One way to achieve such feedback is by asking students on all assignments to describe the breadth, depth, and voice of feedback they prefer. Through such actions, the lead teacher modelled that everyone in the class was on a journey of development, that the journey was long, and that mistakes would be (and even *should be*) commonplace.

Between Co-Teacher and Students

One of the co-teacher's roles was to liaise between the students and the lead teacher. That is, the co-teacher's youth and identity as a graduate student made it possible to connect to students as a peer while also maintaining a position of authority. Indeed, the co-teacher often provided students with emotional support to a greater extent than an official instructor is able to by recalling her own stories of academic frustrations and disappointments. She was also able to share with students the many strategies she used to succeed in her academic work.

By developing this combination of friendship and respect with students, the co-teacher was able to gain insight into their struggles and anxieties. She emphasized that anything they said during consultations would remain confidential unless they wanted it to be shared with the lead teacher. Thus, students were able to discuss issues that they may otherwise have been hesitant to share. Note that a "shared friendship" between three people does not entail a license to share *all* information. This relationship of understanding allowed the co-teacher to provide students with help tailored to their specific needs. However, it is important to note that the individual rights and responsibilities of each co-teacher depend on their specific contexts. Indeed, not all co-teachers will have the same allowance of confidentiality. Therefore, it is important for lead teachers and co-teachers to discuss such issues beforehand and establish ground rules.

Rapport With Auto-Peer

Auto-Peer was treated as an equal member of the instructional team. Students were given opportunities to respond to the feedback provided by Auto Peer in the form of a report where they either showed how they addressed the concerns raised or discussed why they disagreed with it. Note again that Auto-Peer is designed to highlight "possible" writing issues, rather than "absolute errors." For example, Auto-Peer highlights "long paragraphs" (e.g., those of more than 15 sentences). The system points out that while long paragraphs are possible, the student would be advised to check whether the text could be better expressed using multiple paragraphs. Through the Auto-Peer report requirement, the human instructors are provided with insight as to students' misconceptions and can provide further feedback where necessary.

Although Auto-Peer certainly *provides* extensive feedback, like any member of the teaching team, it must also *receive* feedback. After all, the software is only seeking to become an improved version of itself. Accordingly, students were continually encouraged to suggest improvements to the system. In fact, such was the appreciation of Auto-Peer that students often reported that they were using the tool in their own discipline-specific courses. Such feedback, and subsequent discussion, led to the realization that Auto-Peer could be developed further so as to more specifically address some of the nuanced issues of writing requirements across the campus. Indeed, within a year, designs had been made, and the *discipline specificity analysis tool* (DSAT), the next generation of Auto-Peer, was underway (McCarthy et al., 2022). This development, we would argue, more than demonstrates the importance of rapport at every level of the multi-agent teaching team.

Reciprocal Zones of Proximal Development

The benefits afforded by the collaboration within the multi-agent teaching team and between the team members and students can all be considered examples of bridging the *zone of proximal development* (ZPD).

As defined by Vygotsky (1935/1980), the ZPD is the distance between students' achievements *without* assistance and their achievements *with* assistance from someone more knowledgeable. The most obvious examples of such assistance are the support provided by instructors to students and the support provided by the lead teacher to the co-teacher. However, upon closer inspection, we see that each member of the classroom environment makes valuable contributions to the shared goals of the class. For example, the *curse of knowledge* that can be attributed to a highly trained lead teacher can be circumvented by taking into consideration the co-teacher's objective feedback. Similarly, student perspectives on the feedback provided by Auto-Peer are used to improve various aspects of the tool, including the interface, the issues addressed, and the phrasing of the explanations provided. As such, all members of the classroom environment contribute to optimizing one another's performance.

Data Collection

Another strategy used for improving student outcomes was collecting data. Primarily, the data was used to evaluate students' understanding of the material through a variety of methods, such as formative evaluations, engagement measures, feedback analysis, and informal assessments conducted during individual meetings.

Formative Assessments

The use of formative assessments to understand the general skill levels of students is a relatively recent strategy. As Dodge (n.d.) explains, traditional *summative assessments* grade students and judge their performance as a measure of their success or failure. By contrast, *formative assessment*, also referred to as "assessment *for* learning" (para. 1) focusses on assessments as a tool for gauging students' command of the course material, which allows the instructor to determine which students (or classes) are most in need of help. Such *differentiated assessment* based on formative assessments provides tailored assistance to individual students or classes (Dodge, n.d.; Subban, 2006; Tomlinson & McTighe, 2006).

For our study, we used a variety of formative assessments, including open-book quizzes and short assignments. These assessments provided students opportunities to receive feedback from the instructional team. Students were regularly informed that these formative assignments are designed to maximize the amount of feedback they receive on their work. Additionally, the lead teacher often emphasized that the tests and assignments were as much for assessing the students as they were for assessing the instructional team. That is, students were frequently reminded that if most of them performed poorly in a test or assignment, it reflected the teaching, rather than the learning. For example, if fewer than 33% of students received above 90% in a test or quiz, then the quiz would not be counted in the calculation of final grades. The lead teacher's reasoning was that if too many students find a question difficult to comprehend or respond to appropriately, then the real issue is that either the question needs to be rephrased or that the specific element needs to be retaught. As such, the lead teacher also used these assessments as opportunities for feedback on his own teaching.

Although formative assignments did not greatly impact anyone's overall grade, students were encouraged to take them seriously to maximize their benefit from the feedback. While the lead teacher was responsible for grading students' formative assessments, Auto-Peer and the co-teacher provided students with pre-submission feedback to better develop their best work for submission.

Another form of formative assessment was the final report generated from Auto-Peer feedback. For this report, students were instructed to provide their honest thoughts about the feedback provided by the system and the degree to which they implemented corresponding modifications. If students did not agree with any particular piece of feedback, they were asked to explain their reasoning. Providing students this opportunity allowed them to think critically about the feedback and generate their own reactions without simply implementing changes to receive higher grades. Furthermore, by offering students the opportunity to discuss their thoughts and concerns about the feedback, the instructors were able to address any misconceptions and provide individualized guidance and support.

In-Class Discussions and Participation

Data concerning student progress were also collected by analyzing engagement, which is important because engagement tends to correlate with higher achievement (Fredricks, 2014). However, as Mercer et al. (2021) point out, teachers are not necessarily the best judges of student engagement. This is because students can seem to engage on the surface while not thinking deeply about the material. As such, the co-teacher played an important role in evaluating engagement, which was largely determined through participation. Increased student participation was elicited through a mix of *display questions*, where the teacher knows the answer, and *referential questions*, where the teacher has no set answer in mind (Hugh, 1979). The lead teacher initially took responsibility for asking questions while the co-teacher noted the frequency, accuracy, and depth of student responses. However, over time, the co-teacher also began to ask questions, usually via the written chat box. The co-teacher also noted the frequency, accuracy, and depth of student responses. In this way, both teachers could see which students needed further encouragement. The co-teacher would also respond to the lead teacher's questions, particularly at the start of a class to stimulate student engagement.

The polling feature was initially used to provide students a convenient way to respond to comprehension checks. Because classes were conducted online, students primarily responded by typing into the shared chat box. However, the large volume of responses received in a short span of time made it difficult to keep track of each student's stance on a given question. Thus, the polls provided a concise record of all students' responses. Moreover, perhaps because the poll responses are anonymous, students were honest about their comprehension of course material. The co-teacher recorded students' responses and informed the lead teacher during meetings. Another purpose of polling was to check if students were attentive. One of the main drawbacks of conducting online classes is that some students may sign in but fail to engage in class activities, either by leaving the room or using their computers for other purposes. Frequent polls with the question "Are you still here?" allowed the instructors to email those students whose active attendance needed attention.

Individual Meetings

All students were encouraged to meet with either the lead teacher or the co-teacher outside of class hours if they had questions or concerns. During these meetings, the instructor could gauge the quality of each student's work and their motivation levels. Based on this information, the lead instructor was able to tailor feedback to individual students. Additionally, students were instructed to process their drafts through Auto-Peer and address the feedback provided by the tool prior to these meetings. Accordingly, students were able to utilize the meetings to ask the instructors deeper, content-related questions.

Meetings between students and the co-teacher were important for giving students a chance to speak their minds without fear of judgement. Indeed, during these meetings, students were much more open about what they found difficult in the course. Furthermore, students who were struggling (based on their performance in initial assignments) were encouraged to meet with the co-teacher on a weekly basis to maintain accountability. During these meetings, the co-teacher ensured that their understanding was sufficient by listening to questions, elaborating on class topics, and reading updated versions of their drafts. After these meetings, and with the students' permission, the co-teacher wrote a summary of the discussion that was sent to the student and the lead teacher. As evidenced by final grades and course review feedback, these weekly meetings benefitted these struggling students.

Student Feedback

To ensure students were comfortable with the course structure, the instructors sought formal and informal student feedback. Accordingly, at the beginning of the course, the lead teacher surveyed the students about their opinions on integrating a co-teacher and an AWE into the class. Students were asked to take a similar survey at the end of the semester to gauge changes in their comfort and trust in these agents. Additionally, records of student grades were used to assess their experience. Finally, students were asked to write short reflection papers on their experiences.

Survey responses suggest that the multi-agent approach led to increased student comfort (see Table 1). Perhaps more importantly, this approach improved student outcomes, with average student grades higher than previous semesters for the same course taught only by the lead teacher. Furthermore, students' reflections on the course indicate their appreciation of the opportunities provided[1].

Table 1

Changes in Student Attitudes Toward Co-Teacher and Auto-Peer

Pre-semester survey items	Average scores	Post-semester survey items	Average scores
I often seek out the services of a writing tutor to help me with my writing assignments.	3.61	I will seek out the services of a writing tutor to help me with my writing assignments more often.	4.67
I am comfortable emailing my written drafts to a writing tutor for feedback.	4.88	I am comfortable emailing my written drafts to a writing tutor for feedback.	5.48
I am comfortable using technology (e.g., Grammarly) to review my paper.	4.55	I am comfortable using technology (e.g., Grammarly) to review my paper.	5.21
I am confident that using technology to review my paper will be beneficial to me.	4.33	I am comfortable using technology (e.g., Grammarly) to review my paper.	5.15

Note: All differences between pre and post evaluations are statistically significant at $p < .05$

Results and Discussion

Unsurprisingly, the multi-agent approach was a great success, with 67.67% of students receiving an A grade and a further 13.25% receiving an A-. University administered anonymous course evaluations provide a perhaps more objective analysis. In this respect, one class assessed the teachers with an overall rating of 4.95/5.00 and the second class provided 4.83/5.00. Given that the students were in a compulsory class and none were English majors or minors, these evaluations are noteworthy, especially when compared to the English Department's average rating (4.52) and the College of Arts and Sciences as a whole (4.37). Students' anonymous course review comments were also reassuring, with one student writing, "I loved the Professor and Anuja's constant support to us. They were always ready to give feedback and that was really helpful." Another student noted, "I love how the professor and Anuja make the class really fun. Whenever I send my work on email or submit it on ilearn, i quickly get feedback on my work."

Despite the obvious benefits of a multi-agent approach, we acknowledge that there are some potential drawbacks and difficulties associated with implementing it. For example, many departments and schools are unlikely to be able to provide every classroom with a co-teacher; however, our study, providing suggestions for a multi-agent approach, may diminish expenses while facilitating assistance. Furthermore, regarding technology, many AWE tools such as Auto-Peer are free. As for human assistants, it may be possible to share graduate education students across multiple classes to optimize limited resources. Another potential source of concern with this kind of teaching model is lack of cohesion between lead teacher and co-teacher. However, this issue can be mitigated by encouraging lead teachers to interview prospective co-teachers to ensure that they can work well as a team.

Case studies such as ours are a useful point of departure; however, considerable future research is needed if multi-agent teaching is to achieve its full potential. Such future research includes observing a wide variety of lead-teacher/co-teacher/technology teams. Quantitative analyses will also be needed to better assess the development of student writing skills and student feedback literacy. We also acknowledge that even the term *multi-agent teaching* will need further assessment. For example, the students themselves are also agents, and their contribution to the development of the instructors and the technology needs to be fully considered.

Although this chapter can only offer an introduction to multi-agent teaching, we believe the evidence offered here reinforces and develops the team-teaching approach. That is, our differences in experience, abilities, and goals can be strengths that serve us all to be better versions of ourselves. Presumably, if a development such as multi-agent teaching is to gain widespread acceptance, established teachers need to be receptive to the needs of the many agents that comprise the teaching environment. After all, in areas as varied as medicine, plumbing, hospitality, and air traffic control, the previous generation of novices guide the next generation of experts. Thus, as *older-hands*, established teachers have as much of a duty to student-teachers as they do to students themselves. Such a responsibility may first appear as extra work in an already exhausting schedule. However, if approached as a reciprocal relationship, then the benefits are clearly abundant.

Acknowledgement

This research was supported in part by The American University of Sharjah (FRG22-C-S70). The authors would also like to acknowledge the contributions of Ayah al-Harthy, Angel Merchant, and Nicholas Duran.

Author Bios

Anuja M. Thomas is completing her M.S. in Psychology at Arizona State University, after which, she will join Florida State University as a Ph.D. student in Cognitive Psychology. Her research focus lies at the intersection of language, cognition, and learning, with an emerging interest in computational methods.

Philip McCarthy is currently an Associate Professor at the American University of Sharjah, UAE. He has been a teacher for over 30 years, working in locations such as Turkey, Japan, Britain, the United States, and the United Arab Emirates. McCarthy's research focuses on applied natural language processing and discourse science.

---

1. For full student reviews of Auto-Peer, see https://writingtheresearchpaper.com/student-reviews/auto-peer/

7
Students from Asia and Teachers in Paranational Classrooms: Co-Constructing Identities Amidst Stereotypes

Mark A. McGuire and Zhenjie Weng

A paranational space is never without culture but is instead a dynamic blend of cultures. In contrast, transnational spaces have a dominant cultural framework being moved into or from, such as when a classroom is located in the United States and the students are from Asia. According to Faist (2010):

> Transnationalism is often used both more narrowly—to refer to migrants' durable ties across countries—and, more widely, to capture not only communities, but all sorts of social formations, such as transnationally active networks, groups, and organisations. (p. 9)

Transnationalism is more easily applied to situations involving immigration or individuals seeking to assimilate into a host culture as an explicitly identified community or network. These communities or networks may exist among people who perceive common interests; as Kivisto and Faist (2010, p. 139) put it, "a *singular* social space [emphasis added]." ESL classrooms are considered paranational spaces without a singular source or destination. Such spaces may not even exist in a physical location. Transnational spaces, on the other hand, involve linear expectations about the occupants' cultural identity and a clear relationship between places or persons. Most ESL students are not from the host culture but participate in it. Their relationship with it may be ambiguous, even to them, as they may not consciously define that relationship. If classrooms are viewed as co-constructed learning environments, they are paranational and not transnational. There is no neat guest and host relationship in these spaces. For example, an American teacher in an ESL classroom with students from all over the world in a sense becomes a guest on American soil. Categorizing students as "Asian" is unproductive considering language learners' complex identity construction. In non-traditional classrooms, complexities are amplified when there are no representatives of the host culture (e.g., non-Americans teaching English in the United States) or physical travel (e.g., online classes).

A paranational classroom reflects the larger purpose of language education as it is an open space for students to assert agency over their identity and interactions, and in so doing, challenge stereotypes. While teachers may have eschewed making vast generalizations about student ability based on perceived deficits from their language backgrounds (Larson-Freeman, 2019; Ortega, 2017), these generalizations have taken on more cultural bias. For example, the authors have heard these: "the Chinese students are more likely to cheat", or "the Japanese students are less likely to participate in class discussions," or "Asians are better at taking tests". This chapter therefore aims to explore the impact of stereotypes on paranational students from Asia studying in the United States by analyzing student writing and teacher reflections. The study includes student writing collected at various points in their courses, with some explicitly reflecting on their identities while others briefly mention identity. Through their writing, students reveal the challenges of navigating their identity-construction in a paranational space, where stereotypes held by themselves and others affect their personal and academic development.

Literature Review

Under the effects of globalization, language, power, and culture are fluid and dynamic (Canagarajah, 2007a), "featuring transnational affiliations, diaspora communities, digital communication, fluid social boundaries, and the blurring of time-space distinctions" (Canagarajah, 2007b, p. 924). In a globalized world, individuals must develop a shared language for practical purposes. *Global English* or *Lingua Franca English* has arisen for such purposes (Canagarajah, 2007b). Even though some scholars are concerned that generalization and linguistic hegemony are camouflaged by globalization, English language users can utilize English as a tool for global interactions and contextualize its use for situated functions in local contexts (Canagarajah, 2007a). To expand on this concept, we propose that paranational spaces are without transitional boundaries, where people from different backgrounds meet and negotiate social practices. In these spaces, each language user brings their linguistic resources "to find a strategic fit with the participants and purpose of [the] context" (Canagarajah, 2007a, p. 94). The sense of community must be "achieved situationally through language" (Canagarajah, 2012, p. 82) and the "language based on negotiation can be developed only through and in practice" (Canagarajah, 2007b, p. 927). This process of negotiation results in a shared resource that is mutually recognized and intelligible.

In paranational spaces, students reconstruct multilingual and multicultural identities. Their negotiation of the space and language development relies on the agency granted to them (Canagarajah, 2007b; Larsen-Freeman, 2019). Language awareness, rather than language form, becomes essential to language development. Linguistic competence therefore depends on whether students' language resources meet the needs of the communication situation (Canagarajah, 2007b), with meaning socially constructed through practice (Canagarajah, 2007b; Gergen, 2015). Teachers can allow students to reconstruct classroom norms, modelling co-construction among students and teachers (Lee & Canagarajah, 2019).

Increased global mobility has brought students from different parts of the world into U.S. classrooms (Israel & Batalova, 2021). Additionally, with greater availability and changing economic forces, there has been an increased demand for English language education, resulting in more students seeking language instruction than before. More recently, the COVID-19 pandemic has resulted in a shift from traditional physical classrooms to non-physical, online spaces that are paranational rather than transnational, as they do not favor one nation over another and participants may not necessarily be geographically mobile. According to McGuire et al. (2022), digital spaces are more prominently paranational than transnational, as they do not necessarily involve a change in national space.

In paranational classrooms, one encounters diverse Asian cultures that can lead to cultural tensions and conflicts among students struggling to negotiate shared and conflicting identities. Due to the diverse backgrounds represented in paranational spaces, teaching innovations emphasizing student agency (Vaughn, 2020) in the learning process may be more important. Hence, this paper also explores the challenges faced by two ESL instructors when teaching mostly Asian students and the innovations they implemented to address these challenges. Innovations in the classroom included voluntary and reflective assignments, unstructured student interactions, and class projects with culturally relevant topics.

Put together, this study, informed by CDST, or *complex dynamic systems theory* (Larsen-Freeman, 2019), relied on a qualitative analysis of assignments and reflections from students and instructors to address the following questions:

1. How did Asian students view their role as co-constructors of their Asian identity? How was that influenced by the institution or larger cultural expectations?
2. How did instructors position themselves as co-constructors of Asian identity?
3. How did the paranational environment affect the co-construction of classroom norms?

METHODOLOGY

Participants and Setting

The study is situated in a large, Midwestern U.S. university that had many international undergraduate students in 2020 and 2021. Most took the ESL Composition Placement Test for international students, administered by the ESL Composition Program (Weng et al., 2020). Depending on their test scores, students may be required to take up to two ESOL writing courses in addition to a full load of other university courses, which typically consists of around five to six courses per week (McGuire et al., 2022). The 15 participants in this study were enrolled in two ESOL writing courses taught by instructors with extensive teaching experience in both China and the United States: Rufus, an American instructor, and Xiu, a Chinese instructor. Their classes had 33 and 35 students respectively. The majority of the students were Chinese, making the latent process of co-constructing Asian identity ongoing in both classes, albeit with some variations.

Data Collection

Throughout the classes, students were encouraged to reflect, as a complex writing exercise, about the role that language, culture, and identity played in their lives while studying abroad in the United States. As part of the study, students were asked to reflect on their experiences in the classroom and their perceptions of how they were viewed by others. Specifically, they were asked what they thought their classmates and instructors thought of them and whether they believed that people had incorrect stereotypes about them. There was no specific mention of Asian identities in the prompts. They were also asked about whether they felt mastery of English was something that they could attain or whether English was forever bound to the idea of "native speakers" as the true masters of the language.

Drawing from writing assignments throughout the classes, 20 texts from the recruited students were deemed relevant to this study. The assignment was open enough that students could have written about several things. Some wrote about language or identity-based stereotypes in only a sentence or two, with others writing about a page. These student reflections offer evidence of the ongoing process of co-constructing Asian identity in a paranational classroom. Most of the students identified themselves as Asian, but they came from diverse backgrounds. The classroom was taught by instructors who had experience teaching in both Chinese and American contexts, and who incorporated both teaching styles in their approach. Additionally, throughout their teaching and after the classes, both teachers wrote reflections on their teaching experiences, primarily from the classes in question, but also drawing on their wider teaching experience insofar as it informed their classrooms in this study. In total, there were 14 reflections from Xiu and five reflections from Rufus.

Data Analysis

The data were analyzed thematically (Braun & Clarke, 2012), with a specific focus on statements related to Asian identity and behavior, as well as comments positioning the self in relation to stereotypes about Asian people. Seven themes emerged from the analysis. The teacher reflections were also analyzed for common themes and interpreted within the context of the themes identified through analysis of the students' reflections. The paranational spaces in which students and teachers participated provided opportunities for reconsidering their identities.

FINDINGS

The study identified seven themes from the reflections, which were analyzed in relation to the three research questions. The identified themes were: Asians are Smart/Hardworking, Asians are Good at Math, Asians are Introverted, Asians all have Similar Knowledge/Experience, Asians are Suspicious About Other Countries, Asians come from Suspicious Countries, and Asians are Bad at English. These themes were then used to explore the relationship between students and stereotypes. In addition, the reflections of the teachers were analyzed for common themes and interpreted within the context of the student reflections. The paranational spaces of the classroom allowed both students and teachers to reconsider their identities.

Asians Are Smart or Hardworking

One pervasive stereotype alluded to by two students is Asians as smart or hardworking. The hardworking element connotes hardworking in the sense of being studious rather than physical labor. None of the students disagreed with this stereotype, possibly because being perceived as "smart" and "hardworking" is generally seen as positive. For instance, Student 10 explicitly affirmed the stereotype by saying, "In [non-Asians'] minds, Chinese are smart. Actually, we are." Notably, this affirmation was made on behalf of the group as a whole ("we") rather than solely as an individual ("I"). Circumstances in which students speak not just for themselves but also for groups are discussed further at the end of this Findings section.

Asians Are Good at Math

In a similar example of students speaking on behalf of their perceived group, three students mentioned Asians as good at math (Students 6, 8, and 10). Whether this is distinct from "Asians are studious" is a matter of interpretation, but if they are interrelated, then the "studious" and "mathematically proficient" side of Asians were the most often cited stereotype that students mentioned about themselves. Reactions to this stereotype were mixed. Student 10, who affirmed that Chinese people are smart, also affirmed that Chinese are good at math. This was distinctive because they spoke for all Chinese: "we are [good at math]." Student 6 did not explicitly state whether the stereotype is true generally or if it applied to them. The third, Student 8, rejected the stereotype despite the potentially positive perception of "being good at math": "I want other people to see me as an Asian people but I do not want they think that I am good at math."

While these two stereotypes concerned the intellectual ability of Asian students, the remaining five stereotypes focused on how Asian students interact socially. As a student can be talented at math and socially outgoing, or struggle with math and be introverted, it is notable how images of Asian students arbitrarily fit together through stereotypes into images that many Asian students rejected.

Asians Are Introverted

Student 14 captured the stereotype of Asians being introverted when reflecting on a conversation with a friend: "However, I didn't have anything to say, and she neither. She said: 'You are not a talkative person.' At that moment, I felt complicated because I'm a talkative person when I'm with my Chinese friends." Unfortunately, little additional context was given, but the incident clearly made an impression. This stereotype interrelates with language skills, perhaps in contrast to mathematics, as if students cannot fluently represent themselves in English, English speakers may think that they are not sociable.

Two other students mentioned a stereotype about Asians being "quiet" or "introverted." One student explicitly contradicted the stereotype in their reflection, while the other student, Student 1, acknowledged it. Though not directly referring to the introversion stereotype, Student 1 mentioned that "Chinese prefer to hang out with their peers. It's true because we are in a foreign country." Through the opportunity afforded by their paranational context, Student 1 spoke for Chinese people as a group, suggesting another reason for the stereotype; that Chinese prefer to spend their time with other Chinese. This pattern is revisited later in this Findings section.

Asians All Have Similar Knowledge or Experience

Another stereotype that emerged in the students' reflections was the assumption that all Asians have similar knowledge or experience. Student 6, for instance, mentioned that many people assume that since "I am an Asian … I know all the languages of 'Asia.'" This stereotype, which comes from non-Asians, was not affirmed by any of the students as it is clearly unrealistic. Student 1 also seemed to have experienced a similar stereotype, writing that "Even for Chinese, there are still tons of things to learn in Chinese."

There was apparently one common experience that the Asian students shared:

> I am [Asian] and [Americans] start to think what my background story would be. (Student 2)

> Stereotype is usual in my life, since I am classified as Asian or "Chinese" in U.S. In U.S, many may have few ideas about how China or Asia is really like. And people may conclude how I am like based on their belief on Asian. (Student 3)

Four students referred to being stereotyped as Asian or a culture associated with Asia. Student 13 was unusual, observing, "… people can easily recognize me as a Chinese. … I think they may not be wrong or misleading stereotype." However, from the context, it seems Student 13 may have mistyped when writing that the stereotypes "may not be wrong," perhaps having intended to write "may be wrong." Either way, four out of 15 students explicitly referred to how swiftly Asians are stereotyped.

Asians Are Suspicious About Other Countries

One unique feature of paranational spaces is that the construction of perceived groups overlapped, excluded, or contradicted each other. For example, some students reflected that Asian students have strange ideas about other countries, or that they had no interest in other countries, a hostility or ambivalence which contributed to how they chose to operate in paranational spaces and how their identities were constructed within them. This marks a shift in the reported stereotypes, as they were not held by non-Asians about Asians, but by Asians about Asians, specifically Chinese students, concerning what is appropriate for Chinese students when outside of China. The stereotypes are complex because, being Asian, the students have greater agency over stereotypes associated with Asians and may feel compelled to affirm or reject them. For example, Student 7 reflected:

> Before I came to America, I almost think I need to struggle in a welter of blood and bullets cause in a country like China some people may not get in touch with a gun for a lifetime. It seems ridiculous, but gun crime in the United States has indeed become an important consideration for many Chinese students who will study abroad.

In this case, the student implicitly acknowledged this stereotype about Asians by Asians by admitting that they themselves had held that view. In contrast, Student 12 reported how they were the target of stereotypes by other Asians who were surprised they were (suspiciously) interested in international affairs:

> …people, especially Chinese people, might think I am a weirdo because I am a person who have many identities seemed to be opposite to most teenagers in China. For example, it is rare to find a Chinese teenager to care world politics and social problems, but I am one of them…

The relationships these students have with stereotypes are dynamic, with some students claiming to have "always" rejected stereotypes and others that they came to reject certain ones. This relationship with stereotypes was not determined simply by participants' identities; whether they rejected a stereotype about Chinese people was not only on account of them being Chinese. Rather, they gradually became aware of the stereotypes and then positioned themselves to resist or benefit from them. For example, Student 12 reflected that she was defying a stereotype by subverting what she and other Chinese viewed as traditional norms of propriety in favor of enjoying Japanese animation, "… which might be unacceptable to many girls and women in China because Japanese animations are highly possible to have sexual contents." In this and previous examples, students took various positions relative to the stereotypes applied to them: this student resisted the stereotype concerning Chinese women's propriety, while the students who were mentioned previously conceded that they perpetuated some stereotypes held by Asians about the United States but acknowledged those stereotypes as false.

One particularly colorful example is Student 6 reflecting on their dynamic relationship with their American host culture:

> I think I am a "diverse" person. Since I am here, USA, I learn some skills that Chinese will not easily learn in China: skateboard, hip-hop rap, hip-hop dance. I do not mean that China do not have those things but those things (rap, dance, skateboard) are born in USA. At here, I learn original rap dance, and skateboard. My identity are a rotten [sic] pot which combine American subculture and Chinese culture.

Presumably, "rotten" was intended as "melting" here. China "had those things" but the student only mentioned their affinity for them upon arriving in the United States, where they considered them to have been "born." Note that little mention is made about their life prior to being in the U.S. and whether "defying stereotypes or expectations" may itself be something about them that changed after arriving in the United States. It may be that they were always interested in American culture, and thus had strong potential for developing a multicultural identity. Or their multicultural identity may have been acquired in the process of forging it, with the potential for development and development occurring simultaneously.

Geography also played a role in the development of the students' identities, as noted by Student 11, who shared how moving within China and between different regions affected others' perceptions of them, even among other Chinese individuals who identify as Asian: "I was born in the northeast of China, and three years ago I went to live in the most southern part of China. If asked, I still say I'm from the northeast, but I got a lot of habits which could only be found at the southern people." The role of active self-identification here is notable. Students also used geography to reinforce stereotypes. For example, Student 2 implied that Asian students, or perhaps international people in general, had a uniform impression of America: "If others are foreigners [in the United States], they also think same way I do." This idea that two people from the same culture, or even continent, such as Asia, would look at something as complex as an entire foreign culture, such as the United

States, all in the same way is itself a stereotype about Asians, in this case held by an Asian person.

Asians Come From Suspicious Countries

This stereotype is directed at Asians by non-Asians, although Student 12's previous comment about Japanese animations being improper for Chinese women could be interpreted as Asians holding suspicious views towards one another's cultures. Student 7 recorded one humorous example of non-Asians holding odd views about Asian countries: "…many foreigners who believes that there is no electricity in most parts of China. I can understand this, but it is still funny." This was a specific, saliently false stereotype about China. Another stereotype was more subtle in its vagueness: "Due to some negative news, a relative of my roommate still think that China is a dangerous place" (Student 1). It is notable in this case that "dangerous" does not have a clear meaning—the American roommate may well feel their sense of China being dangerous is entirely justified if they observed China firsthand, unlike the easily falsifiable idea that China largely lacks electricity or that Americans are routinely involved in firefights. As this stereotype concerns China not feeling safe to Americans, this Chinese student may not be able to assess accuracy. However, as a Chinese, the student felt that China is not dangerous. These vagaries may be part of what sustains stereotypes since they are often not easily contradicted.

Asians Are Bad at English

An extremely common stereotype was that Asians are "bad" at English. This stereotype was not only held by non-Asians about Asians, but also by Asians about Asians, to the point that it developed into a perceived marker of social class. As Student 5 observed:

> In China, before my generation, English users are still considered "smart" and "full of knowledge" since not everyone back in time has a chance to learn English. However, if a person does not know any

English, he or she will be considered illiterate. In fact, a lot of my high school teachers do not know much about English, but they expertise in other fields, which I still admire them a lot. But people will generally think that they may not be so literate since they do not know a foreign language very well. This way of thinking is definitely changing over time. It would finitely disappear in the future.

This account is notable because: (1) it represents the stereotypes and their role in society as dynamic, changing according to needs and participants; (2) it suggests that generational differences may be an important contributor to these stereotypes; and (3) the role of English as a social marker transcends racial or ethnic boundaries, meaning that Asians and non-Asians may develop their English knowledge as a form of social mobility. This contrasts with the perceived static nature of "race" and is enabled by the flexibility of paranational spaces. That said, regardless of how accurate Student 5's description is of changing Chinese attitudes toward English, Student 5 has clearly rejected the stereotype that proficient English is associated with higher education, intelligence, or social class. This is not the same as saying that Asians are bad at English, but it is related, as English could only be so important if it is a marked feature in society.

Four students reported being stereotyped as being bad at English on account of their being identified as Asians. Student 9 reported: "So, my accent is not the same as the State, I'm lacking vocabulary and cultural understanding during the conversation." This reflects Student 9 already being aware of perceived differences between themselves and non-Asian users of English, perceiving and affirming these differences. Student 9 also noted, "I do not want to make people judge me with lacking English," thus sensing that this was a threat to their identity as a competent member of society. This fear proved justified: "They [American] employ[ee] thought I cannot speak in English" (Student 9). In this case, there was foreknowledge and participation in the stereotype, followed by anxiety relating to the student's identity, leading into fulfillment of the student's fear as Americans assumed they were not able to communicate effectively.

Two other students echoed these concerns. Student 14 saw this in the classroom, theoretically a space where students should be respected as competent despite the stereotypes held by wider society: "For those English teachers, English as a second language limits and even distorts some of our personalities." This was not, unlike Student 9, a process of anticipating stereotypes, attempting to prevent them, and feeling that the attempt failed. This is rather an observation of what Student 15 viewed as somewhat unavoidable: "When people see me, they assume that I can't speak English. I think that they made a right stereotype. Because native Asians people don't speak English." Student 15, instead of resisting the stereotype like Student 9 or problematizing it like Student 14, articulated and affirmed the stereotype as "right." It is worth noting that this student referred to Asian students as a monolithic group, which suggests a lack of English competence in Asians generally, rather than their own personal English ability. This generalization, although not necessarily intentional, could be seen as perpetuating a stereotype and may have implications for the student's sense of identity. On a more positive note, Student 2 intrinsically articulated, rejected, and suggested that the stereotype could be overcome: "…if I speak English really fluently, people is going to see me different way."

Summarizing the Relationship Between Asians and Stereotypes

The students had two important types of relationships with stereotypes. Firstly, out of the 15 students who referred to or articulated some stereotype targeting them, most rejected the stereotypes. This response to stereotypes had two significant features: (1) the students did not appreciate the stereotypes and asserted their agency against them, and (2) this deployment of agency was effective at countering the stereotype, at least on a personal level. Even if students said that they were still stereotyped by others, most did not identify with the stereotypes and even challenged them. A minority of the participants mentioned stereotypes without explicitly rejecting them. Others affirmed the stereotypes or created their own, such as implying that all Asians are somehow the same. These sometimes echoed existing stereotypes, such as "…native

Asians people don't speak English" (Student 15) and were sometimes new, such as "Chinese prefer to hang out with their peers" (Student 1). In this way, they created a group for whom they could speak, a product of the paranational space in which they were negotiating their identity.

Reflections From the Instructors

As part of the study, the two instructors, Xiu and Rufus, reflected on their respective teaching experiences. Xiu, an Asian Chinese English instructor, found that her identity as an educator was often ambiguous in the classroom, where the majority of her students were also Asian or Asian Chinese. This made the tension of the co-constructive process more personal for her. For example, Xiu reflected on the challenges of balancing her students' cultural norms with the expectations of the academic institution. Rufus, a White American who had lived and worked in China for several years, observed that there was often a perceived conflict of co-constructed educational norms in the classroom. For instance, he reflected on instances where he had to navigate differences in communication styles between himself and his students. It was clear from their reflections that the paranational classroom had higher stakes for Xiu than for Rufus, which informed their perspectives on the co-constructive process.

For both, there was a conflict in how classroom norms should be co-constructed, as American and Asian classroom norms were perceived to contrast, such as concerning whether students should speak up and ask questions during class. For example, Xiu recalled that "my students... would ask me questions on *WeChat* [a Chinese social media application] at midnight or send me their drafts"; "[social media] would easily blur the private and professional boundaries between me and my students." Rufus avoided social media as he was unwilling to compromise what he perceived to be American norms in the co-construction of student-teacher communication, preferring email or teleconferencing (e.g., *Zoom*) over social media. Negotiating the use of technology was not a simple matter of preference for Rufus and his students. They had to navigate different communication styles, with students expecting immediate responses to emails, while Rufus preferred to respond at his own pace. This negotiation reflects the paranational co-construction between students and teachers in the classroom, where cultural norms and expectations were in constant flux. Despite the challenges, Rufus chose to be flexible about meeting times, recognizing the importance of accommodating his students' needs. However, he did not embrace social media or change his email response times. By negotiating the use of technology and communication styles, the students and teachers were able to establish a productive and collaborative learning environment.

Although both Rufus and Xiu were co-constructing their classrooms with their students, as is the nature of diverse, paranational spaces, the resulting co-constructions were very different, as the issue of using social media with students exemplifies. Similarly, there were clear differences in how they approached the use of language and cultural references in class. "When I could use an authentic example of Chinese to explain an idea, it provided an opportunity for me to show that I was interested in their culture," said Rufus, who felt that this enhanced his professionalism rather than detracting from it: "I wanted to model having a multicultural identity as much as I could [and show that] identities can and should be unique." In contrast, Xiu was more hesitant to use Chinese in the classroom: "Sometimes I did not want to use Chinese or [was] conscious about using Chinese because I was afraid that my [American] supervisor or students not from China would perceive me as not professional." In this way, the identities of Xiu's students and supervisor affected the co-construction of her professional identity differently from how Rufus' assumptions and observations about his students contributed how he represented his professional, multicultural identity.

The decision of whether or not to socialize with students outside of class was also a difficult one to make. As Xiu observed: "...a lot of times, I rejected my students' invitation [for hanging out], which really broke their heart as they might think I did not like them." Rufus reported different feelings, perhaps lacking the awareness Xiu described: "Chinese students were used to hanging out [with] their teachers outside of class; however, as an instructor in the U.S. context, I was not comfortable and aware that it might not be seen as professional here." Rufus did not allude to social invitations from students; it is possible that Xiu's Chinese students responded to her Chineseness by inviting her to social events. Meanwhile, Rufus' students, making observations similar to Xiu's, perhaps did not think it appropriate to invite American teachers to social events. Thus, Rufus did not interpret the situation in the same way, and even when there was similarity between Rufus' and Xiu's co-constructed paranational classroom norms, the gravity and feeling about that co-constructive process differed. Thus, the importance of the co-constructed norms was not merely their outcomes but also the process of co-construction.

A final note about the teachers' reflections relates to the course material. Both Rufus and Xiu collaborated in planning their courses, intentionally introducing real-world, difficult topics that were potentially unfamiliar to students from Asian cultures. For instance, they covered topics such as the fraught history of queer rights and the struggle against overt and systemic racism in the United States. Rufus found it difficult to approach these topics at times, observing, "it was risky to bring these things up, because even when students were not deliberately seeking to be racist or homophobic, they may not know when they seem racist or homophobic, especially in a new language" and "this is not their fault personally, but a larger problem of dialogue in their cultures." Xiu felt challenged differently, as she was concerned about representing these issues "because I did not feel confident and competent to talk about this…as I am not an insider." Her meaning of "insider" is complex and rooted in her and her students' identity as co-constructed in the classroom. There was an unexpected tension in that students may perceive these topics as "talking about their own experiences" when they "wanted to know more about American culture." Xiu and Rufus both felt they were talking about American culture, but their sense of "American culture" did not neatly meet their students' expectations. The interpretation of American culture in U.S. classrooms can vary among international students who are in a paranational culturally observational situation rather than a transnational culturally adoptive one.

Discussion

Some of the themes discussed here are transferable to wider conceptions of Asians as a race or ethnicity and the stereotypes that affect them. Despite common assumptions, race is not static. Rather, in the coconstruction of paranational spaces that Asian students engaged in together with their non-Asian peers, stereotypes lose meaning as definitions change. For example, does the "Asians are good at math" stereotype apply to Asians in general or are people referring to a subset of Asians, such as the Chinese? While national or cultural boundaries themselves can be loose, they are generally supported and maintained by their governments. For example, the Chinese government issues Chinese passports to its citizens and employs its military to protect China. While the protection and definition of geographical states is the responsibility of their respective human representatives, conflicts arising in non-geographical places, like online classes or international corporations, are intrinsic to paranational interactions. However, Asia is not protected by a state, and so its meaning is in a liberal state of flux: Americans who never set foot in Asia can be Asian (manifested in how the same stereotypes applied to Asians from Asia can be applied to Asians not from Asia). Meanwhile, none of the 15 students reflecting on the definition of Asian seemed to include Russia, South Asia, or the Middle East. Rather, it was their experiential perceptions that constructed what being Asian meant for them as opposed to Asians being represented by neatly defined national boundaries.

Further, several students spoke for what Asians are or do. The irony is that they participated in perpetuating sometimes novel stereotypes, such as that Asian students spend time with Asian students specifically *because* they are not welcomed by others. Other times they perpetuated more common stereotypes, such as saying "we actually *are* good at math." It may seem strange that conscious subjects of stereotyping would promote it. However, this may be a consequence of the indeterminate definition of Asian: if who Asians are and what they do is changeable, can false stereotypes about Asians be rejected? Fundamentally, in questioning stereotypes about Asian students, there are tacit assumptions about how Asian students behave that may lead to trouble. Thus, any discussion of Asian-ness represents a paranational co-construction, as the concept of Asian cannot be encapsulated by a single national identity or geographical region. The Asian students' efforts to avoid negative stereotypes could be a double-edged sword, potentially trapping them. If Asians do good things rather than bad, then does not doing those good things make them a bad Asian or a non-Asian? For the students, if one affirms that Asians are good at math and disinterested in divisive politics, does that mean that someone not good at math or interested in divisive politics is not Asian? There is not a clear authority for these matters like there may be for a national or cultural identity, so members of the Asian diaspora may quickly lose their Asian-ness when those perceived as more Asian act as experts and wield more power in the process of socially constructing Asian-ness.

Most student reflections rejected stereotypes about Asians and asserted their individuality or non-conformity by strategically employing different labels, such as Japanese, Chinese, or Korean or by contrasting themselves with Asians. However, even when stereotypes are rejected, the students' need to reject them showed that the stereotypes have influence, and in some ways rejecting the stereotype can make that influence more apparent. Racialized stereotypes about Asian students affected their self-perception and well-being in largely negative ways, as manifested by their frequently utilizing their paranational classroom space to explicitly reject stereotypes, demonstrating their perniciousness. Further, these stereotypes were not invented by non-Asians to foist upon the Asian students. Rather, the Asian students participated in their co-construction, giving different accounts of their own Asian-ness in ways contradictory or deleterious to the identity of other Asian students. There are no simple faults or villains here. Rather, choices are made to counter imbalances of power in the paranational co-construction of Asian identity that result in consequences which lead in turn to further choices that counter newly developed imbalances of power in a fluid and dynamic fashion, as students strive to "find a strategic fit" in their new context (Canagarajah, 2007a, p. 94).

The teacher reflections demonstrate how Xiu and Rufus co-

constructed their classrooms differently based on their and their students' identities, highlighting the potential for diverse outcomes in unpredictable paranational classroom spaces (Lee & Canagarajah, 2019). These differences extended beyond simple acceptance or rejection of certain practices like using social media or accepting social invitations, but also in how such decisions were reached, as exemplified by Xiu and her students' varied perspectives on rejecting social invitations from Rufus. Embracing and accepting the development of unique norms in different classrooms is crucial for creating positive and socially healthy paranational spaces.

Conclusion

This study can inform future teaching in similar paranational spaces and in more traditional classrooms by demonstrating the importance of teachers being attuned to the interests of their students rather than tacitly assuming that Chinese, Japanese, Korean, or Asian students share fundamental values in general. "Asian", or any term, is insufficient to encompass the whole of any person. Our analysis reveals that while some students enthusiastically adopted new approaches to traditional classroom structures, others resisted, deeming anything not aligned with their cultural norms or not leading to higher test scores as unproductive. These variations can be difficult to navigate, and it may take some time for teachers to comprehend the complexity of their students' diverse perspectives and attitudes towards learning.

On a theoretical level, cultural exchange merely acknowledges differences, such as students imagining how others thought of them as Asian. Here there can be multiple perceptions that do not necessarily correlate with observable behaviors such as stereotypes. Where paranational spaces may become obvious is through behavior in cultural exchange. Behaviorally, things will be done one way and not another, such as by communicating via WeChat instead of email. How this is arrived at matters. Was power simply asserted by the instructor, in this case to accept the American norm according to the transnational model, or did the students and instructor acknowledge cultural differences and negotiate best practices for their classroom? This demonstrates and measures a paranational space: How much active co-construction is occurring?

Language education must take greater account of how students develop their identities as language users in diverse ways, shed simple categories and transnational models, and encourage students to be open-minded about who they can become through language learning. Students can accomplish this by shedding their own simple categories of who they are told they are, which is enabled by recognizing classrooms as paranational spaces. As Student 8 put it, "... I think I need to just be myself and not follow others blindly."

Author Bios

Mark A. McGuire is a doctoral candidate at The Ohio State University. He has been teaching university EFL and ESL courses for more than ten years, in China and in the United States. His interests include the identity and pragmatic development of English users according to usage-based theories of language.

- **Email**: mcguire.375@osu.edu
- **ORCID**: https://orcid.org/0000-0003-4329-0450

Zhenjie Weng is an Assistant Professor of English Language at the Language and Culture Center at Duke Kunshan University, China. Her specialization is in second, foreign, and multilingual language education, and her research mainly focuses on language teacher education. She has published articles in leading journals in the field, such as *TESOL Journal*, *International Journal of Qualitative Studies in Education*, and *Teaching in Higher Education* on language teacher identity, emotions, agency, and expertise.

- **Email**: zhenjie.weng@dukekunshan.edu.cn
- **ORCID**: https://orcid.org/0000-0002-2639-7822

8
Re-Envisioning Teacher Research by Questioning Assumptions: Gaps and Overlaps

Theron Muller & Colin Skeates

Relatively small-scale teacher research that seeks to address an issue of interest (Jarvis, 1999) has become commonplace in English language teaching, resulting in part from calls to involve language teachers in the field's processes of knowledge production (Nunan, 1990). This has provided a healthy focus on applied language teaching and learning research (Santiago Sanchez & Borg, 2015). One label given to such investigations is action research (Nunan, 1992), which has come to represent a genre of teacher investigation that involves the research process informing and being informed by pedagogy (Altrichter et al., 1993). An example of such research is the investigation of students' improvement in spoken fluency during a semester of EFL classroom study conducted by Talandis, Jr. and Stout (2015). However, action research has been criticized for a tendency to focus on relatively narrow, technical classroom concerns (Santiago Sanchez & Borg, 2015). In this evidence-informed chapter, we illustrate how a focus on technical aspects of classroom pedagogy may mask important insights about how students engage with classroom assignments. These include how they participate in group work and how they perceive the interrelatedness of their larger curriculum. We argue that teachers may benefit from widening their perspective toward what is researched from a technical focus to larger issues of student processes of participation and learning. We illustrate this through discussing how student learning histories, such as language learning histories (Murphey & Carpenter, 2008), influence how they engage with language classrooms, or how in-class student language is shaped by social interactions outside the classroom.

In presenting this argument for teacher-researchers to broaden the research questions they ask, we reference an action research investigation we had planned into students' textual knowledge production through student-created business case studies. We had planned for Google Documents to serve as a social space for students to compose and revise their business case study texts over a semester at a prestigious private university in Tokyo, Japan. The assumption we had made was that students would use the course Google Documents introduced by the teacher to construct their business case study texts. As Google Documents tracks the revisions made to a given document, we had thought this would facilitate a detailed text history investigation of how their case studies were composed and revised. We had planned to apply a translanguaging lens (Lee & Canagarajah, 2018) to analyze how the texts were produced, comparing the original source material and how students represented and negotiated knowledge claims from that source material in their texts. However, as we analyzed the course Google Documents' revision histories, it quickly became apparent that students had not composed their texts using those documents, but rather produced their texts outside our view as teacher-researchers. This dilemma is common in applied research, where participants' engagement with activities often differs from expectations.

This chapter presents a description of how we broadened our research perspective as teacher-researchers to include an investigation of students' engagement with assigned activities, rather than solely focusing on their collaborative knowledge production in the case study texts. This is compatible with an academic literacies perspective toward investigating student writing (Lea & Street, 1998), as it involves focused interviews about how they completed classroom tasks and discussing the larger purpose of the assignment. We illustrate how the original narrower research focus would have led to fewer insights about how students engage with and complete classroom activities. It was only through approaching the research with a sense of curiosity, a willingness to be surprised by the process, and flexibility in our approach that we were able to glean the insights that we share here.

In this reflective chapter, we illustrate how encountering unexpected student responses is a natural part of the teacher-researcher experience. Through data analysis, these surprises can yield valuable insights into the teaching and learning process beyond the scope of initial research plans. We explore issues important to fellow teacher-researchers, who play an essential role in the action research tradition (Nunan, 1990; 1992). We link this study of our classroom investigation to the wider practitioner-research literature and illustrate how encountering unexpected student responses in our teacher-research project led us to widen our research lens. We hope that this example will inspire other teacher-researchers to remain open to surprises and to consider broadening their own research perspectives when unexpected findings arise.

This chapter begins with a short review of some key concepts important to our discussion, including academic literacies (Lea & Street, 1998), translanguaging (Gallagher & Colohan, 2017; Lee & Canagarajah, 2018; Toth & Paulsrud, 2017), and English for specific purposes (Watson Todd, 2003). This is followed by a description of the research methods we applied in our investigation. As this chapter is not a traditional presentation of research, we then discuss several issues we encountered during the research process and how we responded to them. Finally, in our conclusion, we share how the insights we gleaned through our research process could potentially inform other teacher-researchers in dealing with surprises in data from their own investigations.

Review of Key Concepts and Terms

We had initially planned to investigate case study creation processes using translanguaging (Cross, 2016; Gallagher & Colohan, 2017; Toth & Paulsrud, 2017) and academic literacies perspectives (Lea & Street, 1998). Encompassing this more theoretical underpinning was an English for specific purposes (ESP) orientation toward teaching and learning English (Watson Todd, 2003), with a focus on business content in language lessons. These concepts are important to our insights regarding the problematic assumptions we made going into the investigation, so here we present a brief review of them and how they inform our study.

According to Lea and Street (1998), academic literacies challenges the problematic assumption that academics possess a set of skills that students lack. This view, sometimes called a *deficit view*, suggests that students need to improve their writing in order to meet the expectations of higher education. Academic literacies takes a different approach, recognizing that writing is a complex social practice that involves multiple perspectives and contexts. The foundation of academic literacies is a socialization approach toward learning higher education's conventions. That is to say, academic literacies does not approach the curriculum as represented by a discrete set of definable skills that students lack and thus require training to acquire. Academic literacies characterizes such a view of higher education as the conventional approach to teaching writing (Lea & Street, 1998). An academic literacies approach views the learning of higher education's textual conventions as an inherently social process in which some students have readier access to than others, based on a variety of sociocultural factors (Lea & Street, 1998). Thus, in academic literacies, students are seen as coming to the curriculum with a variety of backgrounds and life experiences that differentially prepare or hinder their readiness to engage in the social conventions of university knowledge production (Lillis, 2001). An academic literacies approach addresses disparities in student preparedness for university-level writing by focusing on their experiences and socialization into its textual conventions (Lea & Street, 1998). This approach emphasizes the importance of developing students' awareness of the social and cultural context of academic writing, and helping them to navigate its specific requirements and expectations. Academic literacies has typically been used to investigate university learning in Anglophone contexts such as the UK (Lea & Street, 1998). For example, how first-generation college students' experiences differ from continuing-generation students in terms of "weaker academic preparation, tenuous social support, and high risk of attrition" (Penrose, 2002, p. 437). In the context of learning English in Japanese universities, it offers the advantage of acknowledging that students enter the classroom with learning histories that likely shape how they engage in the classroom in important ways. For example, how students have been taught to compose texts in their previous learning is likely to influence how they approach textual production in their later learning (Lillis, 2001).

Just as academic literacies views higher education conventions as social practices, translanguaging sees language use as inherently social and multifaceted (Lee & Canagarajah, 2018). The implications of such views for educational practice are that learning cannot be broken down into discreet, rarefied skills that can be taught outside of the larger social context in which those skills are used. Translanguaging and academic literacies both push against a reductionist, deficit paradigm that learners lack some identifiable ability that can be taught to them separate from the larger socialization inherent to higher education schooling.

Therefore, a translanguaging lens (Lee & Canagarajah, 2018) is compatible with an academic literacies approach toward learners' socialization into higher education. Translanguaging views languages as inherently interconnected and interdependent, especially at the level of individual language users, rather than as separate and discrete (Lee & Canagarajah, 2018). From a translanguaging perspective, language users are not using disconnected, nameable languages such as Japanese or English. Rather, they are using language to pursue social communicative purposes (Lee & Canagarajah, 2018), employing all the language resources at their disposal that they consider socially appropriate. In this investigation, that includes Japanese and English as inherently interrelated language systems at the individual and social interactive levels. In other words, a translanguaging view of language production focuses on the message conveyed rather than the language medium (in this case, English or Japanese) that it is conveyed in (Lee & Canagarajah, 2018). Attention is paid to the social semiotic space in which interaction occurs and how the languages in use in that space facilitate conveying meaning (Lee & Canagarajah, 2018). The advantage of applying such a translanguaging lens to the analysis of students' language learning is that rather than seeing the use of students' first language (in this case, Japanese) as a hindrance to their English learning, it represents a social semiotic resource that assists them to successfully communicate their intended meaning.

Finally, as the classroom we investigated is a business English class, this study intersects with issues raised in the ESP literature. One criticism leveled against ESP is that it tends to concentrate more on what should be taught, or concerns with vocabulary and forms (Skeates, 2016), to the detriment of how it should be taught, or the best methods for teaching vocabulary and forms (Watson Todd, 2003). For example, Hyland's (2011) concept of specificity argues that teachers should focus on language associated with the target genre/register of a course, or that the target language taught should be based on analysis of student needs. However, how to use the results of a needs analysis to inform instructional methods is left to teachers. By adopting an academic literacies and translanguaging-informed investigative approach, we discuss social processes of student knowledge production in ESP business English lessons. Specifically, we explore the implications for ESP pedagogy of how students engage with classroom assignments.

Methods of Investigation

Here we separately discuss the pedagogic and research methods applied in this investigation, paying attention to our perspectives going into the research project, how these came to be seen as problematic as the research progressed, and the new perspectives that these problems inspired through the widening of our research lens.

Pedagogical Methods

As this is a reflective piece, it is important to acknowledge the roles we play in the research narrative as teacher-researchers. In Colin's year-long course, he concentrated on academic writing in the first semester and on developing business case studies, the focus of this chapter, in the second semester. He has published on earlier incarnations of student-created case studies, including his approach to needs analysis (Skeates, 2015) and the necessity of focusing on factors other than language, such as different student language proficiency levels in the same class in an ESP course (Skeates, 2016). Theron's contribution to this project was in negotiating the research design and assisting with the data analysis, topics which are discussed in the next subsection. Theron is an English language teacher-researcher who practices and investigates the teaching of student writing (Muller, 2012, 2014, 2015), so his interest in researching individual contexts of language use informed this investigation in important ways.

The course's final assessment was an end-of-term group oral presentation of a student-created business case study that students were expected to produce using self-identified sources. As part of the preparation for this assignment, the class included intergroup discussions about every two weeks. In general, case studies exhibit considerable diversity (see Yin, 2014, for a general overview, and Myers, 2013 for discussion specific to business). In this instance, students were asked to organize their case studies using a 5-section scaffold adapted from Swiercz (n.d.). It includes an introduction, background of the problem, analysis of what the company did, missing information that would have meant a deeper exploration of the issues related to the case, and references. As Yin (2014) explains, a case study seeks to explain the why and how of the problem investigated. Consistent with how students learned in the first semester, they were asked to use Google Documents to organize their case study texts. As researchers, we had initially envisioned these as online spaces that would facilitate, host, and archive student collaboration. Within a shared course Google Drive folder, each group was provided a template file to copy and use to develop their case study. Students were asked to add information as the course convened and develop the case study together in their groups. With three to five members per group, the expectation had been that over time, the case study documents would increase in length and word count as group members synthesized information from in-class lectures and insights relevant to their business case study investigation.

Research Methods

Colin was responsible for the collection and initial analysis of data. The planned text history analysis of students' business case studies was based on Theron's doctoral research into the writing for publication practices of Japan-based authors (Muller, 2018). In that research, he examined the changes made to manuscripts as they underwent peer review and revision along their trajectories toward publication. We hoped that the methods Theron applied there could be used to analyze the students' texts in this investigation, albeit in pursuit of different research goals. Thus, the initial analytical framework we planned to employ was best understood by Theron, who would guide Colin in applying it to the students' business case study data. However, as we next describe, our initial plans concerning the collection and analysis of students' business case studies had embedded within them several problematic assumptions that form the basis for our discussion in this chapter.

While our initial intention was to do a "text history" (Lillis & Curry, 2006, p. 8) analysis of the business case study texts, it became apparent as we analyzed our data that students did not extensively revise the texts. In response to this and to better understand how the students engaged with the class assignments, Colin decided to conduct three focused interviews after the course finished asking how students completed the assignments. Through these sessions we came to better understand how they approached the assignments and why the Google Documents and their revision histories did not yield the richly detailed revision work we (problematically) assumed they would. How these insights inform our understanding of some of the problematic assumptions we made going into this research is discussed next.

DISCUSSION OF KEY ISSUES ARISING THROUGH THE INVESTIGATION

As we were interested in how students worked on the class tasks outlined previously, their completing them in an unexpected way led us to want to better understand how they approached the assignments. The next three sections outline issues that emerged during our investigation, shedding light on the assumptions we initially had about student work. We hope these insights can inform other teacher-researchers interested in investigating their own practice.

Problematic Assumptions About How Students Use Technology

An early issue that emerged was our assumption that students would use course Google Documents to revise and discuss their manuscripts, which turned out to be incorrect. We gradually came to this realization as we examined the word counts from week to week along with textual changes. Students appeared to add text in chunks, likely copying and pasting from elsewhere. Further, once text was added, it tended not to be revised.

As we conducted the post-course interviews, we found that students did indeed collaborate to construct their case study texts, albeit outside the class Google Documents set up for them to use. Rather, the interviews revealed that they used communication technologies they had more control over to discuss and prepare the assignment texts. These included *Line*, a popular social messaging application in Japan, along with creating their own Google and Microsoft Word documents. Regarding production processes, some students reported writing first in Japanese then translating into English (Interviews 1, 2, and 3). In these interviews, participants reported finding Japanese information online. They copied and pasted it into word processing software, then translated it into English themselves or with translation software. They focused on using English that their group members would understand, as other group members needed to read and synthesize the text to develop the case study (Interviews 2 and 3). Students reported further modifying the English text for the benefit of students in other groups, who were audience members for the end of term presentations (Interviews 2 and 3). This demonstration of students' social awareness through paying explicit attention to using language other students would understand within and outside their group helps illustrate how the social context of production influences the texts, even though how it influences them was not visible to us as researchers. This also shows how students may complete an assignment while only superficially engaging the resources specified by their teacher, in this case the course Google Documents. We observed that the course Google Document text was largely a by-product of socialization processes, rather than the medium through which students socialized. A potentially important pedagogical insight is that interviewing students about how they engaged with the class assignments demonstrated that they did indeed devote time and energy to them, as teachers might expect. However, the tool we had planned to use (to make how they completed their assignments visible to us as teacher-researchers) did not fully capture the work they put into their assignments. Teachers may want to keep such limitations of their observational tools in mind when assessing student effort; in this instance, concluding that the students had not spent time or effort, and basing assessments off such conclusions, would have been problematic.

From a teacher perspective, neither of us had anticipated students not using the course Google Documents, particularly since the students had used them in the first semester and because they are so commonly used in our own professional experience. For example, we used them to compose this chapter and our previous co-authored work (such as Muller & Skeates, 2022). Theron regularly uses them with co-authors and editors, including for preparing many of the documents involved in publishing this edited book. In addition, as this was an online class, the need for a structured means of collaboration contributed to our thinking that students would use the course Google Documents. However, from the students' perspectives, they were a place to put completed texts, which gave them a more archival than textual construction role. Notably, up to 50% of sources cited in students' end-of-year case study presentations did not appear in the course Google Documents, a further indication that students did not use the documents as Colin had intended.

Concerning this research, had we kept to our original data analysis plan, we would have found little evidence of student textual production processes. Rather, most of the text would appear to have been copied and pasted from elsewhere, whether that elsewhere was student-composed text, the result of translation engine use, or some other source. Studies on student appropriation of language—an alternative term for plagiarism—have been fruitful, revealing how it can be part of the learning process rather than a practice to be punished and banned (Abasi, et al., 2006). Investigations that examine finished student writing for some features or characteristics are not atypical, such as word count (Muller, 2014) and reference language source (Adamson and Coulson, 2015). However, focusing solely on students' final writing products may overlook the dynamic processes of textual production, where changes are made to texts as they are developed and refined, a phenomenon that has been illustrated in the context of writing for publication (Muller, 2018). However, in this instance, analyzing such production processes proved more difficult than we had anticipated.

Our experience described here offers a cautionary tale for teacher-researchers. Seemingly straightforward changes to classroom procedures and technologies, such as introducing a new online platform for collaborative writing, may be viewed as disruptive or confusing by students. Thus, in this instance, a better initial research question may have been to ask how students compose written texts for any collaborative writing assignment. Once students' standard compositional processes have been established, then questions could be asked about how we as teacher-researchers could investigate them.

Teacher Versus Student Conceptualizations of Group Work

One aspect of having students create business case studies was the intention to promote collaboration. Colin assumed that, similar to past students who took the course, current students would discuss and negotiate the textual content together. However, upon examining the course Google Documents, it became clear that students had largely worked on their own parts of their documents separately, with little to no interaction, such as marginal comments or text mixing. Had we not broadened our research perspective, we might have concluded that the students largely did not interact with one another's texts. However, through the interviews, students shared how they understood the course Google

Documents helped foster collaboration and deeper understanding (Interviews 1, 2, and 3). Asking about how the students collaborated led to discussion of different group strategies. One group indicated how they had worked alone until toward the end of the semester when they needed to prepare their presentation (Interview 1). As noted previously, another group reported using social messaging applications (e.g., Line) to discuss their case study text (Interview 3). Finally, as we previously discussed, members of a third group worked individually to translate Japanese texts into English using Microsoft Word before adding their translated text to the Google document. This group took into account the comprehensibility of their text for classmates as the final presentation approached (Interview 3).

At the outset of this project, we assumed that students would work together in similar ways, but our findings revealed a heterogeneity of collaborative practices. This issue highlights the need for a more nuanced understanding of how students engage in group work. The three groups interviewed employed three different group work strategies, demonstrating that these students differentially implemented class instructions. Thus, group work should not have been assumed to be a jumping off point for this investigation. Rather, the investigation would have been more robust if it had made the phenomenon of group work a topic of investigation, asking how students collaborate instead of problematically assuming homogeneity across the different groups.

This issue has broader implications for teacher-researchers, highlighting the need to go beyond simply stating that students worked in groups or pairs, and instead examine the specific processes and strategies employed when students collaborate. To achieve this, teacher-researchers can use conversation analysis-style examinations of student classroom interactions, as demonstrated in Muller & DeBoer (2012), to explore how students negotiate classroom activities and meaning. It may be that while group work is popular in active learning-oriented classrooms, students could be unsure about how to effectively work together. This means that, for example, they may complete activities such as gap fill exercises in different and unexpected ways from one group to the next. Thus, understanding the processes students employ when doing group work may help to illuminate important insights about how educational outcomes could be improved.

Implications of Students' Perceptions of the Interrelated Nature of Their Curriculum

The third issue that emerged was how students interacted with and understood the marketing terms and concepts covered in this class and their business education in Japanese. Previous research has shown that students see links between content they learn in Japanese and in English, which helps them draw useful inferences in understanding (Adamson & Coulson, 2015), an essential aspect of a translanguaging perspective toward student learning. However, because of the nature of the lesson content Colin teaches in this course, he assumed there would be little or no crossover between it and the broader curriculum, as he intentionally covers concepts from business education no longer contemporary in the field. For example, none of the marketing reference texts (e.g., Tuckwell, 1997) used on the course mention social networking sites, despite the central role they play in current-day marketing research (e.g., Wang, et al., 2021). Further, to the extent there was crossover, Colin had assumed it would be one-way, from Japanese into English. One such example of this was a student who said, "Because I already know it (the word / concept) in Japanese, it is easy to translate into English" (Student 1, Interview 1). This reflects the kind of crossover observed in Adamson and Coulson (2015), where learning concepts in Japanese assisted students' English understanding, or a one-way process of learning in Japanese informing student learning in English. However, in this investigation, students experienced this crossover in both directions, as Colin summarized following Interview 2:

> Students then spoke about the translation of meaning going both ways—sometimes the Japanese helped them better understand the English and sometimes the lecture content in English helped them better understand what they were learning in Japanese. (Interview 2 Summary)

This idea was further elaborated upon in Interview 3:

> The Japanese marketing classes helped us to understand the English class. For example, we studied the 4Ps [a marketing concept] in Japanese. That said, the English lectures were really easy to understand. (Student 8)

Concerning how their English lessons helped them understand their Japanese lesson content, Student 8 noted that:

> In Japanese classes, we had lectures, and sometimes videos; there was no discussion about the ideas. In Colin's class, we could talk with each other and, therefore, better understand the content. (Interview 3, Student 8)

Thus, the key to the two-way crossover, at least for this student, was that in their English lesson there was a space for students to interact with one another to better understand the different concepts covered in both their English and Japanese lessons. In this instance, it is not the language medium of interaction that the student flags as important. Rather, it is the opportunity for interaction that is valued, i.e., the social space for drawing inferences between concepts in common between their English and their Japanese lessons. In addition to facilitating their understanding of the English content, this interaction gives students opportunities to more deeply comprehend concepts covered previously in their Japanese business lectures. This insight highlights the inherent interrelatedness of language, which we gained by adopting a translanguaging lens to understand how students used their languages in two-way knowledge interaction.

Another insight concerns the importance of giving students space to discuss and come to their own common understandings of course content. Without this opportunity, it is likely that learning across both courses would have suffered. Creating the case study required the application of concepts, not only demonstrating understanding, which helped students further integrate the content. Of particular importance here is how the previously hidden socialization process (students discussing key concepts) challenges the teacher's assumptions (Colin thinking that the English and Japanese lesson content were mostly unrelated). This suggests that teacher-researchers may benefit from asking themselves what commonalities students see in their curriculums rather than treating courses as standalone experiences. After all, most students are taking more than one course per semester and are therefore more likely to see opportunities for crossover than teachers, who may not have a comprehensive view of students' curriculums. This is particularly true for adjunct, part-time teachers, as in Colin's case.

One effective approach for gaining insight into student experiences of learning is through student reflective writing. As Muller (2012, 2015) discussed, this method allows for a thorough exploration of how students perceive the connection between their medical English lessons and the broader medical curriculum. Specifically, students mention the tension between needing to master medical terminology to successfully navigate the curriculum requirements of medical school and the need to communicate with patients in a language they can understand, whatever the language medium may be.

In summary, the investigation revealed that Colin's assumption that the content of the Japanese course was mostly unrelated to the English course was incorrect, as students identified areas of overlap between the two courses. This suggests that it would have been beneficial for Colin to inquire about the areas of overlap and how students perceived them. Additionally, Colin assumed that student discussions in the English course were only related to that course, but students identified connections between different courses they were taking. This highlights the importance of seeking to understand students' experiences and perspectives to gain a more comprehensive understanding of their learning.

Conclusion: How Gaps and Overlaps Help in Theorizing the Research Process

To conclude, we have described how our initial plans for our practitioner-research project included problematic assumptions about how students engage with course assignments. Rather than ignoring these issues and following through with our planned analysis of data, we saw this as an opportunity to expand our approach and gain a better understanding of students' experiences in the course. Doing so yielded important insights regarding problematic assumptions we had made going into the research. These assumptions included: first, that students would use Google Documents in the manner intended by the teacher; second, that group work would be homogeneous across student groups while in fact it was heterogeneous; and third, that the English course content would generally not overlap with students' Japanese language curriculum while students did, in fact, identify such connections. Further, keeping an open mind facilitated important insights that we otherwise would not have been able to make. Specifically, this re-envisioning of our research reaffirmed the following three insights: first, the importance of students' learning histories to their approach to course assignments, consistent with an academic literacies approach to higher education socialization processes; second, group work showed surprising diversity of student implementation, including different ways of producing texts and translanguaging strategies that as teacher-researchers we could not easily see; and third, how higher education socialization fosters student understanding, including two-way insights between curricular content taught in English and Japanese. We interlink our insights concerning these issues with how other teacher-researchers may widen their own research lenses, thereby investigating less technical and more fundamental issues of relevance to classroom language learning.

Author Bios

Theron Muller is an Associate Professor at the University of Toyama, Japan. His doctorate is from The Open University, UK, research exploring the publication practices of Japan-based language teachers. He has published and presented widely on writing for academic publication, English language teaching and learning, and teacher development.

Colin Skeates is an adjunct professor at various universities in Japan. He has a master's in teaching English and a bachelor's in marketing research. He is currently exploring the uses of panoramic technology through a company he co-founded, limex360.com.

9
Effects of Extensive Reading on Japanese Learners' Writing Ability

Kiyomi Yoshizawa, Atsuko Takase, and Kyoko Otsuki

Extensive reading (ER) has been reported to help language learners develop their cognitive skills for reading comprehension, reading fluency, vocabulary acquisition, and grammar (e.g., Beglar et al., 2012). Moreover, ER has been proven to positively impact the development of language learners' affect, such as motivation and attitudes towards reading in a foreign/second language (Takase, 2007). Previous studies also report that ER improves learners' writing skills (e.g., Tsang, 1996). Improved writing skills through ER can be particularly advantageous for EFL learners, who may have limited access and exposure to large amounts of the target language. In addition, the number of instructional hours in class is limited in formal educational contexts, so teachers must be selective in the contents of their lessons while meeting institutional and societal expectations (Mermelstein, 2015; Watanabe & Ohba, 2018). This study investigates the impact of ER on the development of summary-writing ability in Japanese EFL learners, as summarization is a critical skill required for academic and business purposes (Yang, 2014).

Previous Studies on the Effects of ER on Writing Skills

Previous studies examining ER and the improvement of writing skills differ in terms of participant age, ER duration, writing measures, and learning contexts. For example, in their 1989 study, Hafiz and Tudor investigated the impact of ER on the development of reading and writing skills. During a 12-week after-school reading program, the ER group (who read graded readers) received 42 hours of instruction. Results indicated that the ER group outperformed the control group on both reading and writing assessments.

Lai (1993), Hafiz and Tudor (1990), and Fujii (2020) examined linguistic characteristics in participants' writing. Lai (1993) examined the number of words (e.g., fluency), error-free T-units, sentence structures, error types, as well as overall impression of content and style of participants' essays. Student writing at the end of the program was significantly higher in number of words, error-free T-units, as well as overall content and style than at the beginning. Hafiz and Tudor (1990) reported that the ER group increased fluency and accuracy of expression (word types, syntactically acceptable T-units, semantically acceptable T-units, and spelling correctness) with no significant difference in lexical complexity or syntactic maturity. In a study conducted by Fujii (2020), participants' writing fluency, syntactic maturity, syntactic accuracy, and lexical complexity were assessed. The results showed a significant improvement in fluency and syntactic accuracy, but not in syntactic maturity or lexical complexity. The study concluded that participants wrote more effectively by using simpler sentence structures by the end of the program.

Other studies used the *ESL Composition Profile* (Jacobs et al., 1981) to assess participants' writing. Tsang (1996) conducted a comparative study of after-school activities with a 24-week duration. Participants were "pre-selected" (p. 216) from high-performing classes based on their academic performance in the previous year and randomly assigned to one of three groups: an ER group, a writing group, or a mathematics group (control group). The ER group demonstrated significant gains in content, language use, and overall improvement in writing quality, while the other groups did not. In Lee and Hsu (2009), the ER group similarly outperformed the control group. Mermelstein (2015) examined the effect of 15 to 20 minutes of ER during class on Taiwanese university students' writing skills, showing that the ER group outperformed their counterparts in all aspects except organization.

While showing promising results, these studies have some potential problems with their internal validity. First, Tsang (1996), Lee and Hsu (2009), and Mermelstein (2015) assessed participants' writing using the ESL Composition Profile, which provides an assessment of ESL test-takers' writing ability based on five analytic scales: content, organization, vocabulary, language use, and mechanics. However, the subscale content is not ability-based yet constitutes 30% of the assessment. Bachman and Palmer (2010) acknowledge that content knowledge is part of language ability in some assessment situations. However, the essay topics Tsang (1996), Lee and Hsu (2009), and Mermelstein (2015) used were all related to the participants. To what extent correspondence is achieved between what is written and what a writer intends to communicate is not clear. Second, only Lee and Hsu (2009), Mermelstein (2015), and Fujii (2020) applied ER in regular school curricula. The remaining studies used extracurricular activities or summer activities when school was in recess. Further, ER was a novel activity for participants, so it is more likely that their motivation to read or attitudes toward reading were higher than in regular classrooms. Third, the writings in Lee and Hsu (2009) and Mermelstein (2015) were assigned as homework, with no information available concerning the time spent on writing or dictionary use. Thus, factors other than participation in ER may have influenced students' writing performance. Finally, Lai (1993) and Fujii (2020) did not have a control group, so it is difficult to judge whether the improvement in the participants' writing was due to ER or natural growth.

Despite some potential problems with their internal validity, these studies suggest that ER facilitates learner writing ability development regardless of age, ER duration, writing measures, or learning context. For example, the ER learners in Mermelstein (2015) outperformed their counterparts in writing at the end of the program even though only a small portion of class time was used for ER each week. The learning context in Mermelstein (2015) resembles that of many EFL programs, where ER is adopted along with a designated textbook in an official reading program.

Additional research is required to determine the impact of ER on the writing proficiency of EFL learners in two particular areas. Firstly, it is uncertain if ER enhances writing ability in genres other than descriptive writing since the seven studies referenced only used essays or descriptive writing samples (Tsang, 1996). Secondly, the extent to which ER enhances writing organization among EFL learners is unclear. Despite employing the same ESL Composition Profile, Tsang (1996), Lee and Hsu (2009), and Mermelstein (2015) obtained varying results. Although Lee and Hsu (2009) observed a significant improvement in writing organization, the other two studies (Tsang, 1996; Mermelstein, 2015) did not report significant gains. This study aims to investigate both aspects, while considering the application of ER in an EFL school context where a designated textbook is used as part of an official reading program to enhance ecological validity.

Study Aims

This study[1] examines to what degree ER improves EFL learners' summary writing skills and influences their writing organization. In the study's design, we referred to Cumming et al.'s (1989) research, which demonstrated that adult English speakers learning French created a mental model of text significance by integrating situational, propositional, and verbatim representations of available information. As reading proceeded, participants' mental models were revised as new information was processed and incorporated. While summarizing, their mental models were further revised based on the "perceived correspondence to the passage and the need to state its most integral elements accurately" (Cumming et al., p. 208). This study analyzes the impact of ER on the development of Japanese EFL learners' summary-writing skills, specifically in terms of the number of correct propositions and coherence. Correct propositions refer to propositional representations following Cumming et al.'s (1989) research, while coherence relates to situational representations that establish binary relations between text segments based on their propositional content (Hobbs, 1979). In this study, coherence primarily pertains to the sequence of principal events in a narrative text since summary writing requires identifying coherence relations.

Method

Participants

A total of 102 Japanese university students participated in this study, 47 in the ER group and 55 in the control group. Their English proficiency ranged from CEFR A2 to B1. Before university, most students had studied English for six years in junior and senior high school, where the main teaching methods were the communicative approach combined with grammar translation. English teaching and learning in Japan often focuses on entrance examinations, especially for universities. Many students prepare for these exams by familiarizing themselves with grammatical structures and memorizing vocabulary. Thus, while students have some knowledge of grammar and vocabulary, they have difficulty utilizing what they have learned in actual communication.

ER was implemented with the experimental group for one academic year, which consisted of two 15-week semesters. The group comprised first- and second-year university students majoring in regional promotion. Each class lasted 90 minutes, with two-thirds of the time spent using *Reading Explorer 3* (Douglas & Bohlke, 2014), a textbook that features passages on natural wonders, interesting places, events, and people. The lessons mainly focused on developing vocabulary, strategic reading skills, and raising textual structure awareness. After working in the textbook, the remaining time was dedicated to *Sustained Silent Reading* (SSR). ER students were also encouraged to read books outside the classroom by checking them out from the university library. The number of words read by the end of the year was 150,000 on average. Books included series from *Oxford Reading Tree*, *Foundations Reading Library*, *Cambridge English Readers*, *Oxford Bookworms*, and *Penguin Readers*. Apart from *Oxford Reading Tree*, books read by the ER participants were graded readers. Following each book, students filled out reading logs with the completion date, book and series titles, word count, readability level, reading time, and a brief comment.

The control group consisted of second-year university students majoring in natural science. They used *Reading Explorer 2* (MacIntyre &

Bohlke, 2014), which featured similar topics to those used by the ER group. The control group's lessons were comparable to those of the ER group, except for the graded reading time. By repeating the same task for pre- and post-tests, the role of the control group was to help determine the impact of the textbook-based teaching method on participants' summary writing.

The two groups shared many similarities in terms of their use of textbooks and teaching approaches, including the use of textbooks in the same series with varying levels and a focus on paragraph reading. Both groups engaged in class discussions, which included inferences, literary effects of wording and sentence structure, and expressing opinions to the whole class. However, the experimental group spent approximately one-third of their class time on SSR, while the control group spent the entire class time on the textbook. Additionally, only the ER group was encouraged to read outside of class.

Materials

The current study utilized the following materials: the *EPER_ppt* (*Edinburgh Project on Extensive Reading Placement/Progress Test*) from the Institute for Applied Language Studies, University of Edinburgh (1995) and a summary writing task.

EPER_ppt

All of the participants took the EPER_ppt Form A at the beginning of the course to assess their language proficiency and reading levels. The EPER_ppt is a cloze test developed by the Edinburgh Project on Extensive Reading (Institute for Applied Language Studies, University of Edinburgh, 1995) to place learners into appropriate reading levels and assess their progress. The test consists of 12 short passages that are approximately 80 words each. They are taken from different levels of obsolete graded readers and arranged in ascending order of difficulty.

Summary Writing Task

Students in both groups completed a summary writing task at the beginning and end of the program. The summary writing task included three steps: First, students read a passage about an American who invented a TV set for 5 minutes. Second, they wrote a summary of the passage for 10 minutes. Third, they answered five comprehension questions about the passage for 3 minutes. The passage was 306 words long (four paragraphs) and followed the main character's life chronologically (Nation & Malarcher, 2007). The *Flesch Reading Ease* score was 76.9%, and the *Flesch-Kincaid Grade Level* was 5.4.

The participants' writing was analyzed for propositions and coherence. For propositions, four proficient English speakers were asked to summarize the story. The propositions common among the four were used as a basis for marking students' writing. Additional propositions were examined, with 16 included at the final stage. Depending on how essential the information in each proposition was, one or two points were assigned to each. Along with the propositions, the summary's overall coherence was also examined, which indicated to what extent the participants could represent the principal events in chronological order, as it was conceivable that students would list propositions from the story without indicating how they were related.

A scoring key was developed through a discussion of the scoring of each proposition. The three authors independently scored all summaries using the key, and any discrepancies were subsequently discussed. A fourth rater scored 21.6% of the participants' summaries using the key. Interrater reliability was calculated using *Kappa statistics* to determine rater consistency, with substantial to almost-perfect agreement found.

Results and Discussion

ER's Effect on Reading Ability: Propositions

Table 1 presents the descriptive statistics for the number of words the ER and control groups wrote in the 10-minute summary writing task at the beginning (Time 1) and end (Time 2) of the reading program. The means for both groups increased by 12 to 15 words. The gain for the ER group was 14.61 and for the control group 11.52. In both, the standard deviations were large.

Table 1

The Gains in the Number of Words in the Participants' Summaries

	ER Group (n = 47)			Control Group (n = 55)		
	Time 1	Time 2	Gains	Time 1	Time 2	Gains
Mean	68.60	83.21	14.61	69.93	81.45	11.52
SD	25.04	27.73	23.62	27.02	27.01	21.87
Minimum	9	20	-52	12	19	-38
Maximum	125	146	63	136	149	65

Table 2 shows the proportion of correct propositions per paragraph and coherence. Figure 1 shows gains in proportions of correct propositions per paragraph and coherence between Time 1 and Time 2. The control group wrote 12% more correct propositions in Paragraph 1 at Time 2 than at Time 1. However, the gains in the propositions in Paragraphs 2 and 3 were 7%, and in Paragraph 4, 3%. The gain in coherence was 4%. The control group showed the largest gain, 12%, in first paragraph propositions; however, gains in propositions in subsequent paragraphs were less than 10%, as was coherence. For the ER group, the proportion of correct propositions in the first paragraph decreased by 2%. Those in the subsequent paragraphs increased 6 to 20%. The ER group also increased their coherence score by 10%. Comparing the control and ER groups, the former increased correct propositions in the first paragraph more than in the subsequent paragraphs and more than coherence; however, the gains in the subsequent paragraphs and coherence gradually decreased. The ER group showed gains about three times more frequently than the control in Paragraphs 3 and 4. A similar pattern was observed for coherence.

Table 2

Propositional Accuracy and Coherence in Written Paragraphs

		P1	P2	P3	P4	Coherence
	Time 1	0.54	0.45	0.45	0.14	0.30
ER	Time 2	0.52	0.51	0.65	0.24	0.40
	Gains	-0.02	0.06	0.20	0.10	0.10
	Time 1	0.45	0.45	0.49	0.08	0.27
CON	Time 2	0.57	0.52	0.56	0.11	0.31
	Gains	0.12	0.07	0.07	0.03	0.04

Note. P1 to P4 refer to the first to fourth paragraphs.

Figure 1

Gains in Propositional Accuracy and Coherence in Written Paragraphs

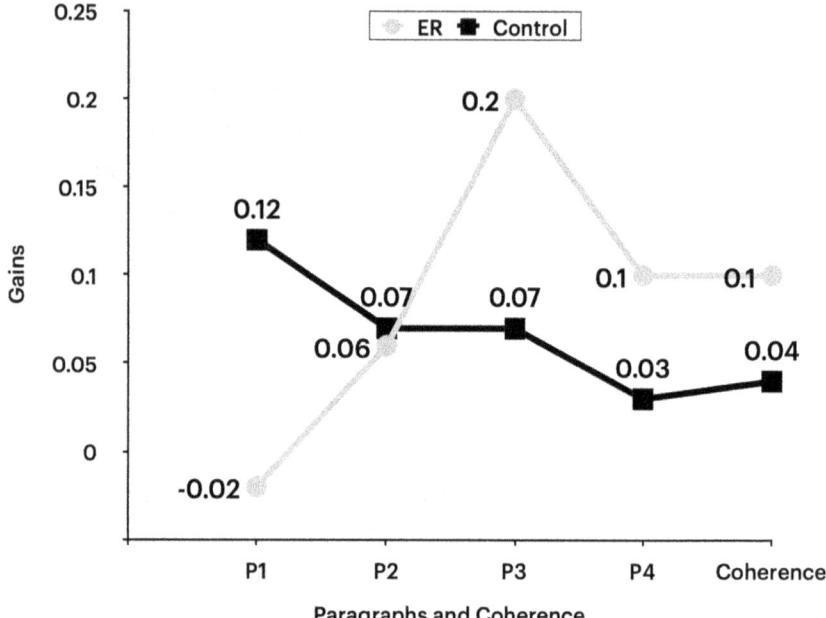

To examine the effect of ER on participants' written propositions, 16 propositions were analyzed using a *Rasch* measurement model to convert scores on the rating scale to an interval scale. One of the results of the Rasch analysis was person ability in logits, which were converted to a scale of 0 to 100. Descriptive statistics of the converted scores are shown in Table 3. Scores improved for both ER and control groups at Time 2 compared to Time 1, with the ER group showing a gain of 12.68 and the control group a gain of 5.41.

Table 3

Descriptive Statistics of 16 Propositions (Converted Scores)

	ER Group (n = 42)		Control Group (n = 49)	
	Time 1	Time 2	Time 1	Time 2
Mean	43.37	56.05	45.31	50.72
SD	15.84	17.96	17.34	17.10
Minimum	0.17	15.81	0.00	14.76
Maximum	75.04	90.33	80.49	90.33

A one-way between-groups analysis of covariance (*ANCOVA*) was conducted to compare the effectiveness of ER on the participants' summary-writing ability. The independent variable was the instruction type (with or without ER). The dependent variable was the converted scores for the propositions written at the end of the program (Time 2). The converted scores for the propositions written at the beginning of the program (Time 1) were the covariate. An ANCOVA examines the impact of an independent variable while controlling for the effects of preexisting variables (Pallant, 2013). Before the ANCOVA, we confirmed that the assumptions for conducting a one-way ANOVA were met. There was no violation of the assumptions of normality, linearity, homogeneity of variances, homogeneity of regression slopes, or reliable measurement of the covariate. After adjusting for the effect of the preexisting variable, that is, the converted scores for the propositions written at Time 1, there was no significant difference between the two groups in the converted scores for the propositions at Time 2, $F(1, 87) = 3.49$, $p = .065$, partial eta squared = .04.

The Effect of ER: Coherence

McNemar tests (McNemar, 1947) examined whether there was a change in the proportion of participants' coherent summaries from the beginning to end of the program. Table 4 shows the crosstabulation of the coherent (1) and incoherent (0) summaries. The underlined numbers show changes in coherence between summaries. For the ER group, six students wrote incoherent summaries at Time 1 and coherent summaries at Time 2. Two wrote coherent summaries at Time 1 but incoherent ones at Time 2. These changes were not significant: $p = .289$. A similar pattern was observed for the control group. Ten students wrote incoherent summaries at Time 1 but coherent at Time 2. Eight wrote coherent summaries at Time 1 but incoherent at Time 2. These changes were not significant: $p = .815$.

Table 4

Cross-Tabulation of Coherent and Incoherent Summaries

		Time 2 (ER)		Time 2 (Control)	
		0	1	0	1
Time 1	0	15	<u>6</u>	18	<u>10</u>
	1	<u>2</u>	20	<u>8</u>	19

Note. 0 = not coherent; 1 = coherent

Summary of the Findings

After one year of instruction, both the ER and control groups showed improvement in the propositions included in their summaries. The descriptive statistics suggested that the ER group improved more than the control group, although statistical significance was not observed, despite the difference approaching significance. Thus, ER may have improved EFL learners' summary-writing skills even when only one-third of instruction time was spent on SSR. The statistical results for the differences between the ER and control groups may be partly due to the weight given to propositions. The first paragraph is short, consisting of only two sentences. It introduces the topic of the passage, the inventor of television, and states that he is not well-recognized as TV's inventor. His biography begins in the second paragraph. For the first summary, 45% of the control group and 30% of the ER group wrote the proposition referring to his recognition nearly verbatim. For the second, 50% of the control group and 28% of the ER group wrote the acknowledgement proposition verbatim (Cumming et al., 1989). In our analysis, verbatim and propositional representations were not differentiated, which may have confounded our results. Another factor which might have resulted in smaller group differences is the amount of writing in each summary. We did not set a minimum amount for students to write because the summary writing time was only 10 minutes, so we anticipated some summaries would be short. As Table 1 indicates, both the ER and control groups showed large variation in summary length at Time 1 and Time 2. If a minimum amount to write had been set and summaries longer than the criterion had been analyzed, a clearer picture might have emerged.

Concerning coherence, neither group showed significant differences between their writing at the beginning and end of the program, like Tsang (1996) and Mermelstein (2015) and unlike Lee and Hsu (2009). One factor that might have affected participants' writing skill improvement is whether they had instruction aimed at improving writing skills. Lee and Hsu (2009) and Mermelstein (2015) incorporated one year of writing instruction. No information is available about how much reading their participants did during that year. Nevertheless, Lee and Hsu (2009) may have showed gains due to the quantity of input and writing instruction. For example, Lightbown et al. (2002) compared the second language development of children in a comprehension-based ESL program to those in a regular ESL program over six years, showing that the former outperformed or performed equivalently to the latter on comprehension and oral production but not writing. Lightbown et al.

(2002) concluded that comprehension-based instruction alone does not automatically lead to writing skill development, so these need to be taught. However, this does not explain why Mermelstein (2015) showed nonsignificant results, thus further study is needed.

Another factor that may have influenced the proposition and coherence results is the issue of time on task outside class. The participants used different levels of the same textbook series and were instructed to prepare for in-class study by answering comprehension questions. Each week, the participants spent 30 minutes to one hour on this preparation. Also, vocabulary quizzes were administered each week that they spent time preparing for. Further, ER group participants were strongly encouraged to read outside class. As a rough estimate, the participants in the ER group read about 150,000 words at a reading rate of about 100 words per minute (WPM). They were encouraged to select books they could comfortably read at that rate, and their reading logs showed this was the case. Further, the ER group spent more time reading ER books outside of class than the control group. However, the amount of time spent outside of class was not controlled to ensure an equivalent amount of time between each group (Suk, 2017; McLean & Rouault, 2017). Because the amount of time spent outside of class was not controlled, this lack of control may have contributed to the absence of significant differences between the two groups' propositions and coherence.

Summary Examples (ER Group)

What follows are examples of changes observed in the ER group's writing. Excerpt 1 shows the summaries of Tomi (pseudonym) at the beginning (Tomi 1) and end (Tomi 2) of the program. The numbers in parentheses indicate the proposition numbers. The summaries are presented proposition by proposition and include errors. One change in Tomi's summaries is an increase in the number of propositions. In Tomi 2, the underlined sentences indicate added propositions. Tomi wrote six propositions at the beginning but more than twice as many by the end. The second change in Tomi 2 is the inclusion of Proposition 2, which is considered integral to the text (i.e., how potatoes grew in long lines provided the main character with a hint regarding television). Tomi wrote "The potato gave him the idea. (2)" Although Tomi's proposition 2 is not exactly accurate, we considered its inclusion worth partial credit. The third change is that Tomi was able to use more linking expressions. As a result, the sequence of events is clearer in Tomi 2. The words in bold help to clarify the sequence of events.

Excerpt 1

Tomi 1

> Philo Farnsworth is a man who first invented television. (1)
> Philo Farnsworth was born in 1906 and grow up potato farm. (3)
> He liked science. (4)
> When he was 13, he came up with the idea about television and draw television picture. (5, 6)
> However, he was not rich. So he couldn't try (7)

Tomi 2

> Philo Farnsworth is the man who invented the Television. (1)
> He was born and grow up on a potato farm. (3)
> He loved science. (4)
> When he was 13-years-old, he drew a television's picture. (5, 6)
> <u>The potato gave him the idea</u>. (2)
> But he was poor, so he couldn't make the machine. (7)
> <u>He worked at many kinds of jobs</u>. (8)
> **Then**, <u>two man gave him the money to make television</u>. (16)
> **So** <u>Philo made a first television</u>. (9)
> <u>During the world war II, he helped the US army, and after the war, many company made television</u>. (12, 13)
> **Finally** <u>Philo had to sell his company</u>. (14)

Excerpt 2 shows Hana's summaries (pseudonym) at two time periods: Hana 1 and Hana 2. The former shows a breakdown in the sequence of events: Proposition 7 is written before Proposition 4. Additionally, Hana 1 includes propositions that are not in the original text. For example, the information in the second clause in the third sentence ("so he became...his company") is a distortion of the original text. The main character built his company after he created his first television model. Similar to the distortion of text, one proposition is based on incorrect inference. Hana wrote the following proposition between Propositions 12 and 14: "After the war was over, he had no money." The original text describes the main character as having supported the US army "instead of building up his television company" and states that his competitors were "bigger, richer companies." Hana's proposition is presumably based on her inference, which has less ground. Furthermore, Proposition 4 is repeated at the end of the paragraph.

In Hana 2, the first change is that the number of propositions increases. At Time 1, Hana wrote eight propositions, five of which were counted as correct. In Hana 2, the underlined seven propositions were added. Thus, Hana 2 includes more than twice as many propositions as Hana 1. The second change is that Hana 2 started with a sentence that introduced the topic of the text: "This story about the man who invented TV." Although her expression was a sentence fragment, we interpreted the fragment as introducing the topic of the text. The third change in Hana 2 is the inclusion of an integral element from the text: "One day he came up with a TV idea. When he saw a potato farming, he got an idea of it. (6, 2)" The fourth change is that Hana 2 shows indications of smooth connection between events. For example, "one day" and "after that" were used to clarify the sequence of events.

Excerpt 2

Hana 1

Philo was poor, and he couldn't invent a television. (7)

[*Wrong order*]
Philo loved science when he was a child and he wanted to make television. (4)
But he worked hard, so he became a rich man and he could build his company. (8) [*Information in the second clause is a distortion of the text*]
Some years later, RCA company said "the television" is our company's product". (10)
Philo fought with RCA, and he won the battle. (11)
When WWII began, he spent a lot of money to the army. After the war was over, he had no money. (12) [*Inaccurate inference*]
At the end of the story, he had to sell his company. (14)
Philo loved science when he was a child and he wanted to make television. (4) [*Repetition*]

Hana 2

<u>This story about the man who invented TV. Philo Farnsworth was born in 1907</u>. (1) [*Introducing a topic*]
Since he was a child, he loved science. <u>He read a lot of science books</u>. (4)
One day <u>he came up with a TV idea. When he saw a potato forming, he got an idea of it</u>. (6, 2) [*Insertion of important information*]
He wanted to invent it, but he was poor man. So he started to earn money. <u>He worked a lot of jobs</u>. (7, 8)
One day <u>he's TV idea was founded by two rich men. They gave money Philo to invent it</u>. (16)
<u>In september 7th 1927, he finally invented TV</u>! (9)
After that, he fought with RCE. Because he must get the rights of selling TV. (10)
He won this battle, but World War II began. (11)
He spent a lot of money to army. (12)
When the war finished, he started to sell it again. (14)

Limitations of the Current Study

This study has several limitations. First, since it was conducted in a natural classroom setting, the summary writing time was restricted, which might affect the number of propositions produced. Second, because intact groups were used, generalizability is limited. Third, as mentioned previously, time outside class was not strictly controlled. Fourth, verbatim representations were not differentiated from propositional representations. Despite these limitations, the study's findings indicate the likely positive effects of ER on developing EFL learners' summarization skills in limited input contexts.

Pedagogical Implications

Our findings suggest that even limited use of ER can improve EFL learners' summary-writing skills. Rather than teaching reading and writing as separate skills, ER can be used to enhance EFL learners' integrated skills (in this case, reading to write). At the same time, we agree with Lightbown et al. (2002), who emphasize the need for instruction geared toward the improvement of writing skills. Summary writing requires the following processes: comprehending textual contents and recognizing the order of primary events. Additionally, since paraphrasing is inevitable in summary writing, learners need to have a wide range of vocabulary, which is facilitated through ER (e.g., Krashen, 1989; Suk, 2017). Previous studies have demonstrated the omnidirectional effects of ER on improving learner English skills, indicating that instruction combined with ER has a greater potential to enhance students' summary writing skills compared to instruction alone.

Finally, our study suggests several strategies for implementing ER in the classroom. First, it is important to provide learners with even a short period of time to read in class, as this can encourage them to read outside of class. Second, while in-class SSR is essential, teachers can maintain learners' motivation by incorporating book-related activities or tasks, such as writing reviews or giving book presentations. Finally, teachers should monitor students' reading behavior regularly through tools such as reading logs to ensure learners are not stuck in a cycle of disfluent reading or a decrease in reading motivation. We hope these suggestions can aid teachers in successfully implementing ER in their classrooms.

Author Bios

Kiyomi Yoshizawa is a professor in the Faculty of Foreign Language Studies and Graduate School of Foreign Language Education and Research, Kansai University, Japan. Her research interests include language testing, reading in a foreign language, and extensive reading. She has incorporated extensive reading in her reading classes for more than ten years.

Atsuko Takase is a teacher at Iwano Private English School in Japan. She has received an Ed.D. in TESOL. Her research interests include extensive reading/listening (ER/EL), motivation to ER/EL, and language acquisition, including grammar and vocabulary through ER/EL. After having practiced ER/EL at high schools and universities for 30 years, she is now practicing ER/EL with students at various age groups, from children to adults. She is currently a board member of the *Extensive Reading Foundation* and the *Japan Extensive Reading Association*.

Kyoko Otsuki is an associate professor at Nara Prefectural University in Japan. She has received a PhD in applied linguistics. Her research interests lie in extensive reading, English grammar, pragmatics, and discourse analysis. She has practiced extensive reading for more than ten years at various universities.

Acknowledgements

This study was supported by JSPS Grant-in-Aid for Scientific Research (C) Grant 18K00766. Furthermore, we are very grateful to Professor Alister Cumming for his insightful and supportive suggestions.

---

1. This chapter is based on a presentation given at the *Extensive Reading Around the World 2021 Conference* (August 21, 2021).

10
Humor Competency Training with Japanese Learners of English

John Rucynski and Caleb Prichard

Humor in L2 communication is a complex skill that can be elusive (Shively, 2018; Wulf, 2010), despite it being used ubiquitously to break the ice, bond, and diffuse tension (Holmes, 2000). Meanwhile, failure to detect or understand humor can lead to confusion, embarrassment, or conflict (Lems, 2013). As humor varies from culture to culture, learning its mores in target culture(s) can empower language learners to benefit from its use and to avoid the pitfalls of not being able to use it in communication. However, making room to develop learners' L2 humor competence in already busy language curricula can be a challenge. Pomerantz and Bell (2011) argue that foreign language classrooms are a "safe house" (p. 150) where learners should have the freedom to experiment with L2 humor. Additionally, language education researchers advocate incorporating humor competence instruction into language teaching curricula (Kim & Lantolf, 2018; Shively et al., 2022; Wulf, 2010).

Two obstacles to making humor competence a component of language education are: First, the lack of teacher awareness about the potential role of humor in language learning (Banas et al., 2011; Bell & Pomerantz, 2016). Literature on humor in education tends to focus on its affective benefits, perhaps leading teachers to believe that humor's only role is as something fun or different to enliven lessons or improve the class atmosphere. Second, there is a lack of understanding about how to incorporate humor into language teaching curricula (Bell, 2011; Wulf, 2010). Although there has been a gradual increase in a focus on humor in English language teaching materials (Gardner, 2020), instructors generally need to look beyond textbooks to include humor instruction in their curricula.

This chapter explores the possibilities of incorporating humor competency training in the language teaching curriculum by examining the question: Does humor instruction lead to gains in learners' humor competence? More specifically, this chapter focuses on verbal irony. We first explain the goals and benefits of humor competency training. After summarizing the results of two previous studies designed to improve Japanese learners' ability to *detect* verbal irony (Prichard & Rucynski, 2020; 2022), we describe follow-up research on how the training affected participants' willingness and ability to *produce* ironic comments in online communication. Finally, we share learners' quantitative and qualitative impressions concerning the effectiveness and usefulness of the training.

Although the frequency and function of verbal irony varies between cultures, it serves a range of purposes, including bantering (Jobert & Sorlin, 2018), bonding (Attardo, 2002), and diffusing tension (Gibbs, 2007). Despite this, there remains little research into language learners' *production* of verbal irony. In one study of Dutch learners of English (Smorenburg et al., 2015), explicit instruction was effective in improving their prosodic ability to express sarcastic utterances. In a more recent study of Spanish language learners (Shively et al., 2022), 2.5 hours of pedagogical intervention improved irony detection and increased the frequency of ironic responses. In contrast to those studies of students' oral production of irony and sarcasm in Dutch learners of English and English-speaking learners of Spanish, the focus of this study is the production of irony by Japanese learners of English in online communication.

Goals and Benefits of Humor Competency Training

In defining humor competence in foreign language education, differentiating between teaching *with* humor and teaching *about* humor is important. Teaching *with* humor refers to using humor to enhance language learning through helping learners relax or by making language learning more interesting and memorable. Teaching *about* humor involves deepening learners' understanding of humor in the target culture(s). To achieve this, Wulf (2010) suggests a generalized approach to teaching humor that incorporates "microskills" (p. 162) training to help learners understand and (possibly) produce L2 humor. Other researchers have focused on increasing learner understanding of specific forms of humor, such as detecting and comprehending English jokes (Hodson, 2014), sarcasm and verbal irony (Kim & Lantolf, 2018; Shively et al., 2022; Smorenburg et al., 2015), in addition to satirical news (Prichard & Rucynski, 2019).

Improving learners' humor competence is not easy. Humor instruction sometimes fails for lack of clear goals, such as what instructors hope learners will be able to *do* with humor. Bell and Pomerantz (2016) propose using a backward design model, first establishing goals or end results of humor instruction before designing activities or materials. They outline four L2 humor goals of helping learners: 1) recognize, 2) understand, 3) respond to, and 4) produce it. All four goals are not necessary for all humor instruction. Choosing which goals to focus on requires considering factors such as learner language proficiency, course curriculum, and appropriateness of humor production. For example, in our previous studies on satirical news (Prichard & Rucynski, 2019; Rucynski & Prichard, 2020), we did not task students in our English reading skills courses to write satirical news; instead, we provided strategies to help them detect and understand satirical news connected with curricular goals to improve critical reading skills and media literacy.

Regarding verbal irony (the focus of this chapter), the four goals outlined by Bell and Pomerantz (2016) can be illustrated through the following examples:

- *Recognition*: On a drizzly day in London, English language learners (ELLs) can detect that the question "Lovely weather, isn't it?" is a sarcastic joke.
- *Understanding*: ELLs can comprehend that the intended meaning is actually "What awful weather!"

- *Response*: ELLs can appropriately reply to the question with a statement such as, "Yeah, just lovely!" (with a sarcastic tone).
- *Production*: ELLs can initiate verbal irony by making a statement such as "Another lovely day, isn't it?"

In addition to establishing clear goals, humor instruction should provide value beyond the humor taught. While humor presents benefits through improved class atmosphere and increased learner motivation, humor instruction should not be limited to providing learners with occasional laughs. As an example, we provided humor competency training on verbal irony in our university English courses in Japan to yield the following three benefits.

First, teaching verbal irony provides learners with insights into the humor of the target culture(s). In Japan, learners may struggle to comprehend verbal irony in English in part because Japanese culture tends to use this kind of humor less often. As conversation analysis has revealed, verbal irony is used more frequently among speakers in predominantly English-speaking countries than in Japan (Gibbs, 2000; Fitzgerald, 2013). This lack of understanding extends to written verbal irony on social media platforms such as Facebook and could be exacerbated by the traditional *yakudoku* (grammar-translation) approach to secondary school English education in Japan (Herder & Clements, 2012). A deeper awareness of how verbal irony is used in English can thus improve learners' pragmatic competence in face-to-face and online communication.

Second, understanding *online* verbal irony (the focus of the second and third studies described in this chapter) is an important component of digital and media literacy. Being able to effectively read and respond to online discussions is an increasingly important media literacy skill (Moon & Bai, 2020; Tsang, 2019). Furthermore, the use of verbal irony, including sarcasm and jocularity, is ubiquitous on social media platforms (Peled & Reichart, 2017). These platforms provide English language learners with free opportunities to interact with countless others in English, but failure to understand and respond appropriately to humor such as verbal irony can result in confusion or embarrassment (Bell & Attardo, 2010; Rucynski & Prichard, 2020).

Third, exposure to verbal irony can improve learners' ability to understand (and produce) non-literal statements, an integral component of pragmatic competence. The inability to detect an interlocutor's intended meaning is a form of "pragmatic failure" (Thomas, 1983, p. 91). Wulf (2010) argues that "being an accomplished L2 speaker involves not only using language for literal statements of fact, but also expressing oneself creatively, including humor" (p. 167). Verbal irony provides invaluable opportunities to practice creative language use, as it focuses on non-literal statements such as hyperbole, jocularity, and sarcasm. Additionally, verbal irony has several useful functions, including lessening or strengthening criticism, strengthening bonds, and amusing others (Gibbs, 2007; Dynel, 2014).

Humor Competency Training for Detecting and Understanding Verbal Irony

While this chapter focuses on the response/production of online verbal irony, we first summarize our previous studies on the detection/understanding of verbal irony (Prichard & Rucynski, 2020; Prichard & Rucynski, 2022). When implementing humor competency training, it is imperative to check learners' ability to detect and understand a given form of humor before expecting them to respond to it or produce their own.

Before planning humor instruction on specific genres of humor, it is first important to ensure that you can answer yes to the following five questions (criteria based on Rucynki & Prichard, 2020):

1. Are learners likely to encounter this form of humor when communicating in English?
2. Are learners likely to struggle to detect, understand, respond to, and/or produce this form of humor?
3. Is there a clear connection between this form of humor and the goals of the course?

4. Are there sufficient authentic materials available to make humor competency training viable?
5. Can the instructor provide instruction on this form of humor through engaging, communicative-based class activities?

Concerning the first question, verbal irony is ubiquitous in English communication, both spoken and written. For example, Gibbs' (2000) analysis of conversations by Americans found that up to 8% of statements include verbal irony. Further, its widespread use extends to English posts and comments on social media platforms (Peled & Reichart, 2017).

Identifying gaps between the humor in learners' native culture(s) and target culture(s) is key to incorporating humor instruction. Just as differences in L1 and L2 grammar or pronunciation can create obstacles to language acquisition, differences in humor can impede smooth L2 communication. Although Japanese does have verbal irony such as sarcasm, or *hiniku*, it differs from English verbal irony in form, function, and frequency (Erickson et al., 2002; Okamoto, 2007). Previous research suggests that Japanese learners of English struggle to identify ironic and sarcastic utterances in English (Fitzgerald, 2013), with Japanese participants in one study only able to identify about half of the sarcastic utterances in English speakers' recordings (Erickson et al., 2002).

Showing that learners will encounter and have trouble understanding humor does not ensure curricular compatibility with teaching humor. Considering the widespread use of verbal irony in English communication, however, a deeper awareness of it can help learners improve their pragmatic competence and avoid confusion or embarrassment. Verbal irony has a range of forms and functions, including *sarcasm* (generally positive words with a negative meaning), *jocularity* (negative words with a positive intent), *surrealistic irony* (illogical or unexpected statements), and *hyperbole* (greatly exaggerated statements). Sarcasm is used to criticize or ridicule and to, for example, bond or sympathize (Gibbs, 2007; Dynel, 2014).

As previously noted, one barrier to humor instruction is the lack of readily available materials. Additionally, a challenge in implementing humor instruction is making it accessible to learners. However, teaching English humor can employ scaffolding and creating modified examples, the same tools used to teach complex grammar and vocabulary. Through compiling resources (e.g., memes and other images, GIFs, audio and video recordings) and teaching microskills (e.g., recognizing different sarcasm cues), we have helped our learners make significant gains in recognizing verbal irony (Prichard & Rucynski, 2020). Verbal irony production is discussed later in this chapter. After finding suitable resources, they need to be used to create engaging, learner-centered class activities that highlight real-world humor applications. In the next section, we provide details about material and class activity design.

Study 1: Detecting Spoken Verbal Irony

Our first study on humor competency training for sarcasm and other verbal irony focused on learners' ability to detect spoken ironic utterances (Prichard & Rucynski, 2020). By examining the effect of classroom instruction, it was built on earlier work by Kim and Lantolf (2018) that focused on private training sessions. The study followed three steps:

1. Participants ($n = 94$) took a pretest measuring their ability to detect spoken verbal irony in short, recorded dialogues. The scores were compared with the scores of L1 English speakers.
2. We provided verbal irony humor competency training for participants in the experimental group.
3. Participants in both the control and experimental group took a posttest to measure improvement in detecting spoken verbal irony.

To compare Japanese learners' ability to detect verbal irony with L1 English speakers, we received permission to use a database prepared by Rothermich and Pell (2015) that features short vignettes of two or three-line dialogues in which listeners determine whether the final utterance is sincere or sarcastic. Rothermich and Pell recruited 38 L1 English speakers to test their ability to detect sarcasm. From the results, we selected the 40 most valid items in which participants could correctly identify sarcasm or sincerity with a success rate of 95.40%. We played them for 94 students in four required English courses. Students from English speaking and listening courses were selected because recognizing spoken verbal irony is important to real-world oral English communication. Our students' ability to distinguish between sarcastic and sincere statements was only 80.35%, indicating that Japanese learners may struggle to recognize sarcasm in English. This difficulty can persist even in short dialogues that include basic vocabulary, although a Japanese translation was provided for more challenging vocabulary items.

For the humor competency training component of the study, experimental group participants ($n = 46$) from two courses received humor instruction on detecting verbal irony, while control group participants ($n = 48$) received no special training. We devoted about 30 minutes per class for three class periods to the humor instruction. The humor competency training consisted of an overview of sarcasm and its various functions, a focus on microskills for detecting spoken verbal irony (including visual and prosodic cues), as well as opportunities for collaboration and communicative practice.

For visual cues instruction, we shared examples of GIFs, images, and memes with faces to compare sarcastic (e.g., averted gaze, blank stare, rolling eyes) and sincere expressions. For instruction on prosodic cues, internet audio and video clips were shared. Students were provided cues to identify sarcastic statements (e.g., elongated vowels, exaggerated speech, negative tone for positive words). When demonstrating visual and prosodic cues, linguistic terms such as "averted gaze" and "elongated vowels" were simplified (e.g., "looking away" instead of "averted gaze") to fit the learners' English proficiency.

After completing the humor competency training, both groups took a posttest where they were again tasked with differentiating between sarcastic and sincere statements using different recordings from the Rothermich and Pell (2015) database. Scores for the two groups were similar on the pretest, but the experimental group gains (humor competency training) on the posttest were significantly higher than those for the control group (no humor competency training). Despite the complexities of foreign language verbal irony, studies (Kim & Lantolf, 2018; Prichard & Rucynski, 2020) show that English language learners can improve their ability to detect verbal irony through research-informed humor competency training.

Study 2: Detecting Ironic Online Comments

For our latest studies on humor competency training (Prichard & Rucynski, 2022), we shifted our focus to online verbal irony. The ability to understand and respond to online discussions is an increasingly important component of digital and media literacy. Further, verbal irony is frequently used in English social media posts and comments (Peng et al., 2019). Additionally, as all our required English courses at the time of these studies were conducted online due to the COVID-19 pandemic, focusing on this type of communication was appropriate and important.

For our first study on detecting online verbal irony, we followed the same steps as our study on spoken verbal irony. First, the ability of Japanese learners of English to detect online verbal irony was compared with that of L1 (or proficient) speakers of English using five fictional Facebook posts that we created. Each of the posts included an original comment accompanied by an image (e.g., meme) or a news headline and blurb. Each post was followed by nine "friend" replies, a mixture of 30 sincere comments and 15 ironic comments. For example, one post featured an image of a dog sitting by a pile of shredded papers that it presumably destroyed (see sample images later in the chapter). Participants rated each comment on a scale of 1 (sincere) to 6 (ironic).

To validate the instrument, we recruited 145 L1 English speakers and highly proficient L2 speakers to pilot it. Participants distinguished the sincere and ironic comments 95% of the time. We then recruited 148 students from our required English courses at our university. The students could identify whether comments were sincere or ironic only 76% of the time, suggesting again that Japanese learners of English struggle to detect verbal irony in English, whether spoken or online.

Next, 129 students from our required English reading and writing courses took either of two versions of a pretest at the beginning of the course to determine their ability to recognize online verbal irony. Participants had an average score of 289 on the *Global Test of English Communication* (GTEC), the proficiency test used by the university to stream students into English classes by proficiency level. As with the previous study, participants in the experimental group ($n = 78$) received humor competency training on detecting online verbal irony while participants in the control group ($n = 51$) did different class activities. As these courses were held asynchronously online, training was delivered via a Google Slides slideshow. Reading the slideshow was estimated to take 30 minutes of class time. The slideshow featured an overview of the functions and risks of verbal irony, followed by cues for detecting verbal irony. Attention was given to paralinguistic cues that help detect ironic online comments, including the sarcasm marker (/s), emojis (e.g., eye roll, upside-down face), or alternating caps (e.g., "wHaT a GoOd DoG!").

Other slides considered expectations. For example, a comment such as "I want a dog just like that!" seems illogical after a picture of a destructive canine. Expectations can be based on knowledge of the world, topic, and awareness of authors' viewpoints. This can be done when commenting online with strangers by following author comments on a thread to judge whether subsequent comments are congruent. To ensure that participants read the slides, comprehension questions about verbal irony cues were included as a required assignment.

After completing the humor competency training, all participants took the posttest. Despite limited time for the humor competency training and no opportunities for F2F collaborative activities, participants in the experimental group (humor competency training) made significantly more gains in their ability to detect online verbal irony compared to the control group (no humor competency training) based on between-subjects *univariate ANOVA*. The greatest gains were in detecting *meaning reversal items* (i.e., recognizing that "What a good dog!" means "What a bad dog!"; Kapogianni, 2011). This study again provides promising evidence that even limited humor competency training can help learners make significant gains in detecting L2 humor such as verbal irony.

Current Study: Production of Online Verbal Irony

So far, this chapter has discussed ELLs' ability to detect verbal irony. Some teachers may question whether focusing on producing verbal irony has a place in the English classroom, especially in a Japanese context. Compared to predominantly English-speaking countries, sarcasm is relatively less common in Japan, where it may be viewed as a negative or hostile form of humor (Gibbs, 2007). However, producing verbal irony is an important communicative skill for ELLs provided that the training includes risks and warnings about using sarcasm. Actively engaging in verbal irony is a mark of advanced proficiency that is especially salient for learners who want to study abroad or use authentic English on, for example, social media platforms (the focus of this study).

As sarcasm has various functions, it should not be dismissed as a negative form of humor. As noted previously, sarcasm and verbal irony are also used to agree, bond, or mitigate tense situations (Dynel, 2014). Returning to a simple previous example, the function of saying "Lovely weather, isn't it?" on an overcast day initiates small talk. There could be an expectation to respond with a similarly sarcastic statement, just as an appropriate response to the perennial summer greeting in Japan of "*Atsui desu ne!*" (It's hot, isn't it?) would be to agree with "*So desu ne!*" ("Yes, it is") rather than to counter with a disagreement such as "*Zenzen atsukunai*" ("It's not hot at all"). Previous research illustrates that language learners struggle to engage in L2 humor, which negatively impacts cross-cultural communicative competence (Bell & Attardo, 2010; Shively, 2018). As ELLs may struggle with the appropriate production of verbal irony and sarcasm, the English language classroom is a safe environment (Pomerantz & Bell, 2011) where instructors can provide feedback on whether learners' production of ironic statements is accurate (likely to be humorous) and appropriate (likely to *not* be offensive).

Instruction on producing online verbal irony could be even more salient, as verbal irony is ubiquitous on social media platforms, as learners may have more opportunities (especially during the ongoing pandemic) to use English online compared to in person. Further, instructors can easily provide feedback, anonymously when necessary. For these reasons, instruction on online verbal irony production could be effective for many learners. Thus, this follow-up study examines how humor competency training on recognizing verbal irony affects participants' willingness and ability to produce jocular and sarcastic comments on a sheltered social media platform.

Methods for Investigating L2 Learners' Use of Verbal Irony Online

This follow-up study uses previously unpublished data from our online verbal irony research mentioned previously (Prichard & Rucynski, 2022). Whereas the previous study focused on detecting and understanding ironic online comments, the data collected included written replies that participants produced to the five fictional social media posts in the pretest and posttest. In the original study, before reading and ranking post responses in the verbal irony detection task, participants were instructed to reply to the posts themselves as a warm-up. Participants were asked to comment on each post as if the author were their friend on social media. There was no instruction to be humorous or ironic, and we did not expect participants to write many, if any, ironic posts.

Although described briefly previously, the fictional posts that participants responded to are described in more detail here. There were two versions of the prompts. Participants were randomly assigned to respond to one version for the pretest and the other for the posttest. Two prompts in each version were informal personal posts with a photo, one was a meme, and two shared news articles on serious social issues (Figure 1). Note that all names in this figure are pseudonyms.

Figure 1

Example Prompts From Version 1

Example of an informal personal post (1 of 2)

Informal meme (1 of 1)

Example of a shared news article (1 of 2)

We analyzed whether the participants' comments were ironic. To minimize rater bias, responses were randomized and the fields indicating the experimental or control group and whether the response was from the pre- or posttest were hidden during data rating. The interrater reliability between the two researchers was 96.41%.

For the ironic items, we coded the type of irony used, including *meaning reversal irony*, where the intended meaning is the opposite of the literal message, and *surreal irony* (also termed *meaning replacement irony*), which are silly or absurd statements with no clear intended meaning (Kapogianni, 2011). The irony cues used, if any, were also coded. These included the following paralinguistic cues: CAPS, AlTeRnAtInG CaPs, a sarcasm tab (e.g., /s), an emoji, and indicating laughter (e.g., Ha, LOL). Other cues were hyperbole and incongruent comments (saying one thing then later the opposite, such as, "That's terrible!" then "You must be thrilled...."). Finally, ironic items were rated for their appropriateness on a one to four Likert scale. The week following the pretest, the experimental group had a lesson on detecting verbal irony, summarized previously and described in more detail in Prichard and Rucynski (2022). However, there was no instruction on using irony, as the original focus of the study was detecting irony. For this analysis of productive use of irony, the pre-posttest gains by the experimental and control groups were calculated and compared using *t*-tests.

Pre-Test Results: How Ironic Are Participants Without Training?

The pretest data is valuable in assessing how frequently the participants use verbal irony in English online. It also helps grasping what kinds of irony and what cues were used by relatively proficient Japanese L2 users of English, which can inform instruction on verbal irony (although it was not used in our instruction, as we were focused on irony detection). In the pretest, participants used verbal irony in 41 of the 675 overall responses (6%). They used it more frequently (14%; 19 of 135) in response to the humorous meme posts, which shows that they sometimes responded to humor with humor, an appropriate response.

They used it just 4% of the time for the informal personal posts (12 of 270) and for the news article posts (10 of 270).

Concerning verbal irony, only two uses were meaning reversal variety (e.g., sarcasm). These sarcastic posts were not critical of the author of the post, but rather the situation. For example, one participant responded to a meme about it being Monday again, with "I LOVE MONDAAAAAAAY." Another responded to the photo of the dog who had destroyed the mail with, "Hey, doggy! What a great job you've done!!" The remaining 39 comments were surreal (meaning replacement irony). For example, one responded to the dog photo with "Arrest him!" And one quipped, "Wow, I think you should ask it to clean the house." Participants used noticeable hyperbole three times. For example, responding to the meme of a girl who supposedly killed a spider by burning her house down, one wrote, "I guess the spider was the size of refrigerator [sic]." A participant used paralinguistic cues only one time (adding "LOL" at the end of her post).

Overall, the pretest showed that the participants used more surrealistic humor than imagined and that they used almost no meaning reversal irony (sarcasm or jocular irony) or irony markers, such as the rolling eye emoji. This suggests that this group of learners could benefit from instruction on using sarcastic or jocular irony and on the use of cues to ensure irony is not misinterpreted. However, we advise that instruction on producing irony be accompanied by instruction on its appropriate use, considering factors such as one's relationship with their interlocutor.

Post-Test Results: What Was the Effect of the Training?

Although the training was not designed to enhance learners' use of verbal irony, the experimental group showed a significant increase in verbal irony production, from 22 instances (5% of all 420 responses) in the pretest to 65 instances (15% of all 420 responses) in the posttest. The control group did not show gains; they used verbal irony 7% of the time in both tests (19 in the pretest and 20 in the posttest). Overall, the mean gains made by the experimental group participants (received humor training) were significantly higher than the control group means (no humor training), t (133) = 2.74, $p < .007$. While the humor training group had just one case of meaning reversal irony (sarcasm) in the pretest, there were 37 instances in the posttest. The participants tended to avoid targeting post authors; the criticism was jocular, or it criticized a situation or another target (e.g., spiders or Monday, as mentioned previously). Their use of surrealistic irony increased from 21 instances to 30. Obvious hyperbole use did not increase in the posttest, but the use of paralinguistic cues increased from one instance in the pretest (one use of "LOL") to 33 in the posttest. Emojis or emoticons were used 12 times, all in the posttest, including eight uses of the rolling eyes emoji, three uses of a sad emoji when using positive text, and one laughing emoji. All caps were used five times, and alternating caps were used ten times in the posttest. For example, one participant wrote "I LoVe MOndAy." Sarcasm tags were used five times (e.g., "Very clever dog! /s").

However, the irony used by the experimental group in the posttest was rated by the researchers as somewhat less appropriate than in the pretest. The average ranking of the ironic comments was 3.59 in the pretest and 3.35 in the posttest. For example, one participant sarcastically replied, "You are soooo good at cooking!" to a post where a user criticized brownies he made for his girlfriend. Although the fictional author of the post was critical of his own dessert, it may not be appropriate to sarcastically join in the criticism of one's cooking skills. The post could have been a *humble brag* (self-praise disguised as criticism); if self-praise is the intent, enthusiastic support is the most common social media reaction (Dayter, 2018), even if most people react negatively to self-praise and humble bragging on social media (Mately, 2018). The same participant also sarcastically criticized the dog who destroyed the mail, writing "Your dog is so smart./s." While the fictional dog owner in the original post noted frustration with the dog's act, it is unlikely they would appreciate a suggestion that their dog is stupid.

Although the primary goal of the instruction was not to promote productive use of irony, the fact that participants in the experimental group increased their use of irony, albeit not always effectively, serves as a cautionary note for instructors teaching humor or irony, even in a receptive context. Some students may try to use it, even though they may not understand all the subtleties of effective humor production. Moreover, they may not be fully conscious of the possible detrimental effects of sarcastic comments, even if intended as jocular. Although the instructional materials did inform learners of sarcasm's possible negative effects, perhaps we should have been stronger in advising students that we were focusing on detecting humor and that students may not want to use irony unless they are confident of its effectiveness.

Nevertheless, we are not overly worried about the increased instances of failed humor. It must be acknowledged that the test was not in a real setting with real interlocutors. In real life, the participants may not have chosen to use irony. They may have felt that the class was a sheltered and safe environment to play with what they had learned. While this was not our intent, the task seemed to provide learners with the "safe house" Pomerantz & Bell (2011) have advocated for to practice playing with humor and irony in their own way. Given the limited time allocated for the curriculum and the fact that productive use of verbal irony was not the primary goal, it would require many more practice opportunities to achieve a higher level of proficiency in using verbal irony. Educators who wish to incorporate such training can refer to the *Implications and Suggestions for Educators* section.

Learner Reactions

As humor competency training may be unconventional in language classes, it is important to collect student reactions to it. In addition to checking whether learners enjoyed the activities, whether they found them effective and useful in helping them improve their understanding of L2 humor should also be evaluated. At the end of the course, we collected quantitative and qualitative responses from learners to gauge the effectiveness and usefulness of the online irony humor competency training. The control group also received the competency training after the posttest so they could benefit from deeper understanding of ironic online comments.

For the quantitative component of the feedback, we asked learners to reflect on ten of the cues for identifying ironic online comments that were included in the humor instruction. Learners rated these cues as "Interesting / I didn't know!," "I already knew," or "I still don't understand." 92 students completed the questionnaire. For all ten cues, most students rated that learning about it was interesting and/or new knowledge for them. A selection of the highest-rated cues (interesting or new information) are provided in Table 1.

Table 1

Cues for Identifying Ironic Online Comments

Cue	Interesting / I didn't know!	I already knew...	I still don't understand!
/s = sarcasm	74	9	8
Stressing a word (CAPS). ("I TOOOTALLY love natto.") = maybe sarcasm	64	24	4
Laughing emoji or LOL does not always mean sarcasm....	59	31	2
BiG aND sMalL lEtTeRs = sarcasm	58	29	5
If a person says something very different than you expect = maybe sarcasm	56	28	8
Emoji & comment do not match ("I love rainy days... ") = sarcasm	55	36	1

The last item asked students for final comments or feedback about the lessons devoted to understanding ironic online comments. Although this was optional, many students shared their impressions, which were overwhelmingly positive. Several students wrote that they try to develop their English skills by reading the comments on sites such as Twitter and YouTube, but they are often confused by some of the humor used. Thus, they found the lessons informative and useful.

Returning to the possible limitations of traditional grammar-translation methodology in language acquisition (Herder & Clements, 2012), one student admitted that "I used to read the text without thinking too much about it," but that the instruction on irony was valuable in stressing the importance of reading more deeply. Another student wrote, "I want to be able to make jokes that don't hurt the other person," reflecting the importance of including risks and warnings about humor use in humor instruction.

Finally, several students praised the lessons by producing ironic statements, making use of the newly acquired cues. For example, students wrote that they were very interested in understanding sarcasm, so "THiS leSsON wAS NOt IntEresTinG!" or "ThIs lEsSoN WaS tOo BoRiNg." As we agree that language classrooms should be a safe house (Pomerantz & Bell, 2011) for learners to experiment with L2 humor, we found it satisfying that one student wrote, "I had wanted to learn how to use sarcasm and joke [sic], so I am glad to attend your class. What a bad teacher you are!"

Implications and Suggestions for Educators

Along with the results of the original study on detecting online irony (Prichard & Rucynski, 2022), the results concerning participants' productive use of irony are a positive sign for the efficacy of humor instruction. While many language instructors may have concerns that humor is too complex to teach or that there is no space in their curriculum for it, the microskills we introduced for detecting ironic online comments were straightforward and did not take up a lot of class time. Nevertheless, they led to:

- improved ability to detect verbal irony online;
- increased willingness to try verbal irony and use irony cues; and
- positive student responses.

Although the students in this study were relatively proficient in English, these skills could potentially be taught to lower-proficiency learners to help them understand (and produce) verbal irony on social media. Whether other learners would benefit from such instruction warrants further consideration and research.

While the irony production results suggest that a short lesson on detecting verbal irony leads participants to use irony and irony cues more often (at least in a sheltered environment), the irony used was more often rated as inappropriate. Thus, some instructors may prefer to provide instruction only on recognizing and comprehending irony. As learners will likely encounter ironic statements in English, the ability to detect and understand non-literal utterances is an important language skill. Such instructors may suggest learners not use irony themselves as they may need more instruction on irony production or extensive exposure to target language irony to grasp its subtleties.

For educators who do think their learners could benefit from using irony, more detailed instruction on its use and possible reactions to it is necessary. Students could discuss illocutionary effect, appropriateness, and possible reactions to various ironic comments using structured activities. For example, learners could practice making sincere posts ironic by adapting language and adding paralinguistic cues. Learners could practice making ironic comments with various functions, such as bonding as well as lightening or strengthening criticism. Less structured communicative activities would also be necessary, such as a sheltered social media environment on an institution's learner management system that could provide extensive practice and experimentation as well as allow for peer and teacher feedback.

Conclusion

Humor competency training is a relatively new research area in the field of language education. This chapter summarizes some of its promising possibilities in terms of learner gains and reactions. While a wide range of humor may comprise L2 humor competence, the studies highlighted here focus on verbal irony, largely due to the gap between how it is used in English and in Japan, our teaching context. We have made verbal irony humor instruction a part of many of our English courses to give our learners a laugh and to provide them with the tools to improve their real-world cross-cultural communicative competence. While we have argued that the production of verbal irony is worth exploring, it is up to individual instructors to make informed decisions about what humor to introduce in their own courses and whether learners' goal should be to detect, understand, respond to, or produce humor.

Author Bios

John Rucynski is an associate professor at Okayama University, Japan. His main research interest is the role of humor in foreign language acquisition and intercultural communicative competence. He has edited two volumes on this topic and his articles have been published in journals such as *English Teaching Forum, System,* and *TESOL Journal*. His latest project was editing *A Passion for Japan,* a collection of personal narratives by long-term residents of Japan.

Caleb Prichard is also an associate professor at Okayama University in Japan. He has also taught English as a second or foreign language in South Korea and the United States. He co-edited *Bridging the Humor Barrier* with John and has published several articles on humor in second language education. He has researched reading strategy competency among other areas.

11
Exploring EMI in Ethnic Multilingual Education in China's IMAR

Disi Ai (Adis)

The Inner Mongolia Autonomous Region (IMAR) is in the north of China, bordering Mongolia and Russia. Alongside Mandarin (China's official language), Mongolian is the official regional language and the heritage language (L1) for ethnic Mongols living there. In many ethnic multilingual schools, named Mongolian Ethnic/Nationality Schools in the IMAR, Mongolian is taught as students' first language and Mandarin as their second language from primary school. From ages seven to 16, English is a required course throughout their nine years of compulsory education (see Dong et al., 2015; Yi & Adamson, 2017). However, English is not widely spoken or used in the IMAR (Yi & Adamson, 2017). Due to the scarcity of opportunities to practise language at school and in the community at large, English learning for ethnic Mongolian students is an additional foreign language. Considering the overall linguistic environment and the relationship between the three languages, English as a foreign language (EFL) more accurately describes English teaching and learning in the IMAR. To distinguish the Mongols from Mongolia and other countries, I use the term "Mongol-Chinese" to describe the Mongols who live in China as they have both national identities as Chinese and ethnic identities as Mongols. However, the participants who I refer to here do not use this term, identifying themselves as "Mongol" rather than "Chinese," so when I interpret their stories, I tend to use the same terms they do, such as Mongol.

Thus, Mongol-Chinese and Mongol are both used throughout this chapter depending on the context of their use.

In this chapter, I first briefly overview the traditional and new definitions of bilingual/multilingual education as well as research focused on models of multilingual education and the IMAR. I then move to the research design and findings. As mentioned previously, English is compulsory throughout schooling, so learning English is seen as a long journey for these ethnic minority students. Six Mongol-Chinese individuals were interviewed about their experiences and attitudes toward the different media of instruction in their EFL classrooms at different stages of their schooling. They share a complex and dynamic process of EFL learning and the role of medium of language (both monolingual instruction and translanguaging) in the EFL classroom. I conclude by highlighting some implications for ethnic multilingual education and the importance of developing sustainable translanguaging in ethnic minority areas.

Traditional and New Trends in Multilingual Education

The traditional notion of bilingualism and multilingualism refers to "a plurality of autonomous languages" (García & Li, 2013, p. 11), where language learners add whole separate language(s) into their linguistic repertoires. Therefore, traditional multilingual education isolates languages in the curriculum and maximizes target language exposure to avoid language interference (Cenoz, 2019). However, some schools are referred to as *multilingual* because of the diversity of students' linguistic backgrounds rather than the schools' goal of developing multilingualism and multiliteracy (Cenoz, 2009). Thus, some scholars (Baker, 2007; Cummins, 2008; May, 2008) consider *language of instruction* an essential criterion to define bi/multilingual education, not just subjects or the language itself. As Baker (2007) notes, bilingual classroom education teaches some, most, or all subjects via two languages.

Cenoz (2009) argued that if the definition of multilingualism is only based on the language of instruction at school, there is a vague boundary between bilingual schools that also offer additional foreign language(s) as subject(s) and schools that call themselves trilingual or multilingual. Taking the IMAR as an example, its ethnic education strives for multilingualism (Mongolian as L1, Mandarin as L2, English as L3) but most schools use a bilingual model with instruction in either mixed Mongolian-Mandarin or separate Mongolian and Mandarin languages. English as an additional language of instruction only applies to EFL classes in some cases. Thus, Cenoz (2009, p. 55) defined multilingual education as "teaching more than two languages provided that schools aim at multilingualism and multiliteracy." Although multilingual education is a complicated phenomenon, the medium of instruction has always been an important focus of attention in various studies into different contexts of multilingual education (see Cenoz, 2017; Dearden, 2014; Jones, 2017; Kong & Wei, 2019; Soruç & Griffiths, 2018; Yu et al., 2021; Zhang & Chan, 2021).

Although the traditional notion of bilingualism set a hard boundary between languages, García (2009) suggested bi/multilingualism is dynamic, which means the language practice of multilinguals is interrelated, rather than additive. Baker (2011, p. 288) used the term *translanguaging* to refer to "the process of making meaning, shaping experiences, gaining understanding and knowledge through the use of two languages." In education, translanguaging was first used as a pedagogical practice in a bilingual school in Wales where students' input and output languages were allowed to be different (Li, 2011). As Cenoz (2017) suggested, translanguaging as an emerging paradigm influences the development of many fields, such as bi/multilingual education and TESOL. For multilingual practices, the idea of translanguaging enables multilingual teachers and learners to use their full linguistic resources in teaching and learning an additional language. In other words, translanguaging softens the boundaries between languages and implies that an additional (foreign) language is best taught "in interrelationship with the learner's existing language features and practices" (Cenoz, 2017, p. 194).

However, translanguaging has different aims and impacts according to the situation in which it is employed. As Cenoz and Gorter (2017) note, translanguaging may cater to developing multilingual identities and empowering minority students in some cases, while focusing on improving language skills in others. Thus, translanguaging involving a regional minority language and national majority language, such as Basque-Spanish (see Cenoz & Gorter, 2011, 2017; Leonet et al., 2017) or Welsh-English (see Jones, 2017), may be perceived as either creating opportunities to "empower minority speakers by legitimating their discursive practices in some contexts" or as "a threat for minority languages" (Cenoz, 2017, p. 196) in others. Following the notion of "sustainable biolinguistic education" that keeps both the local identity inscribed to the ethnic language and global opportunity associated with English in bilingual education (MacPherson, 2003), Cenoz and Gorter (2017) advocated the importance of making translanguaging sustainable by making breathing space for the minority language to balance the use of the minority and majority languages in the different contexts.

Models of Multilingual Education and the Medium of Instruction

In recent decades, more research into bi/multilingual education models has become available (Adamson & Feng, 2014; Baetens Beardsmore, 1993; Baker, 2001; Dong et al., 2015; Ytsma, 2001). Baetens Beardsmore (1993) identified nine variables to categorise five different models of multilingual education worldwide, while Ytsma (2001) examined multilingual education from three aspects: linguistic contexts; linguistic distance; and design of school teaching. Baker (2001) distinguished between: (1) strong bilingual education, such as immersion, maintenance, and dual education; and (2) weak bilingual education, such as transitional and submersion education. The bilingual education type is based on medium of instruction in the classroom, students' linguistic backgrounds, societal and educational aims, as well as language outcome goals. Cenoz (2009) proposed the *continua of multilingual education model* to analyse different types of multilingual education, describing its complex and dynamic nature.

Adamson and Feng (2009, 2014) and Feng and Adamson (2018) have conducted research on trilingual (multilingual) education in China, which involves the use of ethnic minority languages, Mandarin, and

English. Their 2014 study identified four trilingual education models, including *accretive, balanced, transitional,* and *depreciative,* and assessed their implementation across ten ethnic minority areas in China, including the IMAR. In the accretive model, the ethnic minority language has strong vitality and is used as the medium of instruction. The balanced model aimed to find a balance in terms of minority and majority language as the medium of instruction as well as between the ethnicity of students and teachers. As Adamson and Feng (2014) noted, these two models sought to develop strong student competencies in three languages and maintain their sense of ethnic identity, also called *additive trilingualism*. In the school context, additive trilingualism refers to "complementary competencies in L2 and L3 that pupils acquire in school and in society while maintaining a high standard of their L1 and their ethnic identity" (Adamson & Feng, 2014, p. 37). In comparison, the main feature of the transitional model was its intention to shift the medium of language in the classroom from the ethnic minority language to Mandarin, gradually assimilating students into the mainstream. The depreciative model swings between bilingual and trilingual because bilingual reflects a curriculum in which only two languages (Mandarin and English) are taught at school, while this model was labelled trilingual due to students' ethnic backgrounds. Baker (2001) saw the latter two models as a weak form of multilingual education. The models for trilingual education in China (Adamson & Feng, 2014) are supported by Dong et al. (2015), who investigated Mongolian Nationality School models in the IMAR. They also found more people sent their children to mainstream Chinese schools (transitional and depreciative models) than Mongolian dominant schools (accretive and balanced model) due to Mandarin's high economic and social capital. As Dong et al. (2015) note, enrolments across the four models reflected language assimilation in the IMAR, evidencing the transition to Mandarin medium of instruction in trilingual Mongolian nationality schools.

Building on previous studies by Adamson and Feng (2014) and Dong et al. (2015), Yi and Adamson (2017) examined the relationship between students' Mongolian identity and language education medium models in city, town, and village schools. They found that pressure to promote

Mandarin and English negatively impact Mongolian language and identity. Moreover, Mongolian identity is under threat because students sinicize as they progress through the education system. Although schools fight against deterioration of the Mongolian language, such as through economic and demographic changes resulting from an influx of Mandarin speakers into the region, the trend is toward increasingly using Mandarin as the medium of instruction at school. For example, Mongolian students at university mostly learn English through Mandarin (L2) with Mongolian seldom used (Wu, 2009).

Research Design

The focus of this chapter shifts from research into educational policy/models and classroom practice to multilingual learners' subjective feelings and attitudes toward the different mediums of language in their EFL classrooms. The purpose is to give educational practitioners and researchers a chance to "stand in multilingual speakers' shoes" to understand how they make sense of their EFL learning experiences of different mediums of instruction.

To better understand and capture their changing attitudes toward medium of instruction, participants' English learning is viewed as a long-term (and ongoing) process. The research methodology used is *interpretative phenomenological analysis* (IPA). As Smith et al. (2022) observe, interviewing is a powerful and widely used qualitative research method. Compared to structured interviews, semi-structured interviews allow researchers to prepare a set of questions to follow during interviewing but also give researchers flexibility to modify the sequence of questions and use various probes in each interview. At the same time, they accommodate control of the conversation more than unstructured interviews. The semi-structured interview in this study included 12 open-ended questions and lasted from one to two hours based on the richness of participants' narratives. I positioned myself as an *interviewer-traveller* (Kvale, 2007, p. 36), encouraging them to share their stories, feelings, and opinions.

Six ethnic Mongol-Chinese individuals who graduated from Mongolian ethnic schools and speak Mongolian as their L1, Mandarin as their L2, and English as their L3 were interviewed. The participants were asked to share their experiences and attitudes towards learning English through different language mediums. One of the participants, Geriel, is an English teacher in a Mongolian ethnic school, so she also shared her experience as a teacher regarding the medium of instruction in her EFL classes.

According to the *idiographic mode* of IPA (Smith et al., 2022), data were analysed case by case. Each case was transcribed into the interview language (Mandarin) and then translated into the output language (English). As Smith and Osborn (2008) recommended, each transcription was read repeatedly and analysed line by line. Initial notes on transcription were used to develop themes for each case, which were then clustered into a table of themes. These tables were analyzed and clustered again to generate superordinate themes for the final table, which included all six participants.

FINDINGS

Participants in this study shared their retrospective understandings and subjective feelings about the medium of instruction in their EFL classes from primary school to higher education, which led to the identification of three superordinate themes. The first theme, *teachers' position and students' attitudes*, reflected participants' accounts of the different language media used in their English classrooms, where translanguaging was commonly employed, but the teachers' ethnic identity and language repertoires determined whether Mongolian was used as a medium of instruction. Participants' open attitudes toward different teaching languages were also described. The second superordinate theme, *from scared to expectant to EMI*, explored how students' attitudes towards *English as a medium of instruction* (EMI) changed at different stages of schooling. While EMI caused stress for multilingual learners in basic stages, it was expected by university students as part of the cost of improving their English. The third superordinate theme, *tensions arising from the negotiated identity in translanguaging*, focused on the challenges of negotiating identity through translanguaging practices in the EFL classroom, particularly for Mongol-Chinese students and teachers.

Teachers' Positions and Students' Attitudes

Teachers' Ethnicity and the Medium of Instruction

Based on the retrospective accounts gathered from the semi-structured interviews with the six participants educated in Mongol ethnic schools, teachers' language repertoires were essential to deciding the language mediums adopted in EFL classes. Generally, Han teachers were more inclined to use Mandarin and English for instruction while Mongol-Chinese teachers were more likely to mix Mongolian, Mandarin, and English. One should not assume an absolute relationship between ethnicity and language, as the definition of ethnicity relies not only on objective indicators such as linguistic or geographical factors, but also on subjective characteristics like emotional bonds (Edwards, 2009). Thus, it is possible that someone who self-identifies as Mongol ethnicity might not speak Mongolian and vice versa. According to the 7th national census in 2020, registered ethnic Mongolians in the IMAR account for 17.66% of the population while 78.74% of the population are Han, who are the majority ethnic group in China (Statistics Bureau of Inner Mongolia Autonomous Region, 2021). Although there is no available data on the number of Mongolian and non-Mongolian speakers, an estimated half of ethnic Mongolians have sinicized and lost their ethnic language (Janhunen, 2012). In other words, Mongol-Chinese are becoming more and more reliant on Mandarin. This is also reflected in the medium of instruction in the classroom. From participants' EFL learning experiences, only ethnically Mongolian teachers were able to use Mongolian as a medium of language in their English classes, while Han teachers' classes were either Mandarin-dominated or involved translanguaging between Mandarin and English.

The excerpt below is from an interview with Altan, who described his two high school English teachers and the medium of instruction in their classes:

Excerpt 1
Altan describes his English teachers

> I had two English teachers in high school. One was the Han who taught English in Mandarin of course. Another one was Mongol who also used Mandarin as the main teaching language, but if there was anything difficult to understand, he would explain in Mongolian.

Compared to Altan's Han teacher, whose class was Mandarin-dominated, his trilingual Mongolian teacher had more flexibility in the medium of instruction to scaffold students' English learning. Although there is not sufficient research on comparing the medium of different languages (L1, L2, L3 and bilingual/trilingual translanguaging) in EFL, this finding was consistent with Zhang and Chan (2021), who observed two EFL classes conducted by Uyghur teachers in Xinjiang province. Based on their study, Uyghur teachers translanguaged across three languages to compare similar words or grammatical constructs among them. As they argued, translanguaging with the ethnic minority language (L1) is a successful teaching strategy to enhance student comprehension. However, it seemed that translanguaging across three languages only applied to ethnic minority teachers. With the promotion of Mandarin (Putonghua), ethnic minority teachers must pass a Putonghua Proficiency Test. However, there is no similar requirement for Han teachers at Mongolian-medium schools to learn the minority language, even though it is the official provincial language. Thus, a lack of qualified trilingual teachers is a challenge for the IMAR's ethnic education (Leonet et al., 2017).

The excerpts below further show the role that Mandarin plays in translanguaging in EFL classes for students and teachers:

Excerpt 2
Odsar reflects on translanguaging

> In fact, the mixed language of Mongolian and Mandarin has always been the teaching language in my English classes. I don't remember any

Mongolian teacher have taught us in "pure" Mongolian or Mandarin… If any teacher used the pure Mongolian to teach English, I didn't even think we could understand. For example, it was so natural and common for us to say 主谓宾 [subject, predicate and object] in Mandarin. If it was changed to Mongolian, I don't think I could understand these academic [grammar] terms.

Excerpt 3
Geriel reflects on translanguaging

I definitely prefer to teach in Mongolian, it can better reflect the speciality of Mongolian ethnic education. However, there are some challenges. Students need extra support in learning English via Mongolian and Mandarin. I think this is actually related to the "big" environment [market]. For example, if there are more Mongolian textbooks and materials available, Mongolian as the teaching language in English class could be more realistic.

As Odsar explained, the mixed medium of Mandarin and Mongolian was so widely used that students were unable to learn EFL through Mongolian alone. This also reflected the inadequacies of terminology in the minority language (Cenoz & Gorter, 2008; Lewis, 2008). Although it is a common challenge for minority languages in different educational contexts to face the problem of having a weak tradition in academic language use (Cenoz & Gorter, 2008), the mixed medium of languages in the EFL classes, Odsar's case, seemed to represent a passive choice. As Odsar said, she might not understand if the medium of language is "pure" (monolingual) Mongolian. For the Mongolian teachers like Geriel, they emotionally "prefer(red) to teach" in the minority language, but the lack of learning materials in Mongolian made Mandarin the default medium of instruction. From Geriel's narrative, there was a conflict between what she wanted to do and what she was able to do regarding the medium of language instruction in her EFL classrooms. As Li (2011) noted, multilinguals not only can speak different languages separately but also should use and mix them freely. However, both teachers and students in this case were unable to move freely between languages because they had to rely more on the majority language (Mandarin) for academic vocabulary in their EFL classes.

To maintain and revitalize the minority language, Leonet et al. (2017) emphasized the need to support and provide greater space for minority languages in schools to address the societal imbalance between minority and majority languages and promote their revitalization. However, without external support from government, policy, or the market, how much "space" can teachers create to prevent the loss of minority languages? This was a vicious circle in translanguaging as related to the minority language (Mongolian) in that the lack of learning material and sociolinguistic environment increased students' dependence on the majority language (Mandarin). Even if teachers tried to make more space for Mongolian in the classroom, students' limited proficiency in their L1 would make it hard for them to understand academic terminology, with the result that they would become more reliant on Mandarin as the medium of instruction. This represents the process of linguistic degradation. Odsar and Geriel's cases are worth considering regarding the future of minority languages. Do they need to be "maintained" or "developed"? How minority languages be developed through translanguaging?

Students' Attitudes

The medium of instruction in the students' EFL classes was not the Mongol-Chinese participants' main concern during their English learning journeys. What they cared about were results, as illustrated in the following excerpt:

Excerpt 4
Altan's feelings about the medium of instruction

> I didn't care about it [the medium of language in the EFL classroom] at that time, to be honest. What I cared about was if I could understand the class and had a good score.

For the Mongol-Chinese participants, the majority language (Mandarin) and the minority language (Mongolian) were commonly used in their EFL classes, so there were few differences between learning English (L3) via Mandarin (L2) or translanguaging involving their L2 and L1. Thus, participants emphasised the importance of their scores on exams. Sarnai expressed similar attitudes towards the teaching language in Excerpt 5:

Excerpt 5
Sarnai's attitude toward the teaching language

> **Interviewer**: How did you feel when your English teacher was teaching in Mandarin?
>
> **Sarnai**: Actually, I did not have a special feeling, because the Han teachers just taught us via Mandarin or English, so [I] have already got used to it. I also can understand why [some] Mongols [teachers] were sinicized [teaching in Mandarin or translanguaging].
>
> **Interviewer**: Can I understand that what you cared about more is the quality of the lesson?
>
> **Sarnai**: Yes, the teacher's teaching skills are more important. It is important to understand what the teachers try to teach.
>
> **Interviewer**: Do you feel there is a big difference between different languages as the language of instruction during your English study?
>
> **Sarnai**: No. For me, there is no big difference… hmm… but it is difficult to find study materials in Mongolian, [there are] not as many as Mandarin versions.

Sarnai used the phrase "got used to" to describe her feelings about Mandarin as the medium of instruction. This agrees with Wu (2009), who showed Mongolian students got used to thinking in Mandarin and regarded it as it as an effective way to learn EFL. However, as Wu (2009) also noted, it is essential to discuss why Mongolian students prefer learning English (L3) via Mandarin (L2) or translanguaging (the combination of Mongolian and Mandarin), rather than via their L1. Due to the lack of study materials in Mongolian and unequal language requirements for teachers in ethnic schools (as discussed previously), the Mongol-Chinese students had to learn English via their L2 if their teachers were not Mongolian speakers, and so "got used to" it. According to Cenoz (2013), Altan and Sarnai are *active bilinguals* (of Mongolian and Mandarin) and English as a "foreign language user[s]" (p. 82). From the perspective of teaching and learning effectiveness, participants' open attitudes toward the medium of language can better scaffold their comprehension in their L3 study. In this circumstance, students can naturally become emergent multilinguals by using their full language repertoires when developing their L3 competence (Leonet et al., 2017). However, from the perspective of minority language protection, is it preferable for there to be no measures taken to guide translanguaging classroom practices (Cenoz & Gorter, 2017)?

From Scared to Expectant to EMI

While students' attitudes toward translanguaging in EFL were open, their attitudes toward EMI varied. This superordinate theme focuses on students' changeable attitudes towards English as the medium of instruction. Two participants clearly expressed their feelings on EMI in high schools:

Excerpt 6
Duuren's feelings toward EMI in high school

Interviewer: How did you think about English as a teaching language?

Duuren: If I was taught directly in English at that time [in high school], I don't think I could understand the lesson. Other students would be more confused, so I think this was one of the reasons why teachers chose

Mandarin as the teaching language in the end. I would not be bothered as long as teachers did not teach in English.

With the status of English as a lingua franca worldwide, EMI is a global trend for further improving students' English and preparing them for future academic study (Jiang et al., 2019). However, when students' English proficiency falls short of the requirements for EMI, it can become a source of psychological stress. Like Duuren, Odsar was "scared of" EMI due to her "poor [English] foundations" as shown in Excerpt 7 (stress indicated in bold).

Excerpt 7
Odsar's feelings toward EMI in high school

> **Odsar**: In high school, my English teacher actually tried to teach in English. But she realized our [English] foundation was quite bad, then she stopped using English as a teaching language.
>
> **Interviewer**: Do you mean you and your classmates could not understand and give relevant responses in English-medium class at that time?
>
> **Odsar**: Yes. Our [English] foundation was too poor to understand.
>
> **Interviewer**: OK. Then did the teacher change it to a mixed teaching language of Mongolian and Mandarin?
>
> **Odsar**: Yes.
>
> **Interviewer**: From your personal point of view, which language did you prefer your English teacher to use?
>
> **Odsar**: My personal feeling was… [I preferred] a mixed language of Mandarin and English. [Now, I think] English as a teaching language is the best… When I was in high school, I was particularly afraid of full English classes. My English foundation was too poor at that time… **I was**

really scared when the teacher began to speak in English. I was afraid of the teacher asked me questions [in English] and I did not understand the question. That made me so **nervous** at that time. But after graduating from university, now I really realized how important learning English and my English is getting better. So I think I hope my teacher can only teach in English now.

When students barely understood the lesson and had interactions with their teacher using EMI due to their low English proficiency, Odsar's teacher changed the medium of instruction to Mongolian and Mandarin. From the student perspective, EMI classes caused Odsar psychological stress, as she described feeling "nervous" and "scared" because she was worried she would not understand when her teacher asked a question in English. This finding is consistent with Soruç and Griffiths (2018), who examined the challenges and difficulties EMI learners face in the classroom. Lei and Hu (2014) also questioned the effectiveness of EMI in improving students' English competency. Thus, bringing awareness to teachers and researchers of student difficulties and personal feelings is valuable. However, when Odsar finished her undergraduate study, she realized the importance of English in her master's application, as she was applying for an MA programme that required a minimum English level. She changed her attitude toward EMI from scared to expectant. She wanted to engage in more English immersion classes to improve her English level. In this case, sufficient English proficiency resulted in Odsar preferring EMI. Thus, students' attitudes toward EMI change as their English proficiency improves and they come to want to learn the language. As Dearden (2014) notes, the age of EMI introduction and guidelines on how to teach EMI influence EMI classroom outcomes. For teachers, EMI can maximize students' exposure to the target language. For students it may result in de-motivation if the classroom is over-reliant on it (Wu, 2009). How best to balance these issues in the IMAR trilingual educational context is unclear, as the choice between EMI or a mixture of English with ethnic minority students' L1 and/or L2 depends on individual teachers.

Tensions Arising from Negotiated Identity in Translanguaging

Language, an important indicator of group membership, also influences minority teachers' and students' multilingual practices. In social environment dominated by Mandarin, Mongol-Chinese students not only "got used to" speaking Mandarin as their second native language, but also inevitably mixed their L1 with the majority language. Although the mixed medium of languages (Mandarin and Mongolian) can scaffold their L3 learning, identity tensions arise from translanguaging. Altan admitted that he benefited from Mandarin as a teaching language medium in his EFL experience, but as the following excerpt shows, he also struggled with conflict between his Mongol identity and translanguaging in EFL:

Excerpt 8
Altan's conflict with his Mongol identity and translanguaging in EFL

> It [Mandarin as the medium of instruction] was efficient because most learning materials and lessons are Mandarin versions... but I always feel... why I as Mongol is unable to use my mother language to master another foreign language, but have to rely on Mandarin? ... So I feel like I am more like the Han people rather than Mongol.

Like Odsar, Altan realized his competency in Mongolian was not sufficient to learn English through only Mongolian; he had to rely on the majority language to improve his comprehension of English. Thus, he experienced self-doubt about his identity as a Mongolian-speaking Mongol-Chinese. For Altan, there was a hard boundary between languages, which also related to his feelings about his ethnic identity. However, Altan felt he was not qualified as a Mongol, not because of his capacity to use multiple linguistic resources to learn EFL, but because of his feeling of powerlessness to use his first language. In other words, as a student, Altan felt it "convenient" to learn EFL via Mandarin. However, when his ethnic identity was centred on foreign language learning, he felt himself more like a Han. The perceived conflict between ethnic identity and the medium of language in EFL learning gave rise to language-related identity tension. Although translanguaging involving the minority language is considered useful and creative in some trilingual contexts (Cenoz, 2017; Zhang & Chan, 2021), research on how translanguaging influences students' ethnic identity is under-explored. Current research on translanguaging (García & Li, 2013; Li, 2011; Zhu & Li, 2016) is more relevant to transnational multilingual speakers. Altan's case may provide a new perspective for investigating translanguaging involving minority languages. Translanguaging can create "a social space for the multilingual language user by bringing together different dimensions of their personal history, experience and environment, their attitude, belief and ideology, their cognitive and physical capacity into one coordinated and meaningful performance" (Li, 2011, p. 1223). However, it also might cause tensions for minority speakers concerning how to negotiate their identity as language learners and ethnic minority group members.

On the other hand, the Mongolian teacher Geriel also emphasised the need to reinforce Mongolian more than other languages in the classroom. In order to "balance" linguistic status, Geriel believed it necessary to increase students' ethnic consciousness and give more support to the minority language (Excerpt 9):

Excerpt 9
Geriel's feelings about supporting Mongolian in the classroom

> **Interviewer**: Do you think it [using Mongolian as the medium of instruction] is a way to preserve and develop the Mongolian language?
>
> **Geriel**: Certainly. It is developing this language as long as you use the language to communicate. So I really hope that we can find a balance between Chinese, Mongolian and English learning and use.
>
> **Interviewer**: What do you think is a good balance between these three languages?

Geriel: Hmmm. . . Mandarin is the common language, I don't think people need to learn it hard, because it is something that you can master naturally. [Mongol-Chinese] students should have the consciousness of their own language and culture, and actively speak and learn it. I mean, Mongolian students need to speak and use Mongolian more frequently... Among the three languages, I think English is less important than Mongolian. Well, I mean English is important, but it is not as commonly used as Mongolian [in the IMAR]. I just want to have a balance in Mongolian and Mandarin. English is the language that you need to learn via two languages [Mandarin and Mongolian], so it is definitely the one that needs to be learnt and improved [at the lowest level].

Geriel pointed out the unequal bilingualism outside the EFL classroom and sought balance between the majority and minority languages as the medium of instruction to scaffold EFL learning. Compared to Mandarin, minority languages are in a subordinate position (Gil, 2006). The sociolinguistic environment empowers Mongolian students to "master (Mandarin) naturally" while they need to "actively speak and learn" their L1. As a Mongolian English teacher, Geriel prioritized the importance of Mongolian over English concerning its practical value in the IMAR and wanted to make more "linguistic space" for Mongolian. She negotiated her identities as an ethnic Mongol and English teacher in the EFL classroom to balance the languages to achieve "sustainable translanguaging" (Cenoz & Gorter, 2017, p. 908). However, as Cenoz and Gorter (2017, p. 910) observe, sustainable translanguaging is "a difficult balance between using resources from the multilingual learner's whole repertoire and shaping contexts to use the minority languages on its own, along with contexts where two or more languages are used." How sustainable translanguaging can be achieved is discussed in the following section.

Discussion

This study illustrates that translanguaging of Mongolian and Mandarin is common in the IMAR's EFL classrooms. Otheguy et al.

(2015) argue that translanguaging supports the sustainability of minority languages because it allows multilingual speakers to "deploy all their linguistic resources, both lexical and structural, freely, incorporating new ones and using them without restraint as a part of their idiolect" (p. 304). In this study, students and teachers seem to use multilingual instruction freely in their EFL classrooms. However, if we dig beneath the surface, translanguaging is not truly free as it is largely majority language (Mandarin)-dominated. In other words, EFL learning is based on unequal bilingualism. There is asymmetry between Mongolian and Mandarin in number of speakers and teachers, teaching and learning materials, as well as supportive policies. Translanguaging in EFL teaching and learning contexts, in Odsar and Altan's case, is passive. As multilingual speakers, they have few linguistic options in academic contexts. Mongolian's weaker positioning in academic contexts leads Mandarin to be the main medium of instruction, so ethnic minority students must rely on Mandarin in their EFL classes. The phenomenon of *diglossia*, as defined by Fishman (1967), occurs when the minority language is confined to informal settings while the majority language is dominant in all sectors. In some minority communities, such as the Basque community, efforts are made to improve the status of the minority language in society and normalize it as a common language (Leonet et al., 2017).

Cenoz and Gorter (2017) propose sustainable translanguaging as a way to transform the potential threats of translanguaging into an opportunity for minority languages. Translanguaging can be guided by five principles that aim to normalize and expand the use of minority languages: (1) creating breathing spaces where only the minority language is spoken, (2) establishing a need for the minority language through translanguaging, (3) enhancing students' metalinguistic awareness by activating their pre-existing knowledge to recognize the similarities and differences among languages, (4) understanding the position of the minority language in society, and (5) connecting spontaneous and pedagogical translanguaging. In the unequal bilingualism context of Mongolian and Mandarin with additional foreign language learning in English, external support via government intervention is needed to create breathing space for Mongolian. This support is necessary not only to maintain but also to develop the language. Developing minority languages is challenging under diglossia, making it crucial to break the diglossic situation and normalize Mongolian. These steps are important for achieving sustainable translanguaging in the IMAR. When the minority language and the majority language are given the same status in social and educational contexts, multilingual speakers are truly able to use their full linguistic resources freely, rather than following a passive choice. For example, it is necessary to change the unilateral language requirement for teachers. Trilingual requirements should apply to both Mongolian and Han teachers to make more possibilities for minority language translanguaging in schools.

Conclusions

This chapter expands the focus of multilingual education beyond understanding languages as separate or integrated repertoires, to how multilingual speakers make sense of different languages as the medium of instruction in the EFL classroom. It also examines pedagogical strategies adopted in the classroom and concerns raised regarding participants' ethnic multilingual education. As Cenoz (2009) notes, multilingual education is a complicated individual and social phenomenon. Teachers and learners' attitudes towards the dominant language, ethnic language, and English might be different given their different socio-cultural backgrounds. School settings also define multilingualism differently and have different curricular targets (Cenoz, 2019). Thus, we need to think about why a certain pedagogy, such as language separation or translanguaging, is adopted in the classroom.

The intensive and rich narratives in this study provide several implications for the classroom. First, it is crucial to recognize that EFL learning is a long-term and complex process for students, and that their attitudes towards the medium of instruction in the EFL classroom are changeable. Taking a more holistic and longitudinal view of EFL learning can help teachers and educators support students better. Second, the medium of instruction, especially translanguaging, is not only significant for ethnic minority students' EFL learning experience but also related to their identity construction and negotiation. As García and Li (2013) observed, translanguaging makes visible the complexity of language exchanges among people with different histories. However, the relationship between ethnic identity and the practice of translanguaging in the classroom is underexplored. Finally, promoting multilingual practice in the classroom is a first step towards achieving internationalization in society (Motani, 2002). Translanguaging in the EFL classroom should aim for a more equal bilingualism. Sustainable translanguaging can benefit ethnic students by allowing them to realize their acquired advantages as multilingual speakers and build an assertive bi/multicultural identity.

Author Bio

Disi Ai (Adis) is a PhD researcher at the School of Environment, Education and Development (SEED), The University of Manchester in the UK. Her research interest mainly focuses on multilingualism, identity, translanguaging, ethnic minority language practice and education. This paper is a part of her PhD project of Multilingual Lived Experience and Identity Construction in the Inner Mongolia Autonomous Region of China.

12
Saudi Female College Students' L2 English Learning Motivation

Danya Shaalan

Saudi Arabia is an Arabic-speaking nation that has only recently begun to emphasize second language (L2) acquisition of English, mainly for economic reasons. The chapter aims to present results from a complex, mixed-methods research study consisting of three substudies of female college students in Saudi Arabia learning English through second language acquisition (SLA). The overall research question providing the foundation behind this series of substudies was: Among these female college students in Saudi Arabia, how is motivation to acquire English as an L2 linked to target-like production of English articles? This chapter will describe the design of the substudies used to answer this research question and provide guidance to other linguistic researchers interested in applying these methods.

First, I present a history of the status of English in Saudi Arabia as an L2 along with cultural attitudes and practices associated with Saudis speaking and learning the language. Next, I describe the first substudy, which developed an instrument for measuring L2 motivation in a cohort of female Saudi higher education students learning English. After this, I discuss how I used the instrument along with other research methods to conduct a sociolinguistic analysis to help better understand the connections between L2 motivation and their English proficiency. Finally, I describe the results from the qualitative portion of my mixed methods research, where students provided explanations as to their perceptions, attitudes, and experiences surrounding L2 motivation and SLA success. I end with reflections on using such research methodology in linguistics and provide some recommendations for improving future sociolinguistic research.

History of English in Saudi Arabia

The oil boom in 1930s Saudi Arabia sparked cultural changes that favored English as the language of business and led to the employment of English-speaking expatriates in industry, rather than Saudis (Al-Seghayer, 2011). By the late 1970s, foreign investment had led to the development of extensive hospitals, shopping malls, and restaurants. 90% of the employees in major establishments were English-speaking foreigners, while the other 10% were Arab nationals with a strong command of English (Al-Braik, 2007). Despite interest in these jobs, many Saudis were unable to fill them due to a lack of preparation. As a result, the Saudi government began a *Saudisation* of the workforce in the 1970s (Edgar et al., 2016).

Saudisation led to an increase in the percentage of Saudi workers in industry, which also meant that more Saudis were speaking English regularly at work. According to a 2015 report by the *Saudi Ministry of Health* (2015), of all the non-Saudi medical staff working in the country at the time, 67% were physicians, 39% were nurses, 8% were pharmacists, and 6% were other health personnel, suggesting that by then, many Saudis were employed in the healthcare system.

In 2016, Saudi Arabia officially launched the *Vision 2030* countrywide strategic plan, which provides a roadmap to a wholly reformed Saudi Arabia. Vision 2030 has three main focuses: a vibrant society, thriving economy, and an ambitious national agenda (Saudi Vision 2030, 2020). Ultimately, a principal goal of Vision 2030 is to diversify Saudi Arabia's industry profile, and as part of this trajectory, efforts are being made to calibrate Saudi businesses to meet international standards and norms (Saudi Vision 2030, 2020). Among these goals are increasing the prevalence of fluent English-speaking Saudis so that they can compete internationally. University-educated Saudi women present a large untapped resource that could be deployed toward Vision 2030 goals, which include addressing the gender gap in Saudi employment. Saudi Arabia also has strong economic incentives for employers to hire women in novel fields such as marketing, tourism, and media (Swaantje, 2018).

Given the history of Saudi culture, attitudes about the appropriateness of Saudis speaking English instead of Arabic fall along generational lines (Alqahtani, 2011; Alrabai, 2014; Alrahaili, 2013). Older Saudis are used to associating English with expatriates, who make up 80% of the workforce and 30% of the population (Alistair, 2015). Although English is the main medium of communication between Saudis and expatriates, many Saudis cannot effectively communicate in English and do not necessarily value the ability (Alrabai, 2014). Traditionally, the use of English in speech by a Saudi has been seen as a threat to national and Islamic identity (Alrahaili, 2013) or as lacking pride in the Arabic language (Alqahtani, 2011).

This historical attitude has created a social pressure in Saudi Arabia against Saudis speaking or practicing English with each other. However, attitudes are changing, particularly in response to the international importance of Saudis learning English as reflected by Vision 2030 (Alrabai, 2014). As Faruk (2013) observed, through educational policy evolution, now Saudis generally have a more positive attitude toward English because they see it as helping them navigate different domains and contributing to the country's future prosperity. According to Faruk (2013), Saudi Arabia has undergone three periods of transformation: the first period (1902-1959) saw the establishment of the country, the second period (1960-2004) involved the development of infrastructure, and the third period (2004-2013) focused on the implementation of ambitious projects to develop the knowledge economy. Certainly, these periods have impacted generational attitudes in Saudi Arabia. One study showed that 85% of college-level Saudi English learners believe that English ability will help them land a highly-paid job (Moskovsky & Alrabai, 2009). Other studies have shown that Saudi women have a more positive attitude toward learning English than their male Saudi peers (Alrahaili, 2013; Hagler, 2014).

Learning English in Saudi Arabia

The first English curriculum was introduced into Saudi public schools in the 1950s (Mahboob & Elyas, 2014). The Saudi educational structure follows a sequence that begins with preschool and kindergarten, typically for children six years old or younger. After this, students attend primary school, which covers grades one through six and is designed for those between the ages of six and 11. Following primary school is intermediary school, which spans grades seven through nine and is intended for those between the ages of 12 and 14. Once intermediary school is completed, students move on to secondary school, which encompasses grades 10 through 12 and is designed for students between the ages of 15 and 17. After secondary school, students can pursue higher education in college degree programs.

When initially introduced into the curriculum, English was only compulsory at the intermediary and secondary stages, or grades seven and up (Mahboob & Elyas, 2014). The policy changed in 2004, with English starting in grade six, the final year of primary school. Since its inception, the national English curriculum, standardized by the *Ministry of Education* (MoE) for all levels of education, has been characterized by its uniformity (Al-Mutairi, 2007; Al-Seghayer, 2011). The curriculum promotes standardized teaching in English, emphasizing a particular set of religious, social, and economic values, giving it a clearly recognizable consistency (Al-Mutairi, 2007). The objectives behind this uniformity are to make education more efficient, to ensure consistent standards, and to equip Saudi learners with the skills and knowledge to partake in social and cultural activities (Al-Mutairi, 2007).

Cultural Influence on English Speaking Among Saudis

In Saudi Arabia, the culture has historically been viewed as collective, as maintaining strong ties among family members is emphasized, with group well-being valued over individual desires (Al-Johani, 2009). In Saudi families, adults traditionally view children as passive recipients whose role is to learn from adults, with children directly representing their parents' character and reputation (Al-Nafisah, 2000). Consequently, Saudi society attributes students' academic successes and failures to their parents (Al-Nafisah, 2000). This attitude provides a disincentive for public displays of failure, such as struggling to speak English correctly in front of others. In fact, Saudis are generally expected to confine learning English to the classroom; even if Saudi parents are educated in English, the language is rarely spoken in the household among family members, likely due to strong historical cultural biases against speaking English (Alqahtani, 2011; Alrabai, 2014; Alrahaili, 2013).

In summary, although English has been spoken in industry in Saudi Arabia for decades and has been part of the public education curriculum for many years, only recently under Vision 2030 have Saudis become motivated to adopt L2 English for participation in international business. However, historical cultural biases against Saudis speaking English remain. Given its potential impact on L2 motivation and identity, cultural bias was a key focus of my research on Saudi female students' English language learning motivation.

MIXED METHODS STUDY DESIGN

The original study was focused on understanding the connection between female Saudi college-level learners' motivation to learn English and how proficient they were at using English accurately in a writing sample. The research was split into three substudies. In the first substudy, I developed an instrument to measure L2 motivation in a sample of female college students majoring in English at a Saudi university and used it to gather data. In the second substudy, a subset of participants from the first substudy provided writing samples based on prompts aimed at eliciting written output in English. These writing samples were used to reveal insights about their L2 motivation. Specifically, I planned to calculate how likely the participants were to use *target-like articles*—the correct article for the given context—in their written sentences, such as "I have a sister" vs "I have the sister" (Ionin et al., 2004). My original hypothesis was that those with higher L2 motivation would have a higher rate of target-like articles in their writing, and I was planning to answer this hypothesis through the use of sociolinguistic analysis popularized by Labov (1972, 1984).

However, the planned data analysis could not be carried out due to the poor English proficiency of the participants, as revealed by their writing samples. Their use of target-like articles was inconsistent and too low to support the intended analysis. Their poor written English proficiency was also evident through many missed words and run-on sentences. I am an assistant professor in the College of Languages (CoL) at Princess Nourah bint Abdulrahman University (PNU), which is a large public women's university located Saudi Arabia's capital Riyadh that serves about 60,000 students annually. Although I am Saudi and grew up in Saudi Arabia, I attended college outside the country and now speak target-like English. The CoL, which serves about 2,200 students per year, has three programs focused on teaching English, and I teach in the Linguistics program. Therefore, I was able to design the substudies aimed at this student base with some understanding of their L2 motivation levels and some background knowledge of their English competency. This is why I was surprised to find such a low level of English proficiency in my sample.

Originally, the third substudy, where I interviewed the subset of participants who provided the writing samples, was intended to help me understand the connection between L2 motivation as measured by my instrument and the students' English proficiency in their writing samples. However, given the unexpectedly low English proficiency of the college students, who had learned English through the Saudi education system, the focus of my interviews shifted to investigating the potential relationship between their L2 motivation and English proficiency. I wanted to know why, after many years of study, many had a poor command of English even though they expressed enthusiasm for learning it. Here I present relevant findings from my research that sheds light on this issue.

Second Language Learning Motivation Instrument

Dörnyei (2009) measured L2 motivation through his *L2 Motivational Self System* (L2MSS) framework, which is based on the notion that learners envision a future identity in which they successfully utilize their L2. His framework showcases two aspects of this future identity: the *ideal L2 self* (IL2) and the *ought-to L2 self* (OL2). The IL2 is an internalized self-image of the learner as they aspire to master the target language. On the other hand, the OL2 represents the future self successfully fulfilling duties and responsibilities to meet the L2 expectations of others. Learners, while aspiring to meet these duties and responsibilities, also aim to avoid negative L2 outcomes that would result in not meeting the expectations of significant others, such as parents and teachers. For my first substudy, I developed an instrument to measure the *independent variables* (IVs) of IL2, OL2, and *parental encouragement* (PE). To do this, I first set each of these motivational selves as domains, then developed items based on those domains as statements in Arabic. The IL2 domain measured students' visions of themselves as future L2 users, while the OL2 domain gauged the students' perceptions of L2 learning as an obligation toward significant others (Taguchi et al., 2009). Reflecting the strong Saudi norm of endeavoring to please parents, especially with educational achievement, the instrument also included a domain for PE as a separate construct from IL2 and OL2.

Items were sourced from related instruments and shared with language learning professionals to improve them (Al-Qahtani, 2017; Moskovsky et al., 2016; Ryan, 2009; Taguchi et al., 2009). Respondents were asked to rate each item on a scale of 5 = *totally agree*, 4 = *agree*, 3 = *neutral*, 2 = *disagree*, and 1 = *totally disagree*. There were four items in the PE domain, nine in the IL2 domain, and ten in the OL2 domain, for 23 items in total. To pilot the instrument, I visited the classrooms of female Saudi college students learning English and asked them to complete an anonymous online questionnaire using *Google Forms*. After receiving 47 responses, I analyzed the data and found sufficient evidence of reliability and validity to use the instrument for the main study.

For the main study, I administered the instrument to 207 PNU students in the English program representing three different majors: Linguistics, English Literature, and Translation. All subscale scores were found to be significantly correlated at $\alpha < 0.05$. Additionally, an *analysis of variance (ANOVA)* was conducted to compare the mean scores between the three majors, but no significant differences were observed. Contrary to my expectation that Linguistics majors would be more motivated to be accurate, no significant differences in motivation were found among the three majors.

These findings led me to question whether there were indeed three distinct future L2 selves in this sample. Already, other L2 learner researchers in more collectivist countries (as defined by Hofstede, 2011) had identified a similar difficulty with their measurement instruments in separating future L2 selves in analysis (Papi et al., 2019; Teimouri, 2017). Although Hofstede's model has been criticized, it remains a useful tool to compare countries on levels of collectivism (Hofstede, 2002; McSweeney, 2002; Zainuddin et al., 2018). Even researchers in less collectivist cultures report difficulty identifying future selves other than the IL2, which is why there was no dominant measurement based on the L2MSS for me to use (Kormos et al., 2008; Kormos & Kiddle, 2013).

Based on the results of the first substudy, I did not feel the instrument provided a useful measure of the group's L2 motivation. Given that the participants were enrolled at the same college where I teach, we shared a common background and quickly established a rapport, even though they were not my direct students. Anecdotally, their eagerness to learn English appeared high, as evidenced by their active participation in classroom activities and diligent completion of homework assignments. However, while the instrument I used may have captured certain L2 motivation constructs, the results did not ultimately provide sufficient insight to address my research question.

Data Collection for Writing Prompts

As described earlier, the writing prompts for the second substudy were designed to elicit written output to provide insights into students' views of their future selves and how these views impact their L2 motivation and acquisition (Labov, 1966, 1972). They were classified as *monitored* (vernacular) and *unmonitored* (careful) based on the type of speech they were designed to elicit (Labov, 1966, 1972). The four unmonitored task condition (vernacular style) writing prompts were:

1. What is the best vacation you have ever been on?
2. Tell the story of one of your best childhood memories.
3. Write about what you normally do on your weekend.
4. Describe your favourite place to visit. This might be in Saudi Arabia or abroad.

The four monitored task condition (careful style) writing prompts were:

1. What can English language help you achieve in your society?
2. What does learning English mean to you?
3. How does your family support you in studying English?
4. What kinds of challenges do you think young Saudi women face when they use English in their own country?

25 participants provided writing samples, which I processed into a corpus and analyzed using *VARBRUL*, a sociolinguistic variable analysis approach (Gorman & Johnson, 2013; Labov, 1963, 1972, 1984; Young & Bayley, 1996). As previously described, the low rate of target-like articles precluded this quantitative analysis from yielding useful results. However, in general, the content of what the students provided in the written samples indicated that many had strong opinions about using L2 English. Some examples include:

> My society is Muslim society. It wants people to speak English language to explan islam from other people. (Sarah)

> Englis language is so useful in the time in everything we must learn it. (Shaikhah)

I think most of the women in Saudi Arabia are able to use English language but there is no support them that much. (Doha)

Data Collection for Interviews

As a complement to the quantitative data, I incorporated a qualitative interview design in the third substudy. This approach can be particularly useful in L2 motivation research, as interview data from the same participants can provide valuable insights and aid in the interpretation of the results (Dörnyei & Ushioda, 2011; Rose et al., 2019; Ushioda & Dörnyei, 2012). Therefore, I also conducted semi-structured interviews in Arabic with the 25 respondents who provided writing samples. The interviews elicited description of their L2 motivational trajectories, motivational experiences, and contextual influences on their L2 learning. In typical Saudi Arabic, occasional English words are included, but most of the words in the interviews were in Arabic. I transcribed the interviews in Arabic then translated the sections I felt relevant to the research question into English. Table 1 includes the Arabic questions and their English translations.

Table 1
Semi-Structured Interview Questions

Questions in English	Questions in Arabic
1. What does learning English mean to you?	1. ماذا يعني لك تعلم اللغة الإنجليزية؟
2. Was it your personal desire to major in English or someone else's? Please give reasons.	2. هل كانت رغبتك الشخصية ان تتخصصين باللغة الإنجليزية ام هي رغبة غيرك؟ اذكري الاسباب.
3. Do you imagine yourself using English in the future? Where? Or why not?	3. هل بإمكانك ان تتصوريين نفسك وانت تستخدمين اللغة الانجليزية في المستقبل؟ أين؟ أو لم لا؟
4. How is learning English important for your future? In what ways?	4. كيف تربطين اهمية اللغة الانجليزية بمستقبلك؟ ما هي الجوانب؟
5. What do you think would happen if you did not learn English? What would be the consequences?	5. ماذا تعتقدين سيحدث ان لم تتعلمي اللغة الإنجليزية؟ ماذا ستكون العواقب؟
6. Is there any pressure on you to study English? Please give reasons.	6. هل تشعرين أن هناك ضغط لتعلم اللغة الإنجليزية؟ اذكري الأسباب.
7. Do your parents have a role in your language learning? What is their role? Or why not?	7. هل لديك أشقاء يستخدمون اللغة الإنجليزية؟ هل تمارسين اللغة معهم؟
8. Do you have siblings that speak English? Do you use English with them?	8. هل لديك أشقاء يستخدمون اللغة الإنجليزية؟ هل تمارسين اللغة معهم؟
9. Do you experience any difficulties in learning and using English in your country? Please give reasons.	9. هل تواجهين صعوبات في تعلم و استخدام اللغة الإنجليزية في بلدك؟ اذكري الأسباب.
10. How do these difficulties influence your English language learning?	10. اذكري كيف الصعوبات تؤثر على تعلم للغة الأنجليزية.

Through this qualitative substudy, I aimed to gain a better understanding of the theoretical components that informed the design of my two quantitative substudies. Specifically, I sought to explore the factors influencing L2 motivation in this sample, examine the relationship between L2 motivation and language proficiency (both in writing and speaking), and investigate the motivational component contributed by respondents' views of their future L2 selves. I wanted to understand why the written English proficiency of this group was insufficient for the planned quantitative analysis, despite their prior L2 English study experiences in primary, secondary, and intermediary school. Additionally, I sought to gain insights into the participants' perceptions of their future

L2 selves in their own words, and to examine the connection between these perceptions and the measurements obtained from the developed instrument.

Interview Results

My analysis of the interviews produced several intertwining themes. First, for many participants, L2 motivation was strongly influenced by family and national identity. In addition, many participants expressed an interest to learn English as part of their future employment plans. However, most described challenges to mastering English through Saudi Arabia's education system. They complained of its low quality and a lack of learning experiences outside the classroom. I summarize these themes in the following sections.

Family Identity as a Source of L2 Motivation

Several respondents described being committed to their English program through their collective identity with their family. Unlike in more Western settings, these learners did express independent motivations to learn English or choose it as their academic major. Those who favored majoring in English often cited their family's support. Amani is one such example:

> I chose to study English because it was both my desire and my parents'. My parents supported me, because they themselves couldn't learn English and they wanted me to learn it. (Amani)

Families and students appeared to want to align their motivation to learn English. For example, Jawaher describes convincing her family to agree with her choice of major:

> My parents didn't encourage me to major in English because they believed I had already knew English. They tried to convince me to choose another major. But I'm glad I chose English because it's the best

choice for me. Now they have changed their minds and became proud of me since they saw me studying hard and doing my best. (Jawaher)

Further, students whose parents did not support them learning English expressed difficulty with L2 motivation and learning. One example of this is Hala's experience:

I didn't choose law because my father's approval is more important to me... If I don't get accepted in the [graduate English] programme because of my low proficiency, I would have no problem choosing a field other than English... My dad is like that with everyone. He is controlling. He even decided me and my brother's future, like where we're going to work. (Hala)

Hala's comment reflects the issue with measuring L2 future selves and assuming that the "other" L2 self is somehow independent of the self-concept, which it is apparently not in these learners. Given that learning L2 English has been recently promoted in Saudi Arabia as a desired cultural value, if these families value L2 English proficiency, the students would have provided more accurate writing samples. On the other hand, where family L2 motivation and individual L2 motivation were operating at different intensities, the students experience demotivation, which could lead to lower L2 proficiency. Overall, the students had low L2 proficiency, so differences in the students' expectations for their L2 abilities compared to their families' expectations likely did not significantly impact their proficiency.

National Identity as a Source of L2 Motivation

Several participants expressed motivation to learn English so that they could fulfill what might be considered "ambassadorial" roles; educating English-speakers about Saudi Arabia, the Middle East, and Islam:

> I want a job that will allow me to travel and talk to a big audience about my culture, like traditions, social norms, anything, and share my interactions with English speakers and how I changed their shocking misconceptions about my culture. (Doha)

> Most Western countries have inaccurate perceptions about our religion, Saudi Arabia, and Arabs in general. So, working in tourism would be a good opportunity for me to present the positive aspects of our society to Western tourists and change their perceptions. (Hanan)

A similar ambassadorial orientation was seen in a study of identity and ambassadorial behavior among Hong Kong residents (Wassler et al., 2019). Although this theme was only expressed by a few respondents, it is intriguing and invites future study.

Instrumental L2 Motivation Associated with Living in Saudi Arabia

The ambassadorial motivations described previously were expressed in the context of employment. Some participants envisioned their future L2 selves working abroad, dealing mainly with tourists or other individuals outside of Saudi Arabia. However, with English so ubiquitous within Saudi, some expressed interest in learning the language to improve their prospects for employment and daily living within the country. For example, one participant reported helping an elderly Saudi woman communicate with a non-Arabic-speaking hair stylist in a beauty salon by acting as interpreter:

> I was glad that I was able to help the woman, but I was surprised that she didn't know any English. Doesn't she need it? How does she run errands or go about her day not knowing any English? (Uhoud)

Challenges to L2 English Acquisition in Saudi Arabia

The strongest themes in the third substudy concerned the challenges respondents faced learning L2 English within the Saudi educational system and culture. Naturally, some of this challenge came directly from parental pressure associated with the collective L2 future self identity described earlier:

> Whenever I get a bad grade, I conceal it from my father. Not because I'm afraid of him, but you know how fathers want their daughters to excel. He wants me to be excellent in English. To me, I think it's normal to get a bad grade because I don't expect to perform well all the time. (Amira)

However, family expectations were rarely expressed as a source of demotivation.

The L2 Learning Environment as a Source of Demotivation

Most of the challenges to L2 motivation and acquisition appeared to originate from the L2 learning environment (L2LE):

> I want to become an English teacher in the future because it's not a tough profession to achieve. It's not an impossible dream because it doesn't require high English proficiency. I just have to make the lessons enjoyable for my students. (Nawal)

Nawal's opinion that English teaching "doesn't require high English proficiency" and success can come from making "the lessons enjoyable" reflects problems with low-quality English teaching in Saudi Arabia. Her description of English teachers also reflects her educational experience.

Themes associated with L2 English demotivation arising from the L2LE also concerned poor public school teaching quality that inadequately prepared the students for higher education. Layla described how grade school learning was "too easy" compared to her higher education experience, so she felt unprepared for college:

> The English curriculum at school was so easy. I was excellent in English and my grades were high. That's why I chose to major in English and my

family supported me because they thought I was excellent in English. Now I'm facing difficulties because the course material is hard, and it keeps getting harder. I keep getting low grades. (Layla)

Others provided detailed complaints about the quality of English instruction throughout the Saudi system:

At school, I used to know the composition task in my exam beforehand, because teachers used to give us paragraphs to memorise for the exam. They didn't even teach me how to write properly. Now I don't know how to write a simple paragraph in my writing course. (Aisha)

I could never ask my teachers questions for clarifications in class or by email because they either tell me to ask my friends, or reply that they would not explain something that they had already explained in class. So, I ask my colleagues instead, and they don't even know the answer sometimes. (Hind)

I see how some teachers are biased towards the good students and how they monitor their development because they're already excellent in English. Teachers give them feedback on how to further improve their English and I don't get the same attention on my work. How am I supposed to improve if I'm left to feel that I have a defect for having poor English? (Raneem)

In general, the participants explained that in elementary and higher education levels, English teachers did not speak target-like English themselves, so they could not provide examples to emulate. This is because many are non-Saudi and are teaching on contract from countries where English is not the main language. In addition, many English teachers in higher education lack the teaching and interpersonal skills necessary to be effective in the Saudi higher education L2LE.

Challenges to Practicing Conversational English in Saudi Arabia

Despite the recent emphasis on learning English in Saudi Arabia as part of Vision 2030, conversing with others in English in public is still perceived as boastful or otherwise inappropriate (Al-Qahtani, 2015; Alrahaili, 2018). Although non-Saudi service workers speak English, they generally do not speak target-like English, and they are not sufficiently integrated into Saudi society to serve as English conversational partners for Saudi L2 learners (Alsubaie, 2014). These societal features make it difficult for L2 English learners in Saudi to practice speaking English, as these comments indicate:

> I find it hard to practice English at home because my siblings get irritated with me when I speak English to them. They ask me why I'm using English when everyone around me speaks Arabic. (Huda)

> My brother knows English, but he doesn't encourage me to use English at home. He thinks that I'm trying to flaunt my English. (Doha)

Overall, the participants identified the lack of opportunities to practice speaking L2 English in Saudi Arabia as a significant barrier to acquiring proficiency in the language.

DISCUSSION AND RECOMMENDATIONS

My insights from this research concern the development and selection of appropriate research methods to study L2 English acquisition in Saudi Arabia as well as the importance of the Saudi education system for Saudi L2 English acquisition.

Use of Research Methods

When I first began considering research methods, I realized that measuring L2 motivation using the L2MSS framework (Dörnyei, 2009) might not be very useful for this particular group. This is because they didn't differentiate their future L2 self from their collective identity, which is closely tied to their family. In situations where there was a discrepancy in the intensity of the students' and families' L2 motivation, it was crucial for them to either align themselves towards L2 learning or move away from it. If the student remained committed but the family did not, the student was unlikely to have succeeded. Further, if the family was committed and the student was not, the student often expressed anxiety and fear of failure. For these students, it is crucial to align their L2 identity with the identity that their family has of them. However, the entire sample demonstrated a low English proficiency in their writing samples, in that they could not use articles properly, left words out of simple written sentences, and made long run-on sentences. Therefore, L2 motivation arising from their vision of their future L2 selves may not be a primary influence on their English learning success.

Secondly, in retrospect, I feel my measurement of target-like articles in writing samples based on sociolinguistic research methods was problematic. It appeared to be a marker of proficiency rather than sociolinguistic variation. Further, variation in target article usage between monitored and unmonitored prompts in the same individual would likely have been subtle if they could be detected at all. In a practical sense, this target-like article outcome was probably not sensitive enough to reveal sociolinguistic variation in this group even if it was present.

The Saudi Education System as an Influence on L2 Motivation

Compared to L2 motivation arising from identity, it appears that a much stronger driver of the quality of L2 output in this group was lifelong experiences with a less-than-adequate L2LE. Despite the motivation of many Saudi students to learn English, they have faced significant obstacles due to the lack of support for language acquisition in public schools and higher education institutions. From my perspective, the absence of high-quality L2LE resources is a more potent factor contributing to the lower-than-expected proficiency levels in article usage.

Saudi L2 English education can be improved in three areas: motivating students through effective teaching and curriculum, encouraging families to support their children's education, and considering students' perspectives when making changes. Firstly, the results from the third substudy show that Saudi teachers play a crucial role in their students' L2 learning success. University teachers should take into consideration that they are teaching learners with a low-quality L2 English educational experience in public school. Many students have reported frustration in trying to get teachers to answer their questions. University teachers therefore should adopt strategies that accommodate all learners, such as using Arabic to explain difficult concepts. Research conducted in the Saudi context has recommended this educational approach due to students' preference for Arabic when learning complex concepts in lessons (Almohaimeed & Almurshed, 2018). Instructors should also take into consideration their learners' views about their own learning experience and address them accordingly. Instructors can play a crucial role in fostering L2 learning motivation by cultivating their students' potential future selves and actively supporting these self-guides throughout the learning process. One way for L2 English teachers to accomplish this would be by surveying their students' wishes and interests for the future as well as through learning about their role models, then taking these into account when developing the curriculum. This can be done in traditional classroom settings or online through technological and media sources. By considering learners' hopes and preferences and adapting classroom activities to align with them, teachers can improve their efficacy.

Although this may be an evidence-based policy recommendation, it is unlikely to be implemented on a widespread scale. As described earlier, the MoE controls the curriculum, and it is up to each learning environment to choose effective ways to deliver it (Al-Mutairi, 2007; Al-Seghayer, 2011). Although changes in teaching methods in Saudi higher education are typically implemented locally (e.g., department, college), sharing resources and strategies within and across institutions can still enhance L2 English learning. Thus, teacher training plays a vital role in improving L2 education.

Students also require more exposure and chances to use English beyond the classroom. Teachers should recognize this need and guide their learners toward technological resources and other strategies to boost these opportunities. One example is already in place at PNU, led by the Arabic Language Teaching Institute for Non-Arabic Speakers (PNU-ALI), which teaches L2 Arabic to visiting foreign students at PNU. It is a language exchange dialogue program, where English speakers from the PNU-ALI programs arrange to meet with the Arabic speakers of PNU's L2 English programs so they can practice their respective second languages. Using this program could positively impact the L2 learning experience of the PNU students in both programs. Second, teachers could encourage using communication apps such as Skype to talk to English speakers in other countries. Digital exchange programs could be set up like the traditional one at PNU-ALI to help learners practice their English with target-like English speakers in other countries. Finally, PNU's L2 English programs could seek to deliberately host English speakers for forums in a question-and-answer format where the speaker informally interacts with students in English. If the visiting speaker does not know Arabic, it will force the students to work with what English they have to communicate. Implementing these experiences would increase opportunities for PNU students to improve their English in their current learning environment.

Besides teachers and curriculum, family support also plays a crucial role in motivating students to learn L2 English. Lamb (2013) suggests that a family-level approach should be encouraged to optimize students' learning experience. Parents and family members who have English proficiency can serve as positive role models and adopt strategies to enhance their children's motivation to learn English. By finding constructive ways to maintain their children's motivation and continuing to encourage them even after they choose their major, students can receive much-needed support to persist in their language learning. Family members can also promote positive attitudes towards learning by sharing their own L2 learning experiences. This can inspire students to follow suit and thus feel more motivated to continue learning English.

Finally, as previously mentioned, changes to L2 English education in Saudi Arabia are primarily implemented at the local level, with the MoE responsible for designing the curriculum. However, since the current curriculum is disconnected from learners' interests and needs, having been designed decades ago, local institutions can address this issue by updating their delivery methods and incorporating more relevant and engaging materials. However, this situation has created a stagnant environment in that local institutions are not forced to review and refresh their teaching. This means regular needs analyses and curriculum evaluations do not take place as often as many educators would like. Thus, to ensure the alignment between learners' needs and the curriculum, educational leaders at the local level should conduct regular surveys to obtain learners' feedback and recommendations on their learning experiences, such as preferred teaching methods and materials, as well as seek suggestions on ways to improve the curriculum and teaching approaches. One of the challenges of education in Saudi Arabia is that students are assigned a pre-defined curriculum that does not reflect their interests and needs (Rahman & Alhaisoni, 2013), which can be a source of demotivation. Surveying learners' opinions about the various components of their learning experience might improve L2 learning outcomes and would provide teachers with a stronger foundation upon which to base their pedagogy.

Conclusion

In conclusion, my series of substudies has shown that although many of the female Saudi college students expressed strong motivation to master English, as revealed through instrument measurements and interviews, their motivation did not successfully translate into L2 English proficiency. The reasons for this were identified in the third interview substudy and included navigating familial influences arising from a collective identity experienced between students and their families, as well as the learners' ambassadorial inspirations and influence from a national education system that emphasizes studying English but does not prepare high school students for advanced English learning in college. Recommendations to address these challenges include: finding creative ways for Saudi English learners to practice conversational English that respect social norms, establishing quality teaching standards for college-level English instructors and providing training to meet these standards, and exploring ways to make the college-level English classrooms more student-centered.

Author Bio

Danya Shaalan is an Assistant Professor in Applied Linguistics who is currently serving as the Vice Dean of Academic Affairs in the College of Languages at Princess Nourah bint Abdulrahman University (PNU) in Riyadh, Saudi Arabia. Her current research interests include Saudi higher education students' motivation and second language acquisition (SLA), the connection between SLA and identity, sociolinguistic methods, SLA motivation, the second-language learning environment, and the influence of integrativeness on SLA.

13
Revisiting the Need for Foreign English Teachers in South Korea

Laura Taylor

Wanted. English teacher for a preschool. No experience necessary. Must have a bachelor's degree in any subject and be from an "Inner Circle" country (i.e., Australia, Canada, Ireland, New Zealand, South Africa, the USA, or the UK). Please include a photo with your resume.

I was that "English teacher." I graduated from university with a degree in Economics and Political Science and found myself working in a job that I hated. I was looking for a change and when a friend said they would be teaching English abroad and that it would include housing, lunches, and a decent salary, I asked where I could sign up. Pretty much immediately, that same company that my friend was working for sent me a job application. After sending my resume (which included no teaching experience) and a photo, I was hired. A couple months later I boarded a plane ready for a new and exciting adventure.

I was tasked with teaching preschool, which included children between three and six. There were six of us, four women and two men. We could all be classified as White, from either Canada or the United States. We had shared offices in a special part of the preschool specifically dedicated to "the foreigners." Meanwhile, the Korean teachers, who all spoke English just as well as I did, occupied the room next to the toilets. All four of them crammed into a room that could barely fit 2 desks. On my first day, the Director handed me a book and showed me to the door of my classroom. I walked into a room of four-year-olds who all gawked at me as I entered. I had no idea what I was doing; I could not speak a word of Korean, and most of the children were still at the "Hello, how are you? I am fine, thank you" phase in their English learning.

I always felt a little bit awkward because it was quite clear from the beginning that we were at the top of the hierarchy, clearly above our Korean counterparts. Yet they helped us at every stage—getting bank accounts, posting letters, filling prescriptions, and more. Things that were clearly well outside their job descriptions. Yet, when it came time for the parents to arrive, it was my job to stand outside of my classroom and greet each of the parents. It was my job to be in the front row of our English recitals dressed up in Korean high fashion. Meanwhile, the Korean teachers were behind the scenes wiping noses and taking the children to the bathroom. They all had degrees in teaching and several had been working at the preschool for more than a decade. That was at least ten years more experience than I had, yet I was seen to be the expert because I "looked the part." When I finished my contract, I decided it was time to actually get some real teaching experience so I went back to school to get my Master's and ultimately a PhD. During that process I decided to examine the experiences of pre-service Native English-Speaking Teachers (NESTs) to see if others had similar experiences to me. But it was more than just our teachers, and the Korean teachers, that puzzled me; it was the nature of the wider context of these private English language schools, where it seemed like there was a different option available on every street corner. Why did these schools exist? Why did they need to recruit foreign English teachers when the Korean teachers seemed much more qualified? Why did parents pay significant tuition fees for their children to be taught by someone without any teaching experience? The questions were endless, and so the opportunity for further research presented itself.

Overview

With the challenges that have faced the world over the past several decades, it has become increasingly difficult for recent university graduates to find work in their home countries, especially with undergraduate degrees not directly tied to obvious career paths. Because of this, more and more Native English Speakers (NESs) are accepting positions as English as a Foreign Language (EFL) teachers in South Korea (hereafter Korea). This is not necessarily surprising, as the pay can be good, which is essential to paying back student loans. Other benefits may include bonuses, medical insurance, pension contributions, furnished accommodations, and more. These incentives, paired with potential travel opportunities during vacation periods, make the thought of teaching English an attractive option. Further, with the demand for NESTs ever increasing, jobs are relatively easy to get if potential candidates are NESs, have a bachelor's degree from an English-speaking university, and can pass a criminal background check.

Before delving into the nature of this research, it is worth examining some key terms and how they fits within the wider contexts of this narrative. Throughout this chapter, the terms NESs and NESTs are used to represent a specific group of individuals. It is recognized however, that these terms, along with many of the other acronyms that are used to designate people into groups are problematic. In this sense, the question arises about what it means to be "native" and why this term is chosen over describing these individuals as those having English as an L1. The answer lies in how jobs are advertised in Korea and the need for individuals to be from specific inner circle countries (i.e., Australia, Canada, Ireland, New Zealand, South Africa, the United Kingdom, and the United States). Thus, having English as an L1 is often not sufficient to secure employment in Korea, perhaps justifying the terms NES and NEST for the purpose of this chapter despite their shortcomings.

This chapter examines the roles of NESTs in Korean private language schools, also known as cram schools or *hagwon*. It is evident that while the job advertisements may sound appealing while applicants are in their home countries, actually, upon arrival, there are other tasks and expectations placed on NESTs not advertised by employers (e.g., unpaid hours, expectations to socialize with employers after work, etc.). These additional expectations, primarily related to differences in cultural and social expectations, can lead to increased stress levels and a reduction in motivation among novice NESTs, creating friction between them and their Korean teacher counterparts.

Currently, Korea is primarily a monolingual country, and yet, English is seen as a language that should be studied from a young age. Song (2011) argues that Korea is a society comprised of an important hierarchical structure based primarily on levels of education. Hence, the report that about 82% of elementary students, 93% of middle school students, and 88% of high school students are enrolled in cram schools or other forms of private tutoring is not surprising (Woo et al., 2004). Education can lead to *upward mobility* (Park, 2009), so parents spend a substantial portion of their household income (up to 9%) on private tutoring (Kim & Lee, 2010). Specifically, with respect to English education, Park and Abelmann (2002) note that English cram schools are a multi-trillion won per year industry and that being taught by a "foreigner" is, potentially, one essential component. Despite this clear indication that cram schools are popular in Korea, very little research has been conducted on the inner workings of these schools, their expectations, or how foreign teachers cope with working in them.

English language cram schools are for-profit businesses and competition for students is fierce. To entice parents to enrol their children in these schools, promises of rapid English ability advancement are commonly advertised. Students are often assessed by how quickly they can finish a course book and move to another as student progress is monitored through in-class testing.

A dilemma arises through parents being promised results and expecting excellence but English cram schools being for-profit, meaning they try to keep costs down, so they typically hire NESs who have little or no formal training or experience teaching English. Past studies have suggested that even teachers with at least some teacher training or qualifications experience high levels of occupational stress when dealing with pressures from students, colleagues, and other staff, all of which can lead to a lack of motivation (Adams, 2001; Kyriacou, 2011). Therefore, it is not surprising that when novice NESTs with no qualifications experience these factors paired with other issues, such as their lack of knowledge of the Korean language or inability to effectively communicate with many of their students, their stress levels increase and their motivation decreases. Thus, a gap can be created between parental expectations and NESTs' actual teaching practices.

Arguments might be made about whether the *native speaker fallacy* still exists (Braine, 1999; Phillipson, 1992), and whether NESTs have better oral language proficiency (Tang, 1997). While these are highly debated topics, in this chapter the focus is on Korean cram schools rather than a more generalized examination of NESTs. The current situation suggests that cram schools are widely used and deemed necessary by Korean parents for their children to excel and attend "elite" universities. Currently, the preferred situation in these schools appears to be NESTs teaching English classes to children. Because of this perception that NESTs should teach in these schools, the issue explored here what this represents, and how this might contribute to the wider discussion on private English language schools in Korea.

Rationale

This chapter considers how a lack of experience paired with the influences of a foreign culture affect the role of novice NESTs in Korea with the goal of reimagining English cram school structures. There were two premises underpinning this investigation—that culture would significantly influence NESTs and that stress levels related to teaching would increase as a result. It has been previously noted that novice teachers often use prior knowledge from their experiences as learners in their teaching practice to combat their initially weak understandings of subject-specific content (Ell et al., 2012). The issue, with respect to NESTs, is that they are asked to teach English as a second or foreign language, something that as native speakers they have not experienced from a learner's perspective. Linking to Sinner (2010)'s observation that program delivery is affected by cross-cultural differences, the research question is: "To what extent does culture play a role in the teaching and stress levels of novice NESTs in Korea?"

It is necessary to define some of associated terms. First, *teacher stress* is, "the experience by a teacher of unpleasant, negative emotions such as anger, anxiety, tension, frustration or depression, resulting from some aspect of their work as a teacher" (Kyriacou, 2001, p. 28). This definition accommodates the level of teacher stress increasing if the demands placed on teachers do not fall within their expectations. Second is *cultural adaptation* (or lack thereof), often referred to as *culture shock*. Anderson (1971) suggests that this shock occurs when individuals experience social elements that are not part of their normal social experience. Zhou et al. (2008) take a more proactive view of this term, suggesting that although it is associated with contact-induced stress, it can be managed by individuals, although the level of management will vary.

METHODOLOGY AND CONTEXT

This qualitative study examined the progression of four North American first-time NESTs during the first six months of their one-year contracts at a Korean private preschool. After informed consent was obtained from teachers, school staff, and parents, semi-structured interviews were conducted with the teachers and classes were observed to determine whether the teachers could comprehensively teach English and whether they had negative experiences. Interviews were held pre-arrival, after 1 month, after 3 months, and after 6 months, while observations occurred monthly. The interviews varied in structure but started with questions about general expectations. In subsequent interviews, participants were asked to compare what they had experienced versus what they had expected. Observations examined the chosen tasks and the implementation of these tasks in practice. What quickly became evident was that the teachers were unprepared for some of the cultural and social differences between Korea and their home countries. They were also misinformed about their role within the preschool. The frustration that ensued in the following weeks became so overwhelming that by weeks five and six, teachers had reduced the amount of effort put into each lesson dramatically (e.g., they did not prepare supplemental materials to assist them in teaching and they sometimes were not aware of which page in the textbook was supposed to be taught). This created friction between the teachers and the Korean staff and ultimately led to a breakdown of communication by all parties involved.

FINDINGS

Findings from this study were thematically coded using qualitative analysis software. The main themes generated focused on cultural and social issues alongside the NESTs being seen as not teachers, but rather 'edutainers,' or responsible for ensuring that the children enjoyed their experiences.

Cultural and Social Issues

Differences in culture were evident inside and outside the classroom. While both are important to the NESTs' experiences, the in-house issues are focused on here.

The first set of interviews were the week before the teachers arrived in Korea and were designed to examine expectations toward living and teaching. All four teachers expressed excitement toward their new roles and admitted that they thought difficulties surrounding cultural issues would mainly be associated with food and language. However, this view was quickly replaced after arrival in Korea, with the realization that the cultural differences were much more extensive.

All four teachers noted that their signed contracts specified "37 contact hours per week." However, upon closer inspection these 37 hours were the *teaching* hours and did not allow for preparation time. Further, teachers were expected to be at the school at eight in the morning, have lunch for 45 minutes, and finish at six, meaning nine hours and 15 minutes of work each day. Further, if the teachers did not have a class at the end of the day, they were expected to remain at the preschool and wait for their colleagues to finish before leaving. Moreover, if the Director or Owner had to work late, the teachers were required to wait for them to finish before they could leave. As one teacher noted, "We are not necessarily expected to be doing work during these hours, we are just expected to sit and wait until the boss leaves. When he goes home, so can we. It's not productive."

This is not necessarily unexpected as Korea is considered a collectivist society underpinned by Confucianism (Cheah & Park, 2006). However, the difference between the school's expectations and a more Western style of employment meant that rather than feeling a sense of unity within the school, teachers felt as if time was being wasted.

Some might argue that this idea of collectivism is no longer relevant in Korea (Cheah & Park, 2006), especially since, as previously noted, parents spend a substantial part of their household income on tutoring so that their children will have better opportunities. However, while competition may be perfectly acceptable in one situation, in others, such as with the case of the teachers, the desire for equality and unity also exists.

Another issue that aggravated the teachers was the desire for the Korean staff to avoid conflict. Teachers suggested that when speaking with the Director about classroom issues (e.g., the textbooks being too difficult or the desire to change the way a lesson had been designed), the Director would listen carefully, nod, and agree. However, nothing would be changed. Again, this likely relates to the differences in cultural expectations.

For the teachers, the language barrier, initially thought of as possibly a hindrance to adapting to life in Korea, quickly became monumental. This was true both in and outside of classroom. In the classroom, NESTs were expected to show excitement for upcoming holidays—many of which were specific to Korea. Teachers were often left uninformed as to the significance of these events, as this could not be adequately translated by the staff. Further, the teachers were encouraged to teach "Western holidays," but using handouts designed by the Korean staff members. An example of a Halloween handout was described by a NEST, who noted, "The handout said Halloween is when girls dress up as princesses and boys dress up as superheroes. They can play games and have fun." When she asked about ghosts, pumpkins, and trick-or-treating, she was told that these were not appropriate and that she should teach from the handout. This example was one of many noted by the four NESTs in this study illustrating how they felt as though students were being misinformed and thought that what they, as NESTs, could offer was better than the materials produced by the Director and Korean staff.

As this relates to the NESTs' role expectations, they were initially expecting to provide input related to how their classes would be taught and which books would be appropriate. However, their actual roles were much different. The participants felt this was partly due to a language barrier as well as their perception that the Korean staff were more incentivized to appease parents than to take the NESTs' suggestions into account. Differences in job expectation, language, and business enterprise are examples of cultural differences explicitly linked to the unpleasant, negative emotions described previously as teacher stress.

The NEST as the Edutainer

The word *edutainer* is a common one circulating through the private language school industry in Korea, mainly used by foreign teachers. An edutainer is a NEST whose role is to look presentable by always smiling and ensuring students enjoy themselves so that their parents stay satisfied. For an edutainer, teaching the students is secondary, although that students must complete at least one page in their workbook each lesson so it looks like they have been studying diligently.

The NESTs at the preschool in this study noted that they often felt like edutainers. For example, one teacher recounted how she wore a wedding dress while her class of five year-olds sang *Bicycle Race* by Queen to parents watched adoringly from the audience. She noted that while none of the parents questioned whether the children understood the lyrics, they did approve her choice of attire.

This is not to say that all NESTs working in Korean private language schools are edutainers. It is however, a role that sometimes exists. Moreover, being an edutainer is not necessarily a downfall. It is plausible that some NESTs are content with this. However, for some the lack of academic engagement and the dichotomy between being a "teacher" and putting on an act for show can be frustrating.

Discussion

To evaluate the need for foreign English teachers in Korea, it is important to consider the benefits and drawbacks of the cram school model. One of the first arguments for keeping the status quo includes the "authentic" experience of being taught by a NEST. There is some merit to this as teachers have likely spent a good portion of their lives growing up in English speaking countries and are familiar how English functions there to some extent. This might include knowledge of slang or jargon, strong oral proficiency, and working knowledge of their home culture. In certain circumstances, this can be beneficial, especially for students that seeking to study in high school or university abroad.

However, whether teachers see themselves as edutainers or more important members of the language teaching community, issues of culture and stress seem to consistently arise. Being an untrained teacher may contribute. Further, being unfamiliar with Korean culture has a direct influence on the NESTs' well-being. Certainly, teachers who are comfortable in their environment and who feel valued in their role are less likely to succumb to the same frustrations as those who see their role as primarily symbolic. Then again, for some, a job where there is minimal responsibility and an opportunity to travel countrywide may sound enticing.

As suggested by Park and Abelmann (2002), although Korean parents seem to realize that their approach toward private tutoring is, at best, misguided, it is currently seen as one of the only ways to ensure their children's academic success and desirable future employment. Therefore, while parents are striving to keep up with other parents and private language school owners to earn profits to secure their own status, NESTs are left trying to navigate cultural and social expectations while unable to speak Korean or understand the circumstances around them. Based on this, the increased stress levels indicated by the teachers in this study and the apathy and lack of motivation to create stimulating and enjoyable classes seems appropriate for a system that is not necessarily concerned with the level of English the children learn.

Conclusions and Reflections

This study of four teachers is, by itself, a small and unrepresentative sample. Yet it exists as part of a wider discussion on the nature of inexperienced teachers working abroad, and in this case, in Korea. There has been considerable research on teaching English abroad and the benefits of having NESTs (or contrastively the benefits of having non-NESTs). The findings tend to ebb and flow depending on the circumstances and the nature of the population. What seems to be indisputable is that teachers generally experience high levels of stress and burnout (Richards et al., 2018). These findings relate to trained teachers living in their own cultures and speak the same language as their pupils. Thus, it is not surprising that stress and burnout are present among NESTs working in Korea, and that these emotions occur relatively early in their contracts. In thinking about English cram schools, there is more to the story than just the teachers. One might point to the competitiveness of entry into university or the seeming need for English as it is currently positioned as a lingua franca globally. Korea seems to be placing itself in a precarious position, where more and more responsibilities and demands are placed on students to the point where it has reached concerning levels.

Yet despite all the evidence, it is difficult for me as a White Canadian NES to insert my own views into the Korean cram school context. I spent several years working in Korea as a NEST, but would not claim even a remote understanding of Korean culture, as my own experiences placed me as an outsider looking in. The system is also accepted by many parents and students who willingly spend their time working diligently within these cram schools. After my own experiences in the classroom and externally from a research perspective, the Korean staff in these cram schools have consistently demonstrated that they have both the capacity and the cultural know-how to be much more effective as English teachers than the NESTs in many situations. This, again, continues the debate as to whether non-NESTs are preferable in the classroom. From my own perspective, it seems unequivocal that a trained Korean English teacher would provide far more language benefit to students than an English edutainer, but in many instances, parents are not willing to accept this.

Based on the willingness of parents to spend a significant portion of their household income on having their children educated by a NES, at least to some extent NESTs appear to be the "preferred" option. Yet based on the classroom observations and teacher interviews discussed here, there are clear identifiable issues (i.e., a lack of willingness to engage with the teaching materials and misunderstanding of students' non-verbal cues). As cultural differences impact on teacher stress and motivation, it seems logical to question whether the unpleasant experiences of NESTs are affecting students' desire (or need) to excel to gain a coveted place at an "elite" university.

Although the incentives of moving to Korea and becoming a NEST are enticing, issues can arise when untrained NESs take up employment as English teachers. First, there is the issue of culture. This issue extends much further than the language barrier and encompasses several fundamental differences in working conditions and expectations which can lead to an increase in teacher stress. Second, the limited amount of responsibility that NESTs have (i.e., being edutainers) leads to questions of self-worth and can decrease teaching motivation. While this debate will continue into the foreseeable future, it is important to explore this topic and map the trajectory of the cram school landscape in the Korean context.

Author Bio

Laura Taylor works as an Associate Professor, Teaching Stream at the University of Toronto Mississauga (UTM). As part of the Institute for University Pedagogy (ISUP), Laura focuses her work on the academic needs of English Language Learners (ELLs) across UTM. Her attention is mainly directed toward academic writing, with an emphasis on foundational skills required at the tertiary level. The wider mission of ISUP is to provide interdisciplinary support to faculty, staff, and students, and so Laura works closely with colleagues across UTM to foster the development of innovative, inclusive and accessible pedagogy.

14
EMI Business Programs in a Chinese University: Students' Perspectives, Pedagogical Challenges, and Re-Shaped Practices

Lijie Shao

Currently, within the context of internationalisation of higher education (HE), increasing use of English-medium instruction (EMI) programmes in higher education institutions (HEIs) is evident, as is the fast-growing scholarship of EMI worldwide. This is particularly the case in China where EMI provision has been expanding significantly, driven by national HE strategy and investment (Shao & Rose, 2022; Xu et al., 2021). In the Asian context, EMI provision or dual-medium instruction (Barnard, 2014) exhibits two goals: English improvement and content learning. Numerous EMI studies in the Asian context have investigated the linguistic challenges and controversial content/subject learning outcomes that have been impaired by English proficiency, discussing the pedagogical implications of EMI education (Hu et al., 2014; Sahan et al., 2022; Yuan et al., 2022). Through scrutinizing students' EMI perceptions and experiences among undergraduate business programmes in a Chinese university, this study aims to propose pragmatic pedagogical perspectives and practices that are particularly relevant in an Asian context, with a secondary goal of re-shaping current pedagogy toward the proposed practices. In this study, EMI is defined as "the use of the English language to teach academic subjects (other than English itself) in countries or jurisdictions in which the majority of the population's first language is not English" (Macaro et al., 2018, p. 37). Previously, the disciplines of social sciences, business and law were identified as areas with the most EMI provision (Ferencz et al., 2014). Globalisation and international trade have increased the demand for graduates and human resources (Doiz et al., 2013), thus associating the discipline of business with a high level of international orientation (Baker & Hüttner, 2017), so it is worthwhile to focus on business EMI.

LITERATURE REVIEW

EMI in the Context of Chinese HE

EMI in China emerged around the turn of this century and has developed exponentially in just two decades. In 2001, the Ministry of Education (Ministry of Education of the People's Republic of China, 2001) identified EMI as one of twelve strategies for providing high-quality undergraduate education in China. The student-facing motivation was to enable Chinese students to avail themselves of advanced technologies and expertise in English, as well as gain an international perspective, which would enhance the competitiveness of Chinese talent on the world stage. The institution-facing motivation was to boost universities' world academic rankings (McKay & Hu, 2012). Higher education institutions (HEIs), especially those in Project 985 (39 universities), Project 211 (116 universities in total including the Project 985 universities) and Double First-Class University Plan (42 universities along with 465 disciplines from an additional 95 universities) that replaced Project 985 and 211 since the 2010s (Xu et al., 2021) received financial support and preferential policy investment. Other HEIs such as those identified as key HEIs at the provincial level and lower also received support. Within Chinese HE, programmes with an EMI provision label generally exhibit a Chinese and English bilingual education pattern, in which Chinese and English language mediums are used with various degrees of integration depending on the needs of specific institutions and programmes (Huang & Curle, 2021).

Recent Studies on EMI Stakeholder Perceptions and Pedagogical Implications

More recently, EMI research in China has established itself as a recognisable and independent research topic. From the perspective of EMI motivation and perceived benefits at institutional and personal levels, EMI has been positively welcomed and is linked to expectations of internationalisation, career competitiveness, and improved English proficiency (Botha, 2014, 2016; Hu et al., 2014). However, in pedagogical practice, studies have highlighted issues and concerns related to key stakeholders' (student and teacher) English proficiency, which detrimentally impact learning outcomes and overall satisfaction with EMI (Hu & Duan, 2018; Hu et al., 2014; Zhang & Pladevall-Ballester, 2021). Among studies of HEIs examining student beliefs, perceptions, and attitudes towards EMI in China, Hu and Lei (2014) investigated an undergraduate EMI business program. They found that, although there were motivational and strategic convergences between the national and institutional levels, there was a mismatch between policy and pedagogical classroom practice. Whilst the stakeholders positively evaluated the potential benefits of EMI from national, institutional, and personal perspectives, they expressed concern and anxiety regarding the use of English in the classroom. The students perceived less effective learning outcomes regarding English proficiency improvement and content comprehension, a finding echoed in another of their studies (Lei & Hu, 2014). Another study by Hu and Duan (2018) of teachers' questions and students' responses in 20 subject classes in both English and Chinese further confirmed that it was unclear whether EMI in the form of teachers' questions being answered by students could help learners achieve their English proficiency improvement and content learning goals. A more recent investigation by Zhang and Pladevall-Ballester (2021) examined pre- and post-EMI experience among students of different EMI disciplinary courses, which showed students have mixed attitudes toward their EMI experience with obstacles, challenges, and opportunities presented by their linguistic deficiencies.

Consequently, many studies have investigated the problematic "E" in

EMI and its pedagogical solutions to address such linguistic challenges (Galloway et al., 2017; Hu & Lei, 2014; Kim & Shin, 2014; Sahan & Rose, 2021; Tange, 2010). For example, a study by Jiang et al. (2016) scrutinized how EMI subject teachers delivered content in English and how students acquired *English through English for Specific Purposes* (ESP) courses as a way of facilitation. This finding highlighted the significance of a fine-tuned ESP provision with close collaboration between content and English teachers that considers student needs. While recognising the expansion of EMI in Chinese HE and common pedagogical challenges, Fang (2018) proposed three directions for EMI quality enhancement. Firstly, stakeholders should be given specific and consistent EMI policies. Second, substantial language support is required for effective learning. Ultimately, EMI implementation should aim for a multilingual educational context that acknowledges stakeholders' linguistic diversity. Fang's third point responded to the growing appreciation of the pedagogical potential of *plurilingual* repertoires in EMI settings (Dafouz & Smit, 2016), such as *translanguaging*, which draws on available language repertoires to maximize learning outcomes (García & Wei, 2014; Wei, 2018; Sahan & Rose, 2021). In a study exploring teacher perspectives on professional development and certification amid increasing EMI provisions in China, teachers indicated that teaching must change in EMI, not only linguistically, but also in the overall teaching/learning culture and approach (Macaro et al., 2019). It is thus necessary to provide teachers with professional training and development, not only concerning English proficiency, but also with a holistic approach that embraces EMI pedagogy.

Methodology

Research Questions

Through an inquiry into students' EMI perceptions and experiences, this case study aimed to answer an overall question: How do students perceive their EMI experience?

Specifically, the study scrutinised students' perceptions through the following dimensions:

1. Motivation and benefits of enrolling in an EMI programme;
2. English proficiency and improvement;
3. English competency in content learning; and
4. Linguistic challenges and strategies to address them, including teacher pedagogical practices.

Participating HEI and Participants Sampling

The study adopted a mixed methods research approach, including quantitative surveys and qualitative interviews. In sampling the HEI and participants, the following criteria were applied:

- A tertiary HEI that proactively promotes internationalisation of HE in response to national education strategy and policy;
- A HEI that is situated in the Chinese national HE context and public HE system with a history and reputation of EMI provision.
- Within this HEI there are schools with EMI provision at the undergraduate level related to management and business.
- Within the undergraduate business-related programmes, participants (students) are from the 2nd and 3rd year so they have some EMI experience (at least one year) while at the same time being fully immersed in the EMI curriculum.

The school within this sampled university boasts on its website about its innovative and advanced internationalised teaching approach with seamless collaboration between English language and content teaching, including a combination of ESP, bilingual (interchangeable Chinese and English) teaching, and EMI. Table 1 gives details of the EMI context at this university.

Table 1.
EMI context at the participating HEI

Year EMI established	2003
Curriculum design	Business content curriculum integrated with English language support modules
English language support in curriculum	Compulsory EAP and ESP modules in the 1st, 2nd and 3rd years. Optional Overseas Exchange programme with selection mechanism in the 4th year
Participating subjects / majors	Business Administration, Certified Public Accounting (CPA), International Economics, as well as Business, Law, and Finance
Role of English	One of two parallel mediums of education (the other is Mandarin Chinese) and being used for academic purposes only, such as lecture content, learning activities fulfilling learning objectives, and assessment
Student demographic	100% home Mandarin Chinese or Chinese regional dialect as first languages
Teachers	Content and English support: Mostly Chinese teachers with overseas experience in either English-speaking regions or EMI settings (studying, teaching, visiting, or researching). English skills and culture teacher(s) from English as a majority language countries
Entry English requirement	Based on overall China College Entrance Exam scores in which English is included
Instruction band / rank	Top 10% HE institution in China. Key HEI at the provincial level

Research Ethics

The study carefully addressed ethical issues regarding conducting the research. The institution with which the author was affiliated at the time approved the research ethics application. An informal consent form was prepared that detailed the research methodology and data protection protocols, as well as the participants' rights and benefits. During the field trip, the researcher received either formal consent through a signed consent form or informal consent such as oral permission to conduct an interview or observation. The study administered two research instruments: surveys and semi-structured interviews. Surveys were conducted anonymously, whilst each interviewee was recorded as Interviewee 1 (I1) and so on (I1-I11). Any names and specific information related to the interview participants' backgrounds, such as gender, name of country, region, hometown, and schools other than the case study country, China, were replaced by general terms during the transcription process to maintain their anonymity. For instance, a specific university would be indicated as "University" and a specific module as "Module". Anonymity and confidentiality regarding personal information and data protection were ensured.

Research Instruments and Data Collection

The author conducted field research at the sampled HEI. An anonymous survey was circulated and collected in different classes with teachers' permission. The survey, in paper form and in English, had the Chinese translation of key words/terminology (such as EMI) attached to it. The language used for oral instruction, explanation, and communication during survey administration was Chinese. Survey administration at different classes took place either at the beginning or end of the class time, depending on the teachers' preferences. Table 2 lists perceptual questions, which comprised most of the survey. There were also factual questions asking for demographic information such as native language, age, nationality, programme related questions such as year levels, majors and modules, and English learning related questions such as results of national English proficiency tests, prior years of learning English before college, and ways of learning English. This chapter focuses on the perceptual questions in Table 2. These responses became the base for the quantitative analysis presented here. In Table 2, there are numbers in brackets following statements such as "this sounds a lot like me". Those numbers refer to the statements' numerical values for the purposes of analysis. Those numbers did not appear in the surveys. Participants saw the statements only.

From the qualitative side, face-to-face semi-structured interviews that aligned with the research question dimensions were conducted with students who voluntarily agreed to attend. The language throughout the interviews was Chinese given that both researcher and interviewees were native Chinese speakers. Interview recordings were transcribed into Chinese first then translated into English. Interviews lasted from 10 to 40 minutes and covered the following topics:

- Motivation to enrol in an EMI programme along with its benefits and drawbacks;
- Student English language proficiency along with its relationship to content learning and their progress in English;
- Linguistic and pedagogical challenges related to language difficulties;
- Strategies used to address language and overall EMI learning challenges;
- Recognised language support, the curriculum, and their perceived experience;
- Teacher/student proficiency in English and pedagogical approaches; and
- General suggestions for improvements to their EMI programme.

The field trip concluded with 247 valid surveys and 11 interviews.

Table 2
Perceptual Question Items

	Theme/Variable	Question	#Sub-qs	Scale
1	Perceived EMI motivation	Does this sound like you? By learning business through English, I am trying to... e.g., enhance my career advantages	7	'this sounds a lot like me' (5) 'a little like me' (4) 'undecided' (3) 'not really like me' (2) 'not at all like me' (1)
2	Perceived EMI benefits	Does this sound like you? EMI is beneficial to me because it... e.g., teaches me English	11	'this sounds a lot like me' (5) 'a little like me' (4) 'undecided' (3) 'not really like me' (2) 'not at all like me' (1) 'N/A' (0)
3	Self-assessment of English ability	Ratings on English skills (listening, speaking, reading, and writing)	5	1 (poor) 2 3 4 5 (excellent)
4	Perceived English improvement	Does this sound like you? By studying my programme in English, I believe my...has improved e.g., listening ability	5	'this sounds a lot like me' (5) 'a little like me' (4) 'undecided' (3) 'not really like me' (2) 'not at all like me' (1) 'N/A' (0)
5	Self-assessment of English ability in content learning	How would you rate your ability in performing the following tasks? e.g., reading course materials	11	1 (poor) 2 3 4 5 (excellent)
6	Perceived linguistic challenges	When learning through EMI, how difficult do you find it to...? e.g., preview the lesson	12	'very difficult' (5) 'quite difficult' (4) 'not easy not difficult' (3) 'quite easy' (2) 'very easy' (1) 'hard to judge' (0)

Note: #Sub-qs = Number of sub-questions

Data Analysis

The quantitative survey data was analysed in SPSS for descriptive statistics such as mean and standard deviation (SD) for rating scale questions, such as the perceptual items in Table 2. Results for theme one (Perceived EMI motivation) and two (Perceived EMI benefits) in Table 2 corresponded to the first research question dimension: EMI motivation and benefits. Theme three (Self-assessment of English ability) and four

(Perceived English improvement) corresponded to the second dimension: English proficiency and improvement. Theme five (Self-assessment of English ability in content learning) corresponded to the third dimension: English proficiency in content learning. The last theme, six (Perceived linguistic challenges), offered statistical support for linguistic challenges that are part of the last dimension: Linguistic challenges and strategies to address them, including teacher pedagogical practices.

NVivo was used to process the semi-structured interviews. Analysis procedures involved coding the data into nodes then formulating those nodes into themes (Saldaña, 2013). These themes aligned with the four specific dimensions of the overall research question, thus they also corresponded to the perception theme categories from the quantitative analysis. The node repertoire was established in two directions. From a top-down level, thematic coding (Kvale & Brinkmann, 2009) was adopted using the interview question themes. From the bottom-up level, "eclectic coding" (Saldaña, 2013, p. 188) was applied to conduct an open-ended exploration of the interview transcripts.

Findings

This section presents the findings for the four dimensions of the overall research question: motivation and benefits, English proficiency and improvement, English competency in content learning, as well as linguistic challenges and addressing strategies.

Motivation and Benefits

The survey on students' motivation (Mean=3.2, SD=1.0) for learning business through EMI showed students tended to rate career advantages (Mean=3.6, SD=1.2) and working in an international environment (Mean=3.4, SD=1.2) more positively. Please refer to the first theme in Table 2 for the full rating scale. This suggests the students may be aware of the role English plays in bridging them to prosperous careers, associated with being competitive and international. Such findings echo previous EMI studies in relation to increasing student (and faculty) mobility and employability at the national or institutional level (Chen, 2017; Doiz et al., 2014). Students seemed least interested in academic related aspects such as international conferences (Mean=2.8, SD=1.3) and studying abroad, including moving up to post-graduate level (Mean=2.9, SD=1.3), which might be because it was too early for these undergraduate student participants to consider academics at the research or post-graduate level. It may also be because they did not intend to go into academics but rather business and industry. Having said this, results of these aspects were still close to 3, or undecided (see Table 2, row 1).

The survey on the perceived benefits of EMI (Mean=3.2, SD=0.9) showed a positive recognition of the goal of English improvement. At the same time, students also acknowledged EMI "Gives me a challenge" (Mean= 4.0, SD=0.9), which may refer to its demanding nature in terms of studying in English on top of their native language(s). Students also tended to associate EMI with a quality education (Mean=4.0, SD=1.0). On the other hand, while students acknowledged increased motivation and interest in EMI, they did not necessarily agree that it made problem solving easier or the concepts easier to understand (Mean=3.1, SD=1.2). This may indicate that learning in an English medium presented additional linguistic and cognitive challenges, which have been recognised in other studies (Jiang et al., 2016; Richards & Pun, 2022). Please refer to row 3 in Table 2 for the full rating scale.

The interviews revealed a divided picture of the students' motivation and purpose to attend an EMI business programme. There was a distinct division between initiative choice and passive choice. On one hand, two interviewees, I9 and I2, explained that they chose to study business taught in English because this university has a strong subject reputation in languages (including English). In other words, the school's academic strength and long tradition of English teaching attracted them. For instance, I9 considered academic strength in English as a priority criterion when choosing between business programmes and universities with similar chances of being admitted. As a result, even though the national ranking of the business programme in this university might not be as high as in other universities offering similar programmes, I9 was willing to compromise and chose this university to study business taught in English. In other words, I9 made an initial choice to enrol in this EMI business programme. Interestingly, I2 mentioned trying to read more English articles in an authoritative journal in I2's field, with the purpose of continuing in academia later on. I2 further indicated that using English is inevitable when conducting research that requires going through foreign (English) articles and communicating with others (in that academic field) in the future. I2 was also the only interviewee that indicated studying EMI to "access international publications" in the survey (see Table 3). On the other hand, other interviewees mentioned it was not because this university offered bilingual education in business that they ended up attending; Rather, it was because their entrance exam scores matched the university's entry level and the conditions required of the business programmes that they wanted to study. Hence, in their cases, they did not have a strong motivation to study business through English prior to admission. It seems that, due to the highly competitive National College Entrance Exam system (Zhang, 2016) and restrictive school application system that allows for consideration of only one school during the first round of selection, in most cases, Chinese high school students end up being chosen by their universities. Furthermore, I7 and I11 mentioned it was their parents' decision to choose the programme and the university, indicating the parental pressure that Asian students may face (Li et al., 2017). Such external restrictions might explain why the survey showed uncertainty. Specifically, the means were around "3" concerning college choice and programme motivation, meaning undecided (see Table 2).

Responses to perceived benefits generally fell into three principal categories: English improvement, content learning, and bigger picture benefits, such as a more internationalised worldview and preparation for competitive jobs. Regarding progress in English proficiency, some mentioned that the quality of English classes and the English learning atmosphere improved their English skills. Many used national *CET-4/6* (College English Test Band Four/Six) results as an example. CET-4/6 is a high-stakes national English proficiency-indicating test administered to non-English major undergraduate students in China (Jin & Yang, 2018).

For content learning, some mentioned that EMI helped them better understand content, especially terminology, concepts, and principles, which originate in the West, resulting in enhanced academic performance. As for bigger picture benefits, some mentioned that the programme improved their career prospects, particularly concerning working in foreign enterprises. For instance, thanks to the experience of learning economics in English, I4's internship application was stronger:

> My main goal in the future is to secure a good job, and I am personally not very keen on studying itself. And I believe English gives me such an edge based on my working experience. For instance, in the internship application, you have a much bigger advantage if your academic background is okay and your English level is CET 4 or 6, than students from STEM [Science, Technology, Engineering and Mathematics]-oriented colleges. It is because even though their academic background might be stronger, their English, especially speaking skills, was not good enough. It was quite hard for those students to pass CET 4 or 6 while in our school we got more opportunities and resources to practise.

For the EMI motivation and benefits, students showed their appreciation especially from the perspective of career advancement resulting from a linguistic (English) advantage in the job market. It was evident that students attached importance to the goal of English improvement through EMI. The following findings thus will turn to the problematic "E", in which students' expectations were frustrated.

Self-Assessment of English Proficiency and Perceived Improvement

The self-reporting of English proficiency (Mean=2.4, SD=0.7) showed students rated their English proficiency in the lower half of possible answers, closer to poor than to excellent (see Table 2, row 3). They were least confident in their listening (Mean=2.2, SD=0.9) and speaking (Mean=2.2, SD=0.9), indicating limited exposure to oral English and opportunities to speak English. On the other hand, they had relatively higher ratings for their English improvement over time (Mean=3.3, SD=0.9). See numbered row 4 in Table 2 for the full rating scale. However, such low self-evaluation might relate to their culture, as Asian students tend to have less confidence in their English language abilities than their Western peers (Bradford & Brown, 2017).

Additionally, an independent *T-test* between the year 2 and year 3 groups was conducted to see if students in different years perceived their English ability differently. That is, if students in the higher year evaluated their English skills higher than the lower year students, with no significant difference (p>0.05) identified.

Despite interviewees eventually reaching a conclusion that their English had improved, there was a sense of hesitation and uncertainty. On one hand, almost all pointed out that their English had improved, with the evidence being that they had successfully passed the CET-4/6. I6 specifically mentioned that they had passed those tests faster, or with higher scores, than their friends and peers who had not been exposed to EMI or bilingual programmes in other universities. Holistically, the receptive skills of reading and listening were mentioned the most, as the interviewees believed that they received much more exposure to English than their peers at other universities, where the language immersion style was not as strong.

On the other hand, many of the interviewees did not feel the same way about the productive skills of speaking and writing. The reasons varied from insufficient opportunities, that is a shortage of exposure, such as their writing class being only once a week, not being interested in the writing class because it was not related to their major subjects, a persistent "Chinese mind" when writing in English, to not enough personal effort. A third-year student, I7, who elaborated on why their English skills did not progress, might be representative of similar comments from other interviewees regarding limited progress in specific English skills. I7 claimed their English skills had deteriorated because of a lack of English competency and three external motivations, which were exam pressure, loose requirements from teachers, and the too-familiar Chinese language environment. According to I7, due to perceived low English competency, such as limited vocabulary and "the deficiency in all English skills", they could not learn English as they desired. "After all," I7 commented, "my English base is not as solid as English major students." I7 described the interrupted learning cycle, starting with deficient English proficiency, as follows:

> [because of which] I had to make an effort to look up the words. Gradually it came to teachers' attention. Then teachers sent us [PPT slides or handouts] versions with Chinese translation or notes. [Because of this], I started to resort to the Chinese part and stopped looking up the English... Nowadays I feel that my [English] intuition has become worse than before, or from the exam time. I felt my English was always at my best when exams were approaching. (I7)

Notably, I7 stressed the adverse effects of the limited exposure to an English environment on their English progress:

> [English language proficiency], of course, must come from frequent communication in English and accumulation [of skills]. [But] I would never speak English to you in the dormitory. It is impossible. We are so used to Chinese, so gradually [we lost our English] language intuition.

In summary, students tended not to be satisfied with their self-assessed English proficiency or their perceived improvement. Interviews revealed both positive and negative comments. On one hand, there was evidence-based progress such as passing the CETs faster than their peers studying at other universities with higher scores. They saw progress in listening and reading, as well as increased business vocabulary in content learning. On the other hand, a couple of interviewees reported limited or backward progress due to weak English foundations, increasing dependence on notes and handouts in Chinese, and an absence of exams and assessments in English. Such circumstances reduced students' exposure to English and thus was demotivating in their efforts to improve their English.

English Competency in Content Learning

Regarding various learning tasks (Mean=2.6, SD=0.7), students generally gave themselves low proficiency ratings, with "giving information orally" (Mean=2.4, SD=0.9) and "writing academic papers" (Mean=2.2, SD=1.0) the lowest rated two activities. Please refer to row 5 in Table 2 for the full rating scale. These low ratings suggest a lack of confidence in learning content through English, possibly resulting from the curriculum and teaching approach taken, with English not used as much in content delivery as in English support modules. It further suggests students might not have sufficient opportunities to use English throughout their learning, especially in content learning.

Interviews revealed the reality that most of their programme content modules were either monolingual (Chinese) only or bilingual, resulting in limited exposure to and use of English. The majority stated that they used Chinese for cognitively processing the materials and discussions with others, and "English terminology in English first, and then followed by the explanation for the sake of my understanding in Chinese", as I7 noted during note-taking. Though mentioning that they used Chinese outside the classroom, I8 and I9 did indicate a preference for using English terminology, as the business they were learning was from the "West".

Interviewees also showed their dissatisfaction with the integration of EAP/ESP modules and their supporting roles in content learning. This dissatisfaction came from three main aspects: Loosely integrated English and Chinese, the content, including the teaching materials, and the teachers. Regarding the first aspect, I1 and I10 suggested that the English modules were disconnected from their major subject (content) classes. As a result, they sometimes found that what they had acquired in their English classes was not transferrable to their subject (content) study. Concerning content teaching, several interviewees hoped that more English could be used in the classroom and teaching materials, as they desired a programme with more English as a language of instruction. Regarding the teachers, all interviewees pointed out their teachers' English deficiencies influenced class quality, particularly I9, who hoped teachers would use more English in classes, as there was too little English in them. I9 also mentioned more effort should be made to integrate English and Chinese if English-only is not possible. I5's comments describe how these three aspects influenced each other, together with the gap I5 perceived between the current EMI programme and their ideal one:

> I was on an exchange program at the University and I saw their classes. The whole class was entirely in English, including the class by Chinese teacher. [The teacher] used English throughout the whole class. It might be mixed with several sentences in Chinese, but the point is Chinese was a tiny fragment, not the other way around. Then their PPT[s], including the learning materials, were all in English. In this case, you must think, learn, and ask in English. However, here, it feels like English is additional. Teachers do not mind if you use Chinese to ask or do something. It feels like there is no enforcement of using English, and thus you do not have an environment [where English language use is encouraged].

Overall, students indicated their English was deficient in content learning. Interviewees attributed such deficiencies to the underperformance of English modules that were supposed to facilitate their content learning.

Linguistic Challenges and Addressing Strategies Including Teachers' Pedagogical Practice

Among various English usage scenarios (Mean=3.4, SD=0.6), students rated themselves between 3 (not easy not difficult) and 4 (difficult). Please refer to row 6 in Table 2 for the full rating scale. Overall, students indicated it was not easy to overcome challenges, especially those related to oral communication, such as "explain clearly" (Mean=3.6, SD=0.9) and content learning, such as "translating subject knowledge into English" (Mean=3.6, SD=1.0) and "deal with the assignments, tests and exams" (Mean=3.5, SD=1.0).

The interviews offered more details about specific language obstacles. Interviewees reported a range of language-related problems, with vocabulary the most mentioned, leading to demotivation in some cases. Some interviewees reported limited vocabulary slowing their studies, such as when reading textbooks and course materials. Therefore, their strategy was to read the Chinese version first, then trying to match specific terminology and concepts in English. Listening was another obstacle for some interviewees, not only the English, but also the strong accent of their Chinese English teachers. With teachers, interviewees expressed more concerns than positive attitudes towards their content teachers' English proficiency amid endorsements of a few content teachers. Most interviewees wanted more content delivery in English. Even when there was approval of their teachers' English proficiency, it was only of their pronunciation. Most interviewees pointed out that, because of their teachers' limited English, the classes ended up being Chinese dominant. As I5 commented:

> Overall, I don't think [teaching content subjects in English] is as good as content subjects. What we feel in the class is that, at least in classes of content subjects, if there is English involved, they [teachers] use English only as an assistance, rather than a specialised course. They probably explain it in Chinese for most parts, but listing English translations on PPT for example. You [students] can certainly learn well by looking at the English [on PPT]. But most of the time, Chinese is the dominant use, so English is not applied widely.

Despite the risk of compromised content delivery, I5 and others still wanted more classes taught in English. While recognising the necessity of Chinese in facilitating content learning, interviewees noted translanguaging practices that they approved and disapproved of. They favoured classes delivered in English and summarised in Chinese, either orally or in writing. For learning handouts or textbooks, they preferred original English texts with notes explaining key concepts and terms in Chinese, or Chinese texts by Chinese scholars rather than Chinese translations of foreign texts. I4 referred to a content delivery approach that I4 found effective in a module related to international investment:

The good side of Module is Content Lecturer would give us a new case each week, in the paper form, such as Company and how Company conducts its global investment. [The lecturer] first gives us English texts to preview to grasp the gist of the case. Then they explain key points or paragraphs to give objective input, but such input of knowledge was mainly delivered through Chinese. (I4)

Interviewees tended to prefer content in original English (rather than in Chinese translated from English) with a parallel addition of Chinese for explanation and summary. Interviewees frowned on delivery in Chinese (including when readings were done in English but explanations were given in Chinese) and complete delivery in English without Chinese explanation and facilitation. They also objected to materials that were significantly adapted from originals. For instance, I9 believed that compared with original materials that presented significant linguistic challenges, it was even worse if the textbooks were translated from English to an adapted Chinese version containing English notes and vocabulary lists because of the asymmetry of the translation between the two languages. The result was that the concepts and meanings of business subjects were obscure when reading the Chinese translation. It was also tough to recall and match those concepts from the reading to other English materials.

While most interviewees called for more use of English, it is worth noting two interviewees' opposing opinions. I7 generally approved of teachers' English capabilities and blamed their own English ability for not being able to keep up. Therefore, I7 found the current teaching arrangement challenging enough. I1 was happy with the percentage of Chinese and English in the curriculum from a class attendance point of view. I1 used the analogy "it would be too high and too cold" to create worse class attendance because of more English use.

So far, this chapter has presented findings investigating students' EMI experience with a focus on their perceived motivation and benefits, English proficiency and progress, impact on content learning, and linguistic challenges. While students generally acknowledged their English progress and other benefits through EMI, they tended to be dissatisfied with their English proficiency and how this impacted their content learning. They also reported that performing learning tasks in English was difficult. The interviews showed a clear gap between expectations and realities. Though students had faith in EMI, they indicated three pedagogy-related concerns. First, while satisfied with some lecturers' excellent English delivery, interviewees saw detrimental impacts on learning due to their and their teachers' limited English proficiency. Secondly, though supported with well-established English courses for academic and specific (business) purposes, interviewees felt inadequately and loosely equipped with the English repertoire that they needed for their content learning, such as business terminology and concepts. Moreover, the entire curriculum structure was poorly integrated, as they saw a lack of coordination between their English support classes and their content-based ones. Thirdly, most interviewees wanted to have more classes delivered in English regardless of the linguistic challenges. This study thus concludes that EMI programmes in this business school seem to lack in focus and clarity of implementation, which might result from insufficient support at the institutional level and differing interpretations of EMI among teaching faculty. This study echoes studies done in the East Asia context concerning EMI pedagogical challenges (Galloway et al., 2017; Shao & Rose, 2022; Zhang & Pladevall-Ballester, 2021). The next section will draw on lessons from this case study to discuss general pedagogical implications and recommendations for EMI implementation.

Pedagogical Implications and Recommendations for EMI Implementation

This section examines four aspects of implications and pedagogical recommendations for EMI implementation: EMI goals and strategy at the institutional level, pedagogical approaches in a transformed EMI curriculum and the professional development support necessary for such transformation, collaboration between the language support and content teaching, as well as situating EMI in a multilingual university setting.

Re-Constructing EMI Goals in an Explicit and Specific Way: Content Learning, Language Improvement, or Both

This study identified a gap between "curriculum rhetoric" and "pedagogical reality," as Nunan (2003, p. 589) concluded in his investigation into English taught provision in Asia at the turn of this century, a finding that is still relevant to this study. The relationship between English and content as well as EMI's two-tailed goals, English improvement and content learning, seemed tentative and ambiguous. Students reported their English proficiency having detrimental effects on their content learning while at the same time still focusing on the positive side of EMI. Without explicit statements of EMI goals and specific requirements for its implementation, EMI programmes are likely to end up "ignored or replaced by what the relevant agents believe to be appropriate" (Dafouz & Smit, 2016, p. 406). Therefore, it is important to clearly explain how English improvement and content learning goals can be achieved. Students and other EMI stakeholders, such as policy makers, school management, teachers, and parents, should be made aware not only of EMI's promising benefits but also the issues and challenges that EMI implementation may present. In this way, students can establish a pragmatic and holistic perspective. In other words, it might be time to re-educate stakeholders and re-adjust their assumptions that EMI "kills two birds with one stone." Such awareness is necessary because it helps students to understand it is not a deficiency, shortcoming, or drawback if they cannot achieve both goals perfectly or if one goal is prioritized over the other in implementation. Such a shift or reconstruction of EMI perceptions would allow schools and teachers autonomy in curriculum design and delivery without confusing and frustrating themselves as well as students. Undoubtedly, such perception reconstruction should be justified with explicit explanation of goals, implementation, and strategies to address potential challenges. For instance, information sessions and workshops can run following student enrolment to reconstruct their perceptions of EMI. Institutions can add explicit sections concerning EMI to their existing progress reports to students such as semester reports. EMI can also become a regular agenda item at school meetings.

Pedagogical Approach and Professional Support

As Bradford and Brown (2017) and Bradford (2018) illustrated regarding the transformation that EMI approaches in Japanese universities have been experiencing, a significant change underlying teaching content in English is proactively adopting a communicative approach to teaching. Macaro et al. (2019) also identified a holistic pedagogy change that EMI teachers expected to embrace. Along with the pedagogical shift in both culture and practice, teachers' English capacity is the most controversial and concerning area in EMI implementation, so there have been urgent calls to support teachers' linguistic competence and teaching methods (Doiz et al., 2013, 2014; Macaro et al., 2016; Pun & Thomas, 2020; Shao & Rose, 2022). Efforts can be made from two aspects: English proficiency requirements at the recruitment stage and continuous training throughout teachers' careers. Teachers should be expected to demonstrate their linguistic competence by submitting proficiency certificates or using English in interviews. Such policies can bring tangible benefits, such as student satisfaction and more international recognition for programs. On the other hand, teachers should have access to continuous support for their teaching. Opportunities could include training, workshops, voluntary pursuit of further degree study such as PhD or post-doc positions, and visiting scholar programmes across the world.

Importance Attached to Collaboration Between Language Support and Content

Effective integration of language support into content learning is critical in EMI programmes (Dafouz & Smit, 2016). Galloway et al. (2017), in their investigation into EMI among several Chinese and Japanese universities, recommended that collaboration and transparent communication are urgently necessary for consistent and focused EMI programmes. This issue was raised during the interviews, where students reflected on the opaque collaboration and poor integration of their English and content curriculums. Efficient use of English in content learning is essential to enable students to thrive in EMI, which is only possible when content and English support are seamlessly integrated with English for general, communicative, academic, and specific (business) purposes. This requires sophisticated curriculum design, coordinated collaboration, transparent communication with timely feedback and opportunities for improvement.

Positioning EMI in a Multilingual Setting

In contexts where EMI provision bears the distinct characteristics of bilingual and content/English learning due to linguistic challenges for students and teachers, it is pragmatic and fair that EMI pedagogy embraces multilingual settings and utilizes plurilingual community resources (Sahan & Rose, 2021). The pursuit of EMI is not the equivalent of a forced "English only" or monolingual classroom, especially when these compromise learning outcomes. Different languages and cultures should be valued as assets that benefit HE internationalization (Dafouz & Smith, 2016). However, it seemed that some students during the interviews tended to equate the use of Chinese with teachers' lack of English ability. In pedagogical reality, the inclusion of Chinese might not be a forced choice based on students' and teachers' English proficiency, as students perceived it, but rather a necessary and deliberate translanguaging choice (García & Wei, 2014; Wei, 2018) that attempts to achieve optimal learning results for all students. If this is the case, this needs to be highlighted to students through a process of shifting/re-shaping their perceptions of EMI. Other studies such as Galloway et al. (2017) also point out that such awareness, of both teachers and students, was not strong among the Chinese and Japanese universities they investigated. They recommend that a clear policy should be in place to raise agents' awareness, followed by action and practice. Fang (2018) also calls for support and training for EMI agents in Chinese universities to recognise the potential benefits of multilingual environments. This perspective can be integrated into an explicit EMI goal/strategy statement at the institutional level.

Conclusion

This study investigated students' EMI perceptions and experiences of undergraduate (second and third year) business programmes in a Chinese public university that promotes HE internationalisation through EMI provision. Findings from surveys and interviews focusing on students' motivation for studying EMI and their perceptions of its benefits, perceived English improvement, self-reported English proficiency in content learning, and perceived linguistic challenges indicated various pedagogical challenges concerning EMI implementation. Such pedagogical challenges not only lie in addressing problematic English and compromised learning outcomes, but also in re-constructing the pedagogical approach to EMI context empowered by policy and professional development support. A limitation of this study is that only students were sampled without including other stakeholders, such as teachers. Including additional stakeholders could have made the pedagogical implications more relevant and actionable. Nevertheless, this study helps shed light on the student experience of EMI course implementation within this HEI in China. In seeking to address the pedagogical challenges identified, this study has proposed a pragmatic re-education of EMI's two-folded goals at the institutional level with explicit statements and explanations to all relevant stakeholders, especially students (and parents), who tend to assume English improvement and content learning can be obtained automatically and concurrently. Second, this study has called for a holistic and fundamental pedagogical shift in EMI, particularly from the perspective of a more proactive and communicative learning culture. Such change of pedagogy is more challenging than improving English proficiency and content learning outcomes, but the potential benefits to EMI learning results and delivery are promising. Therefore, updated and comprehensive professional training and development support are essential to empower teachers embarking on the change. Third, guaranteeing EMI quality is only possible with transparent, coordinated, and integrated collaboration between language support and content. This is particularly relevant in Asian contexts where EMI is normally provided through an integrated curriculum of language and content. Last but not the least, the role of English and its relationship with other languages should be re-examined from a multilingual perspective. Such a re-examination is significant as it empowers alternative pedagogical practices, such as translanguaging, that facilitate content learning with minimal detrimental impacts from only "teaching in English".

Author Bio

Lijie Shao is the international language tutor at Dublin City University, Ireland. Her research focuses on English medium instruction (EMI) in higher education in the context of internationalization and globalization, multilingualism in China from the sociolinguistic aspect, and teaching Chinese as an international language in higher education. In 2019, she obtained her PhD in Applied Linguistics from Trinity College Dublin, Ireland. Her doctoral project, comparing EMI across contexts, was supported by the Trinity Postgraduate Studentship. She is an early-stage researcher with EMI-related publications in the *Journal of Multilingual and Multicultural Development* and *Routledge Focus on English-Medium Instruction in Higher Education*. Prior to her academic career, she had six years' full time industry experience in international higher education consultancy in Beijing, China.

15
Re-Envisioning Student and Teacher Educational Partnering: The *Hu-women-ism* of Riane Eisler's Work

Tim Murphey

"Treat people as they could be, and you help them become as they can be."

— JOHANN WOLFGANG VON GOETHE

The anthropologist Riane Eisler's *Domineering versus Partnering* model of cultures and groups (families, genders, businesses, governments, and education) has been around for about 40 years (Eisler, 1984; Eisler & Loye, 1985), but it seems only more recently to have been taken up in mainstream education. Historically, Eisler depicts individuals and groups on a scale from *domineering* to *partnering*. She argues using anthropological-historical evidence that we do not have to be domineering (Eisler, 1987) by showing how, in our historical past, there have been times when humans partnered with each other to our mutual advantage, including in some women-led cultures. Part I of this chapter examines how teachers might adjust their teaching to create more "partnering" with students to share the classroom, content, and community building in more democratically and dialogically respectful partnering styles (Eisler, 2000). We all know the old phrase, *spare the rod and spoil the child*. It emerges from domineering beliefs that we (supposedly) must maintain control (often physical dominance) to teach well. However, the truth is *fear of the rod destroys the child* with unnecessary stress and fear, with the result that students do not learn as much as they could in a mutually respectful group that sees them as partners in which they could become better students and better people (Hirosawa & Murphey, in progress).

In part II, I examine scholarship on cooperative-collaborative-community learning (such as Tomasello, 2009; Egitim, 2021; Hattie & Clarke, 2019) and the advantages it offers to staying healthy (Murphey & Edlin, 2020), socially constructing evaluations (Murphey 2019), and well-becoming (Murphey 2014a&b, 2016; Hirosawa & Murphey, in progress). I then examine several proposals developed with colleagues in Turkey for expanding partnering via *Universal Caring and Sharing Advising* (UCASA), which is a playful take on the idiom *me casa es su casa* (make yourselves at home), a greeting Spanish speakers often say to welcome guests. These represent traditional ways to socially partner among our ancestors. I also introduce *Sanga Stella Ocean Collaborative Intentional Autonomy Learning* (SSOCIAL), a project I am collaborating on with a colleague in Italy. Lastly, in Part III, I discuss seven easy ways for teachers to partner with students in SLA classes, explaining how they can be used in any classroom (ideal classmates, language learning histories, action logging, student presentations, student publications, out-of-class teaching, and social testing and grading). Finally, I discuss the work of Carl Rogers (1961), proposing that we have unconditional positive regard toward students in order to create an emotional bedrock of well-becoming in our classrooms.

Part I
Riane Eisler's Domineering & Partnering (Caring) Model

In her introduction to her first book, *The Chalice and the Blade* (1987), Riane Eisler gives some brief biological information and frames her main anthropological questions:

> When I was very small, the seemingly secure world I had known was shattered by the Nazi take-over of Austria. I watched as my father was dragged away, and after my mother miraculously obtained his release

from the Gestapo, my parents and I fled for our lives. Through that flight, first to Cuba, and then the United States, I experienced three different cultures, each with its own varieties. I also began to ask many questions, questions that to me are not, and never have been, abstract. Why do we hunt and persecute each other? Why is our world so full of man's infamous inhumanity to man—and to woman? How can humans be so brutal to their own kind? What is it that chronically tilts us toward cruelty rather than kindness, toward war rather than peace, towards destruction rather than actualization? (p. xiii)

Figure 1 illustrates how she has contrasted the extremes of domineering and partnering in family, economic, and social structures, examining the use of fear, abuse, and violence that play out in gender roles and other relations, which can be further analyzed through narratives and everyday language. For example, while the women's movement for more equity and peace has been ever more expressed, we are still very far from equity goals and banning fear, abuse, and violence from our male-dominated governments (I am writing as Putin is attacking Ukraine in March 2022). Male domination is not just in government, but also often in business and family organization. Male-dominated corporations can be blamed for the climate crisis that has destroyed much of our planet's nature and the massive consumerism-generated inequality between races and countries. Toxic masculinity also accounts for males dying on average 10 to 20 years earlier than women.

Figure 1

Riane Eisler's Domination/Partnership Social Scale

	Domination	Partnership
Family, Economic, and Social Structure	An authoritarian structure of ranking and hierarchies of domination in family, economics, and society, so children grow up in authoritarian, punitive, male-dominated families where they observe and experience inequity as the norm.	Democratic structure and hierarchies of actualization that empower rather than disempower. Caring is economically valued. Egalitarian and equitable adult relations are the norm. Parenting is not authoritarian but authoritative and non-violent.
Fear, Abuse, and Violence	High degree of fear and violence, from child- and wife-beating to abuse by "superiors" in families, workplaces, and society as required to maintain rankings of domination.	Low degree of fear, abuse, and violence, as they are not needed to maintain top-down rankings. Respect for diversity and human rights.
Gender Roles and Relations	Ranking of the male over the female human form. Rigid gender stereotypes, with "masculine" traits and activities such as toughness and conquest ranked over "feminine" ones such as caregiving and nonviolence.	Equal valuing of male and female, as difference is not equated with superiority/inferiority, dominating/being dominated, or being served/serving. This provides a model for relations not based on in-group versus out-group thinking (as in racism, antisemitism, and the like). Fluid gender roles, with high valuing of empathy, caring, caregiving, and nonviolence in both women and men, as well as in social and economic policy.
Narratives and Language	Beliefs and stories that justify, idealize, and normalize domination and violence.	Narratives that recognize our human capacities for violence but present sensitivity, caring, and mutual accountability as that which makes us fully human.

Center for Partnership Systems, 2023

Eisler published *Tomorrow's Children* in 2000, sub-titled: *A Blueprint for Partnership Education in the 21st Century*. The Standford University elite educationist Nel Noddings wrote in her Foreword the following:

> In *Tomorrow's Children*, Riane Eisler has given us a picture of how education might function in the 21st century. She argues persuasively that the adoption of a *partnership model* in both schools and the larger society is essential for human life to flourish. For too long, a *dominator model* has controlled most of the world's societies and, although it has been accompanied by a vast growth in technology, it has also induced violence, exploitation, and the denigration or neglect of a huge portion of the population. Both partnership and dominator models recognize difference but, whereas the partnership model cherishes difference and actively works to form relationships that enrich individual lives and strengthen communities, the dominator model construes difference in terms of superiority and inferiority. Students need to understand how both models operate, but schools must adopt the partnership model … She wants children to know that the partnership model has actually existed in some societies and that these societies exhibited a high level of cultural sophistication: advanced technologies, art, commerce, religion, and diplomacy. They were marked by peace and human flourishing. The dominator attitude is, thus, not necessary for progress and, indeed, it may endanger our survival … Struggle, conquest, and destruction must be supplanted by cooperation, mutual aid, and respect for creation. (p. ix)

Two years later, in 2002, Eisler published *The Power of Partnership*. In her 2019 book with Douglas Fry, *Nurturing Our Humanity*, they began using the term *partnerism*. I see her as a wonderful hu*man*istic writer who favors equality for all, but the *man* in hu*man*istic bothers me as it does not name half of humanity, and if we count children, even more! Thus, I would dare to challenge us to respectfully and admirably use the term *hu-woman-istic* and *children-istic*, as she skillfully argues for equity rights and partnerships among women, children, and men. She has been herself a *huwomanistic* and *childrenistic* researcher among genders, families, and ethnic groups for nearly 40 years (Eisler, 1984; Eisler & Loye,

1985). She not only was an anthropologist, but studied economics, became a world-renowned lawyer and activist, and started the partner movement in education.

Eisler (1987) shares how throughout history there have been periods when women held positions of power, which were associated with more peaceful times and the worship of female deities. For example, the Mediterranean island of Crete and the Meryet-Nit area in Egypt were once organized around female leadership. Several indigenous Indian tribes in America are also matriarchies (Mann, 2005), along with the Mosuo in China (Kuhn, 2016).

Eilser (2002) also advocates for *partnering the self*, what others might call autonomy, writing that "a foundation of partnership living is to be a good partner with yourself. This means taking the golden rule and looking at its flip side—do unto yourself as you would do unto others—and applying this to your life" (p. 10).

In her most recent work, Eisler (2021) writes from an economist's perspective:

> At present, the field of economics as it is generally taught in universities and textbooks only includes the market, government, and illegal economic sectors. The standard models often ignore the economic contribution of three life-sustaining sectors: the natural economy, the unpaid community economy, and the household economy. (p. 73)

Eisler goes on to describe four cornerstones to changing the economist's perspective: children, gender, economics, along with narratives and language. Through narratives and language we convey our misguided domineering attempts at ruling the world (children, gender, politics, and economics) but are doing a very poor job at ecological sustainability in education, politics, and business. She suggests that we need to follow our Scandinavian role models (Eisler, 2021):

> We cannot ignore the relationship between the status of women and a nation's economic success and quality of life. Yet these findings are frequently dismissed—not only by economics departments and texts but

by the media. The dismissal continues despite the highly visible relationship between gender equity and value systems in nations like Sweden, Finland, and Norway. These countries that used to suffer famine and poverty, regularly score high in the World Economic Forum's Global Competitiveness reports. They have the lowest gender gaps (40 to 50% of national legislators are female), low crime rates, high longevity scores, and sit at the top of the international happiness reports ... The major reason for these nations' ascent from the dire poverty to prosperity is that they pioneered caring policies like universal health care, high quality early childhood education, generous paid parental leave, and elderly care with dignity. They also worked to abandon traditions of violence, for example by pioneering the first Peace Studies programs and the first laws against physical discipline in families. And, as you might expect, they are rapidly shifting to solar and other renewable energy sources to extend these values of care toward Nature as well. (p. 77)

Part II
Other "Partnering" Authors and Course/Project Possibilities

I regularly teach a course called *Positive Sociology* (PS), which stems from *Positive Psychology* (PP). This course examines how groups collaborate and work well together with the intention of creating such a highly functioning, collaborative group in our class. One of the biggest forces in PS, PP, and education is relationships of respect, generosity, camaraderie, collaboration, and meaningfulness. These represent partnerships, partnering, or partnerism among two or more people in which participants learn to thrive in the company of others. Tomasello (2009) reviews the research on why and when young children start helping and supporting others:

> For these five reasons—early emergence, immunity from encouragement and undermining by rewards, deep evolutionary roots in great apes, cross-cultural robustness, and foundation in natural sympathetic emotions—we believe that children's early helping is not a behavior created by culture and/or parental socialization practices. Rather it is an

outward expression of children's natural inclination to sympathize with others in strife. (p. 13)

Thus, we naturally mirror the people in our environments to a certain extent, learn to feel what they feel, and are motivated to help. Altruism is not merely helping others; it helps us better cope with our own emotions. In my classes, I ask students to teach something useful from the class to friends or family outside class and to write about their experiences for a class publication that all can read. They choose themes such as eight ways to reduce stress, seven ways to improvise, five ways to feel happiness in song, and other short songlets. I have found these class publications of considerable value. They are the most read and loved scripts in my classes (Murphey 2021a&b and the examples in Part III). However, Bayer (1990) notes sadly that partnering among students has not been common:

> Unfortunately peer collaboration is not yet a major social structure in our classrooms. As Goodlad (1983, 1984) found, the dominant classroom structure takes one of two forms: Either the teacher is in front of the room giving a lecture to the whole class, or students are working alone on assigned tasks with the instructor checking their individual progress. Given the growing body of knowledge supporting the concept of social learning, I suspect this picture will change … Peer interaction in a problem-solving process promotes cognitive development and the use of critical thinking strategies. Individual group members faced with conflicting viewpoints attempt to clarify, analyze, synthesize, speculate, and evaluate the conflicting points of view as they work their way toward resolution. Individual cognitive reorganization is induced by group cognitive conflict (Barnes & Todd, 1978; Inagaki & Hatano, 1977; Perret-Clermont, 1980; Forman & Cazden, 1985; Bruner, 1987). Johnson and Johnson (1979) have had similar results in their work, which they call cooperative learning. (p. 12)

Two examples of how I've worked to form such communities in my own professional practice follow.

Universal Caring and Sharing Advising: UCASA

UCASA was previously introduced as a playful take on the Spanish expression *me-casa est tu-casa*. This traditional way of greeting neighbors has been a type of survival strategy that employs social partnering. My colleagues in Turkey, Hatice Karaaslan and Pinar Üstündağ-Algın, with whom I developed UCASA, metaphorically invited me into their casa during the pandemic, where we began to develop a small sanga/community to collaborate together. During this time, I was reminded of how a sense of belonging is critical for hu-mans, hu-women, and hu-children.

More than surveying student attitudes, we should aim to encourage students themselves to participate in educational research, deliberations, and decision-making for proactive transformation of their own education. Including more student voices in ELT can increase the value of what we do professionally—teach and learn (Murphey et al. 2009).

Sanga Stella Ocean Collaborative Intentional Autonomy Learning (SSOCIAL)

On March 12, 2022, I had a Zoom call with my friend Manuela Cohen, who was staying with her daughter's family in Majorca, along with her newborn granddaughter Stella Ocean, who was just a few weeks old at the time. My niece Kirsten, whom Manuela had helped learn Italian when she lived nearby in Italy many years ago, and Kirsten's husband Rick, who are both digital nomads, also joined the call. I had not seen any of these people for several years due to the pandemic, but I felt even on Zoom like I was suddenly in a special community. This feeling was so powerful that we took Stella Ocean's name for our *sanga* and decided to work for autonomous groups that wished to make the planet a better place. A sanga is one of the three gems in Buddhism, "the community that lives in harmony and awareness" (Hahn 1987, p. 23). Autonomy often refers to individuals. The epiphany we had on that day of admiring Stella Ocean's smile was that groups, as well as individuals, can have autonomy. As teachers, we hope that you have had the experience of certain classes bonding together with a SSOCIAL feeling and developing a strong sense of community. At these times, saying goodbye at the end of the term can feel bittersweet.

Part III
Seven Easy Ways to Partner through Classroom Activities

Below are seven ways teachers can share their classrooms and courses with their students regardless of what the topics of their lessons may be.

Language Learning Histories (1)

It is difficult to equitably share a classroom without participants knowing about each other. In almost all my classes in the first lesson I ask students to share their language learning histories (LLH) in small groups and later write about them in 50 to 75 words so we can learn about one another. For many years (with students' permission) I have sent them to Vera Menezes in Brazil, who has archived them at:

> https://www.veramenezes.com/nar_tim.htm

Ideal Classmates (2)

In this activity, teachers share a prompt with their students, whose answers can then be anonymously shared so their classmates can see what they want from them. They can discuss the answers to ensure understanding. An example prompt for *Ideal Classmates* (Murphey et al. 2014) is:

> Please describe a group of classmates that you could learn English well with. What would you all do to help each other learn better and more enjoyably?

Here is a Japanese translation of the prompt:

いっしょに親しく英語を学ぶクラスメートのグループがどのようなものかを想像して書いてみて下さい。より上手に楽しく助け合って学ぶにはどうすればいいでしょうか。

Translating the prompt into the students' L1 is recommended to ensure understanding.

Action Logging (3)

Teachers improve by getting feedback from students about what they have and have not understood. Asking students to keep class notes in notebooks or Google Classroom documents allows teachers to check what students understood and did not understand, in Hattie and Clarke's (2019) terms, pointing the teacher to "Where to next?" (p. 1). I have done such action logging for 32 years and cannot imagine teaching without the feedback that comes from reading what students think they are learning (Miyake-Warkentin, Hooper, & Murphey, 2020). Of course, for action logging to work well, teachers need to acknowledge to their students what they learned from the entries. Teachers can also make newsletters from action log comments to share with students so they see their efforts are being taken seriously.

Student Presentations (4)

I usually have students do their own presentations two or three times each semester, first with an assigned reading from a class PDF provided to the whole class at the beginning of the semester. Then I often ask students to hunt with a few key search words for articles that they would like to present on. Shorter presentations may involve making a Power Point slide of their role models or another special person they admire. Through organizing student presentations, I have been able to cut down my teacher-talk time to only about a quarter of the total class time (Murphey, 2021a&b).

Out-of-Class Teaching (5)

Learning materials need not be restricted to the classroom. After all, learning is often facilitated through teaching what one is learning to another person. Since teachers learn better themselves what they teach, why not pass that opportunity on to students? In Japan, one advantage is that many families have three generations living together, so students have precious opportunities to learn from their grandparents, including intergenerational learning with foster grandparents. A successful topic has been to have students ask about what their grandparents' schooling was like, and is there anything they might want to teach them (Freedman, 2020). This shows respect for their grandparents' past and opens them up to better relationships.

Student Publications (6)

Creating class publications can be an effective way to build on student presentations or extend out-of-class teaching. By asking students to write about their experiences, as they may have done with their LLHs (discussed previously), they develop their writing skills and gain a sense of ownership over their learning. Teachers can collate these assignments into a booklet or PDF to distribute or publish. Students are often amazed to see their names in print along with their English essays (Murphey, 2021a&b).

Social Testing and Grading (7)

We all give tests and grades, but maybe it would be better to ask students to evaluate their own work. I have been doing this for many years and have found that I agree with about 50% of my students' grades. About 45% are too humble, so I push them higher. Only about 5% overestimate their class performance or missed too many classes for the grade they give themselves. Figure 2 shows an extract from the bottom of a quiz where I ask students to evaluate themselves.

Figure 2

Example Prompt for Student Self-Assessment

> **SCORE BOX**: Give yourself your estimated grades
>
> **Score 1**: After 20 minutes alone (0-100%): ____%
>
> **Score 2**: After time in breakout groups (0-100%): ____%
>
> **In Breakout Rooms please take turns asking questions.**
>
> Send this as an attached file to Tim after breakout groups **before 12:10 today** (mitsmail1@gmail.com).

Teachers can also ask students to make quizzes and tests or submit questions that they think appropriate (Murphey, 2019). As one student put it, "When we get a job we aren't going to get a grade from our boss, so we need to learn to evaluate ourselves!"

Part IV
Interbeing, Well-becoming, Hu-women-ism, and Unconditional Positive Regard

The Buddhist monk Thick Nhat Hanh wrote *Interbeing* in 1987, with a 4th edition released in 2020. The back cover importantly leads with the following quote: "We cannot just be by ourselves alone; we can only inter-be with everyone and everything else." Thus, we must be concerned about how we exist with everyone and everything. When we accept this interbeing, we see that our health depends on the health of others and the planet. A classroom is equally a complex system in which each person effects everyone else, and we all are interbeing with each other. The 14 mindfulness trainings that Hanh describes help us achieve well-being, but even these trainings have been re-edited (well-becoming) in each of the four editions of the book, as Hanh (2020) wrote that they should change:

> During the revision process, we may need to conflate one or more Mindfulness Trainings in order to make space for a new training if the circumstances in society at that time demand it.
>
> During the forty-five years of his ministry, the Buddha changed his way of teaching and practice greatly. The Wheel of the Dharma needs to turn a little every day. If we look at the history of Plum Village, we see that we are always making progress, always discovering new ways of teaching that are more effective. This is why we need to revise the training from time to time. In the field of information technology, every year there is a new kind of software. In the field of education, there are new methodologies and textbooks every year. It is the same in Buddhism; there has to be progress. The wheel of evolution has to keep turning because only then can Buddhism play its role of spiritual leadership. (p. 25)

Thus, even the Buddha was well-becoming. While the Buddhist mindfulness trainings are about achieving well-being, we might also call this process *continual well-becoming* (Murphey, 2014; Hirosawa & Murphey, in progress) because of the continual efforts needed to keep up with the times, be useful, and remain forever inter-becoming with all the parts of our lives, our world, and our universe. May our language learning also be continually well-becoming as we inter-be each other, nature, and our universal caring and sharing advising, agency, and ardour (Üstünda-Algin, Karaaslan, & Murphey, 2022).

Rogers (1961) emphasized the unconditional positive regard (UPR) that therapists (teachers/leaders) needed to have for their therapy/teaching/leading sessions to be successful. The "unconditional" means specifically that the client (student/employee) does not need to "earn" positive regard. Rather, the therapist (teacher/leader) displays it from the beginning. This is also a good description of what it means to be *partnered* (in therapy, education, or work), or respected with nothing conditional required for the therapist's, teacher's, or leader's positive regard. UPR does not depend upon getting a good grade, coming on time, being quiet, etc. It is offered, shown, and communicated in egalitarian ways, such as daring to ask for help, feedback, and collaboration. Dornyei and Murphey (2003) comment on UPR:

> The concept of 'acceptance' was highlighted by humanistic psychology in the 1950s, referring to a feeling towards another individual which is non-evaluative in nature, has nothing to do with likes and dislikes, but is rather an 'unconditional positive regard' (Rogers 1983) toward the individual, acknowledging that person as a complex human being with many (possibly conflicting) values and imperfections. As Rogers (1983) has put it, acceptance involves 'prizing of the learner as an imperfect human being with many feelings, many potentialities' (p. 124); it could be compared to how we may feel toward a relative, for example an aunt or uncle, who has his or her shortcomings but whom we know well and is one of us. (p. 18)

Author Bio

Tim Murphey has studied and taught 15 years in Europe and 30 in Asia. He most recently has retired to an Oregon farm for horses, River Quest, to study equine therapy and our reconnections with nature.

Appendix
Instructions for Language Learning Histories

Write at least 250 words about your language learning history from when you began learning English (or other 2nd languages) to the present. You can write freely, but you can also answer the following questions if they help you focus. (Due date: xxxxx)

- How did you learn English in JHS and HS? Or elementary?
- What positive and negative experiences did you have and what did you learn from them?
- What were you expecting before you came to the university?
- What were you surprised about in your university classes?
- How have you changed your ways of language learning since coming to the university? What are the things that you found especially helpful?
- What are the areas that you still want to improve in?
- How do you think your future will be?
- What are your language learning plans and goals after graduation?
- What advice would you give to other students?
- Have you traveled or lived abroad? Where and for how long?
- What other foreign languages have you learned, studied, or been exposed to?

Example: Tim's LLH

> I was born in Georgia, USA, the last of five children after my family came back from living about 3 years in Japan. (Dad was in the army.) I lived in Germany from the age of 2 to 5 and heard a bit of German. Then in elementary school in Florida we had to learn some basic Spanish. Later in HS I took 2 years of French. When I was 16 I went to Europe and hitch-hiked for 6 weeks in France, Italy, and Switzerland. Then I went to Switzerland for my 3rd and 4th year of college and I was majoring in French and German. Then I went to do an MA in Florida to teach English

abroad. I went back to Switzerland for my PhD. It took 7 years. I was also a ski-teacher at the time. Then I came to Japan in 1990. But my Japanese is still very bad. (153 words/ need a few more)

IN Class you may be asked to tell your story to partners several times as a warm up to writing it. DO NOT READ IT! You know it, just tell it! Writing it first will help you remember different things in preparation for telling your story. Telling (not reading) will help you remember things different that you might want to put into the final written version.

REFERENCES

Abasi, A. R., Akbari, N., & Graves, B. (2006). Discourse appropriation, construction of identities, and the complex issue of plagiarism: ESL students writing in graduate school. *Journal of Second Language Writing, 15*(2), 102–117. https://doi.org/10.10 16/j.jslw.2006.05.001

Adams, E. (2001). A proposed causal model of vocational teacher stress. *Journal of Vocational Education and Training, 53*(2), 223–246.

Adamson, B., & Feng, A. (2009). A comparison of trilingual education policies for ethnic minorities in China. *Compare, 39*(3), 321–333. https://doi.org/10.1080/030579208024 36258

Adamson, B., & Feng, A. (2014). Models for trilingual education in the People's Republic of China. In D. Gorter, V. Zenotz, & J. Cenoz (Eds.), *Minority languages and multilingual education: Bridging the local and the global* (pp. 29–44). https://doi.org/ 10.1007/978-94-007-7317-2_3

Adamson, J., & Coulson, D. (2015). Translanguaging in English academic writing preparation. *International Journal of Pedagogies and Learning, 10*(1), 24–37. https://doi.org/10.1080/22040552.2015.1084674

Acuña González, E., Avila Pardo, M., & Holmes Lewendon, J. E. (2015). The SAC as a community of practice: A case study of peer-run conversation sessions at the Universidad del Caribe. *Studies in Self-Access Learning Journal, 6*(3), 313–321.

Al-Braik, M. (2007). Performance of major English students at King Faisal University: General trends. *Scientific Journal of King Faisal University, 8*(2), 221–235.

Alistair, M. (2015). *Language-learner motivation in Saudi Arabia*. Sheffield Hallam University.

Al-Johani, H. (2009). *Finding a way forward: The impact of teachers' strategies, beliefs and knowledge on teaching English as a foreign language in Saudi Arabia* [PhD thesis, University of Strathclyde]. http://oleg.lib.strath.ac.uk:80/R/?func=dbin-jump-full&object_id=11539

Almohaimeed, M., & Almurshed, H. (2018). Foreign language learners' attitudes and perceptions of L1 use in L2 classroom. *Arab World English Journal, 9*(4), 433–446. https://doi.org/10.24093/awej/vol9no4.32

Al-Mutairi, N. (2007). *The influence of educational and sociocultural factors on the learning styles and strategies of female students in Saudi Arabia* [PhD thesis]. University of Leicester.

Al-Nafisah, K. (2000). *A study of the curriculum and methodology for the teaching of English in Saudi Arabia with particular reference to learning difficulties encountered by students* [PhD thesis, University of Wales]. https://ethos.bl.uk/OrderDetails.do?uin=uk.bl.ethos. 635703

Al-Qahtani, A. (2015). *Relationships between intercultural contact and L2 motivation for a group of undergraduate Saudi students during their first year in the UK* [PhD thesis, University of Leeds]. http://etheses.whiterose.ac.uk/8279/

Al-Qahtani, A. (2017). A study of the language learning motivation of Saudi military cadets. *International Journal of Applied Linguistics and English Literature, 6*(4), 163–172. https://doi.org/10.7575/aiac.ijalel.v.6n.4p.163

Alqahtani, M. (2011). *An investigation into the language needs of Saudi students studying in British postgraduate programmes and the cultural differences impacting on them* [PhD thesis, University of Southampton]. https://www.researchgate.net/publication/277875733_An_investigation_into_the_language_needs_of_Saudi_students_studying_in_British_postgraduate_programmes_and_the_cultural_differences_impacting_on_them

Alrabai, F. (2014). A model of foreign language anxiety in the Saudi EFL context. *English Language Teaching, 7*(7), 82–101.

Alrahaili, M. (2013). *Predictors of L2 attitudes and motivational intensity: A cross-sectional study in the Saudi EFL context* [PhD thesis, The University of Newcastle].

Alrahaili, M. (2018). Cultural and linguistic factors in the Saudi EFL context. In C. Moskovsky & M. Picard (Eds.), *English as a foreign language in Saudi Arabia: New insights into teaching and learning English* (pp. 85–101). Routledge. https://doi.org/10.4324/9781315688466-4

Al-Seghayer, K. (2011). *English teaching in Saudi Arabia: Status, issues, and challenges*. Hala.

Alsubaie, M. (2014). *An exploration of reading comprehension challenges in Saudi Arabian university EFL students* [PhD thesis, The University of Exeter].ORE: Open Research Exeter. https://ore.exeter.ac.uk/repository/handle/10871/15981

Altrichter, H., Posch, P., & Somekh, B. (1993). *Teachers Investigate their Work: An Introduction to the Methods of Action Research*. Routledge.

Ambinintsoa, D. V. & MacDonald, E. (forthcoming). A Reflection Intervention: Investigating Effectiveness and Students' Perceptions. In Curry, N., Lyon, P., & Mynard, J. (Eds.), *Promoting reflection on language learning: Lessons from a University setting*. Multilingual Matters.

American University of Sharjah. (2021). *Fast facts – fall 2021*. https://www.aus.edu/about/aus-at-a-glance/facts-and-figures/fast-facts-fall-2021

Anderson, B. G. (1971). Adaptive aspects of culture shock. *American Anthropologist, 73*(5), 1121–1125.

Anderson, L., & Krathwohl, D. (Eds.) (2001). *A taxonomy for learning, teaching, and assessing: A revision of Bloom's Taxonomy of educational objectives*. Longman.

Appel, C. (1999). Tandem language learning by e-mail: Some basic principles and a case study. *CLCS Occasional Paper, 54*. Trinity College, Centre for Language and Communication Studies.

Atkinson, D. (1997). A critical approach to critical thinking in TESOL. *TESOL Quarterly, 31*(1), 71–94.

Atkinson, D. (2005). Situated qualitative research and second language writing. In P.Matsuda & T. Silva (Eds.), *Second language writing research: Perspectives on the process of knowledge construction* (pp. 49–64). Erlbaum.

Attardo, S. (2002). Humor and irony in interaction: From mode adoption to failure. In L. Anolli, R. Ciceri, & G. Riva (Eds.), *Say not to say: New perspectives on miscommunication* (pp. 159–180). IOS Press.

Bacharach, N., Heck, T., & Dahlberg, K. (2012). Changing the face of student teaching through coteaching. *Action in Teacher Education*, 32(1), 3–14. http://dx.doi.org/10.1080/01626620.2010.10463538

Bachman, L., & Palmer, A. (2010). *Language assessment in practice*. Oxford University Press.

Badiali, B., & Titus, N. (2010). Co-teaching: Enhancing student learning through mentor-intern partnerships. *School-University Partnerships*, 4(2), 74–80.

Baeten, M., & Simmons, M. (2014). Student teachers' team teaching: Models, effects, and conditions for implementation. *Teaching and Teacher Education*, 41, 92–110.

Baetens Beardsmore, H. (1993). An overview of European models of bilingual education. *Language, Culture and Curriculum*, 6(3), 197–208. https://doi.org/10.1080/07908319309525151

Baker, C. (2001). *Foundations of Bilingual Education and Bilingualism* (3rd ed.). Multilingual Matters.

Baker, C. (2007). Becoming bilingual through bilingual education. In P. Auer & L. Wei (Eds.), *Handbook of Multilingualism and Multilingual Communication* (pp. 131–152). Mouton de Gruyter. https://doi.org/10.1515/9783110198553.1.131/HTML

Baker, C. (2011). *Foundations of bilingual education and bilingualism* (5th ed.). Multilingual Matters.

Baker, W., & Hüttner, J. (2017). English and more: A multisite study of roles and conceptualisations of language in English medium multilingual universities from Europe to Asia. *Journal of Multilingual and Multicultural Development*, 38(6), 501–516. https://doi.org/10.1080/01434632.2016.1207183

Bamberg, M. (1997). Positioning between structure and performance. *Journal of narrative and life history*, 7(1-4), 335–342.

Banas, J. A., Dunbar, N., Rodriguez, D., & Liu, S. J. (2011). A review of humor in educational settings: Four decades of research. *Communication Education*, 60(1), 115–144.

Bandura, A. (1975). *Social learning and personality development*. Holt, Rinehart and Winston, Inc.

Barkhuizen, G. (2017). Investigating multilingual identity in study abroad contexts: A short story analysis approach. *System*, 71, 102–112.

Barkhuizen, G., Benson, P., & Chik, A. (2014). *Narrative inquiry in language teaching and learning research*. Routledge.

Barkhuizen, G. P. (Ed.). (2013). *Narrative research in applied linguistics*. Cambridge University Press.

Barnard, R. (2014). English medium instruction in Asian universities: Some concerns and a suggested approach to dual-medium instruction. *Indonesian Journal of Applied Linguistics*, 4(1), 10–22.

Bawens, J., & Hourcade, J. (1995). *Cooperative teaching: Rebuilding the schoolhouse for all students*. PrEdo.

Bayer, A. S. (1990). *Collaborative apprenticeship learning, language and thinking across the curriculum*. Mayfield Publishing Company.

Beglar, D., Hunt, A., & Kite, Y. (2012). The effect of pleasure reading on Japanese university EFL learners' reading rates. *Language Learning*, 62(3), 665–703. https://doi.org/10.1111/j.1467-9922.2011.00651.x

Bell, N., & Attardo, S. (2010). Failed humor: Issues in non-native speakers' appreciation and understanding of humor. *Intercultural Pragmatics, 7*(3), 423–447. https://doi.org/10.1515/iprg.2010.019

Bell, N. D. (2011). Humor scholarship and TESOL: Applying findings and establishing a research agenda. *TESOL Quarterly, 45*(1), 134–159. https://doi.org/10.5054/tq.2011.240857

Bell, N. D., & Pomerantz, A. (2016). *Humor in the classroom: A guide for language teachers and educational researchers.* Routledge.

Belz, J. A., & Thorne, S. L. (2006). Introduction: Internet-mediated Intercultural Foreign Language Education and the Intercultural Speaker. In J. A. Belz & S. L.Thorne (Eds.), *AAUSC 2005: Internet-mediated Intercultural Foreign Language Education.* Thomson Heinle.

Benali, A. (2021). The impact of using Automated Writing feedback in ESL/EFL classroom contexts. *English Language Teaching, 14*(12), 189–195. ベネッセ教育総合研究所 (Benesse kyōiku sōgōkenkyūsho) [Benesse Educational Research Institute]. (2022). ダイジェスト版: 高3生の英語学習に関する調査<2015-2021 継続調査> (Daijesuto-ban-kō 3-sei no eigo gakushū ni kansuru chōsa 2015 - 2021 keizoku chōsa) [Digest edition: Survey on senior high school students' English language learning, 2015–2021 ongoing survey]. https://berd.benesse.jp/up_images/research/kousaneigo 2021.pdf

Benoit, S., & Lomicka, L. (2020) Reciprocal learning and intercultural exchange in a virtual environment. In C. Horgues & C. Tardieu (Eds.), *Redefining tandem language and culture learning in higher education* (pp. 31–47). Routledge.

Benson, P. (2001). *Teaching and researching autonomy in language learning.* Longman.

Benson, P. (2011). *Teaching and researching autonomy* (2nd ed.). Routledge.

Bhowmik, S. (2021). Writing instruction in an EFL context: Learning to write or writing to learn language? *BELTA Journal, 5,* 30–42. https://doi.org/10.36832/beltaj.2021. 0501.03

Block, D. (2007). *Second language identities.* Continuum.

Bloom, B. (Ed.) (1956). *Taxonomy of educational objectives, handbook I: Cognitive domain.* David McKay.

Botha, W. (2014). English in China's universities today. *English Today, 30*(1), 3–10.

Botha, W. (2016). English and international students in China today. *English Today, 32*(1), 41–47.

Bradford, A. (2018). It's not all about English! The problem of language foregrounding in English-medium programmes in Japan. *Journal of Multilingual and Multicultural Development, 40*(8), 707–720. https://doi.org/10.1080/01434632.2018.1551402

Bradford, A., & Brown, H. (2017). ROAD-MAPPING English-Medium Instruction in Japan. In A. Bradford & B. Howard (Eds.), *English-medium instruction in Japanese higher education: Policy, challenges and outcomes* (pp. 6–12). Multilingual Matters.

Braine, G. (1999). (Ed.). *Non-native educators in English language teaching.* Lawrence Erlbaum.

Brammerts, H. (1996). Language learning in tandem using the Internet. In M. Warschauer (Ed.), *Telecollaboration in foreign language learning: Proceedings of the Hawai'i symposium* (pp. 121–130). University of Hawai'i, Second Language Teaching & Curriculum Center.

Braun, V., & Clarke, V. (2012). Thematic analysis. In H. Cooper, P. M. Camic, D. L. Long, A. T. Panter, D. Rindskopf, & K. J. Sher (Eds.), *APA handbook of research methods in psychol-*

ogy, Vol. 2. Research designs: Quantitative, qualitative, neuropsychological, and biological (p. 57–71). American Psychological Association. https://doi.org/ 10.1037/13620-004

Bruner, J. (1987). *Making sense: The child's construction of the world*. Methuen.

Byram, M. (1997). *Teaching and assessing intercultural communicative competence*. Multilingual Matters.

Campbell, A., Adams, V., & Davis, G. (2007). Cognitive demands and second-language learners: A framework for analyzing mathematics instructional contexts. *Mathematical Thinking and Learning, 9*, 3–30.

Canagarajah, A. S. (2007a). The ecology of global English. *International Multilingual Research Journal, 1*(2), 89-100. https://doi.org/10.1080/15257770701495299

Canagarajah, S. (2007b). Lingua franca English, multilingual communities, and language acquisition. *The Modern Language Journal, 91*, 923-939. https://doi.org/ 10.1111/j.1540-4781.2007.00678.x

Canagarajah, S. (2012). Teacher development in a global profession: An autoethnography. *TESOL Quarterly, 48*(2), 258-279. https://doi.org/10.1002/tesq.18

Canagarajah, S. (2018). Translingual practice as spatial repertoires: Expanding the paradigm beyond structuralist orientations. *Applied Linguistics, 39*(1), 31–54. https://doi.org/10.1093/applin/amx041

Carrió-Pastor, M. L. (Ed.). (2009). *Content and language integrated learning: Cultural diversity*. Peter Lang.

Carson, L., & Mynard, J. (2012). Introduction. In J. Mynard & L. Carson (Eds.), *Advising in language learning: Dialogs, tools, and context* (pp. 247–262). Routledge.

Cenoz, J. (2009). *Towards multilingual education: Basque educational research from an international perspective*. Multilingual Matters. https://doi.org/10.21832/9781847691941

Cenoz, J. (2013). The influence of bilingualism on third language acquisition: Focus on multilingualism. *Language Teaching, 46*(1), 71–86. https://doi.org/10.1017/S0261444811000218

Cenoz, J. (2017). Translanguaging in School Contexts: International Perspectives. *Journal of Language, Identity and Education, 16*(4), 193–198. https://doi.org/10.1080/15348458.2017.1327816

Cenoz, J. (2019). Translanguaging pedagogies and English as a lingua franca. *Language Teaching, 52*(1), 71–85. https://doi.org/10.1017/S0261444817000246

Cenoz, J., & Gorter, D. (2008). Applied Linguistics and the use of minority languages in education. *AILA Review, 21*, 5–12. https://doi.org/10.1075/aila.21.02cen

Cenoz, J., & Gorter, D. (2011). Focus on multilingualism: A study of trilingual writing. *The Modern Language Journal, 95*(3), 356–369. https://doi.org/10.1111/j.1540-4781.2011.01206.x

Cenoz, J., & Gorter, D. (2017). Minority languages and sustainable translanguaging: Threat or opportunity? *Journal of Multilingual and Multicultural Development, 38*(10), 901–912. https://doi.org/10.1080/01434632.2017.1284855

Center for Partnership Systems. (2023). Riane Eisler - A life's work that inspired a movement. https://centerforpartnership.org/partnerism-partnership-systems/

Chanmugam, A. & Gerlach, B. (2013). A co-teaching model for developing future educators' teaching effectiveness. *International Journal of Teaching and Learning in Higher Education*, 25(1). 110–117.

Cheah, C. S. L., & Park, S. Y. (2006). South Korean mothers' beliefs regarding aggression and social withdrawal in preschoolers. *Early Childhood Research Quarterly*, 21, 61–75.

Chen, C-F. E., & Cheng, W-Y. E. (2008). Beyond the design of automated writing evaluation: Pedagogical practices and perceived learning effectiveness in EFL writing classes. *Language Learning and Technology*, 12(2). 94–112.

Chen, Q. (2017). Higher education transition and academic mobility in China. In Q. Chen, *Globalization and transnational academic mobility: The experiences of Chinese academic returnees* (pp. 13–31). Springer. https://doi.org/10.1007/978-981-287-886-1_2

Chen, X. (2020). Pre-service teachers' self-efficacy of interdisciplinary team teaching through the use of collaborative concept map. *International Journal of Technology in Teaching and Learning*, 15(2), 76–94.

Cheng, F. W. (2008). Scaffolding language, scaffolding writing: a genre approach to teaching narrative writing. *The Asian EFL Journal*, 10(2), 167–191.

Choung, Y., & Oh, S. Y. (2017). A systemic functional study of thematic organization in the English writing of Korean college students. *English Teaching*, 72(3), 119–144. https://doi.org/10.15858/engtea.72.3.201709.119

Collier, P. (2017). Why peer mentoring is an effective approach for promoting college student success. *Metropolitan Universities*, 28(3). https://doi.org/10.18060/21539

Colvin, J. W., & Ashman, M. (2010). Roles, risks, and benefits of peer mentoring relationships in higher education. *Mentoring & Tutoring: Partnership in Learning*, 18(2), 121–134.

Cook, L., & Friend, M. (1995). Co-teaching: Guidelines for creating effective practices. *Focus on Exceptional Children*, 28(3), 1–17.

Cornelius, S., & Cotsworth, B. (2015). Genre analysis and genre-based approaches to EFL writing: a critical analysis. *Kansai University Foreign Languages Pedagogy Forum*, 14, 15–21. https://www.kansai-u.ac.jp/fl/publication/pdf_forum/14/2_simon.pdf

Cottrell, S. (2005). *Critical thinking skills*. Palgrave Macmillan.

Cox, M., & Richlin, L. (2004). *Building faculty learning communities*. Jossey-Bass.

Coyle, D., Hood, P., & Marsh, D. (2010). *Content and language integrated learning*. Cambridge University Press.

Cross, R. (2016). Language and content 'integration': The affordances of additional languages as a tool within a single curriculum space. *Journal of Curriculum Studies*, 48(3), 388–408. https://10.1080/00220272.2015.1125528

Cumming, A., Rebuffot, J., & Ledwell, M. (1989). Reading and summarizing challenging texts in first and second languages. *Reading and Writing: An Interdisciplinary Journal*, 2, 201–219.

Cummins, J. (2008). Introduction to volume 5: Bilingual education. In J. Cummins & N. Hornberger (Eds.), *Encyclopedia of language and education, volume 5: Bilingual education* (pp. xiii-xxiv). Springer. https://link.springer.com/book/9789048193127

Curry, N. (2014). Using CBT with anxious language learners: The potential role of the learning advisor. *Studies in Self-Access Learning Journal*, 5(1), 29–41.

Curry, N., & Watkins, S. (2016). Considerations in developing a peer mentoring programme for a self-access centre. *Studies in Self-Access Learning Journal*, 7(1), 16–29.

Cusick, J. G. (2015). *Culture Contact: Interaction, Culture Change, and Archaeology.* Southern Illinois University Press.

Dafouz, E., & Smit, U. (2016). Towards a dynamic conceptual framework for English-medium education in multilingual university settings. *Applied Linguistics, 37*(3), 397–415. https://doi.org/10.1093/applin/amu034

Dam, L., Eriksson, R., Gabrielsen, G., Little, D., Miliander, J., & Trebbi, T. (1990). Group II: Autonomy–Steps towards a definition. In T. Trebbi (Ed.), *Report on the third Nordic workshop on developing autonomous learning in the FL classroom* (pp. 96–103). Bergen University Institute for Pedagogic Practice.

Dang, T. K. A. (2013). Identity in activity: Examining teacher professional identity formation in the paired-placement of student teachers. *Teaching and Teacher Education, 30,* 47–59. https://doi.org/10.1016/j.tate.2012.10.006

Davies, B., & Harré, R. (1990). Positioning: The discursive production of selves. *Journal for the Theory of Social Behaviour, 20,* 43–63.

Dayter, D. (2018). Self-praise online and offline: The hallmark speech act of social media? *Internet Pragmatics, 1*(1), 184–203. https://doi.org/10.1075/ip.00009.day

Dearden, J. (2014). *English as a medium of instruction-a growing global phenomenon.* British Council.

Debras, C. (2020). Tele-tandems are not the online version of face-to-face tandems; here's why. *Cahiers de l'APLIUT 39,* (1). 1–13.

Dee, A. L. (2012). Collaborative clinical practice: An alternate field experience. *Issues in Teacher Education, 21*(2), 147–163. https://digitalcommons.georgefox.edu/soe_faculty/200

de Oliveira, L. C., Jones, L., & Smith, S. L. (2020). Interactional scaffolding in a first-grade classroom through the teaching–learning cycle. *International Journal of Bilingual Education and Bilingualism, 26*(3), 270–288. https://doi.org/10.1080/13670050.2020.1798867

DePalma, R. (2008). When success makes me fail: (De)constructing failure and success in a conventional American classroom. *Mind, Culture, and Activity, 15*(2), 141–64.

DeWaelsche, S. (2015). Critical thinking, questioning, and student engagement in Korean university English courses. *Linguistics and Education, 32,* 131–147.

Dodge, J. (n.d.). *What are formative assessments and why should we use them? Tips for using formative assessments to help you differentiate instruction and improve student achievement.* Scholastic Teaching Resources. https://curriculum.austinisd.org/schoolnetDocs/socialStudies/generalResources/WhatAreFormativeAssessments.pdf

Doiz, A., Lasagabaster, D., & Sierra, J. M. (2013). Future challenges for English-medium instruction at the tertiary level. In A. Doiz, D. Lasagabaster & J. M. Sierra (Eds.), *English-medium instruction at universities: Global challenges* (pp. 213–221). Multilingual Matters.

Doiz, A., Lasagabaster, D., & Sierra, J. M. (2014). Language friction and multi-lingual policies in higher education: The stakeholders' view. *Journal of Multilingual and Multicultural Development, 35*(4), 345–360.

Dong, F., Narisu, Gou, Y., Wang, X., & Qiu, J. (2015). Four models of Mongolian nationality schools in the Inner Mongolian Autonomous Region. In A. Feng & B. Adamson (Eds.),

Trilingualism in education in China: Models and challenges (pp. 65–67). Springer. https://doi.org/10.1007/978-94-017-9352-0

Dörnyei, Z. (2009). The L2 motivational self system. In Z. Dörnyei & E. Ushioda (Eds.), *Motivation, language identity and the L2 self* (pp. 9–42). Multilingual Matters.

Dörnyei, Z., & Ushioda, E. (2011). *Teaching and researching motivation* (2nd ed). Longman.

Dörnyei, Z., & Ushioda, E. (2021). *Teaching and researching motivation* (3rd ed.). Routledge.

Douglas, N., & Bohlke, D. (2014). *Reading explorer 3*. National Geographic.

Droga, L., & Humphrey, S. (2002). *Getting started with functional grammar*. Target Texts.

Dummett, P., & Hughes, J. (2019). *Critical thinking in ELT: A working model for the classroom*. Cengage Learning.

Dynel, M. (2014). Linguistic approaches to (non) humorous irony. *Humor: International Journal of Humor Research, 27*(4), 537–550. https://doi.org/10.1515/humor-2014-0097

Early, M., & Norton, B. (2013). Narrative inquiry in second language teacher education in rural Uganda. In G. Barkhuizen (Ed.), *Narrative research in applied linguistics* (pp. 132–151). Cambridge University Press.

Edgar, D., Azhar, A., & Duncan, P. (2016). The impact of the Saudization policy on recruitment and retention: A case study of the banking sector in Saudi Arabia. *Journal of Business, 1*(5), 1–14. https://doi.org/10.18533/job.v1i5.51

Edwards, J. (2009). *Language and identity*. Cambridge University Press.

Eggins, S. (2004). *An introduction to systemic functional linguistics* (2nd ed.). Continuum.

Egitim, S. (2021). Collaborative leadership in English language classrooms: Engaging learners in leaderful classroom practices and strategies. *International Journal of Leadership in Education*.

Eisler, R. (1984). The blade and the chalice: Technology at a turning point [Paper presentation]. World Futures Society, Washington, D. C.

Eisler, R. (1987). *The chalice and the blade*. Harper Collins.

Eisler, R. (1996). *Sacred pleasure*. HarperOne.

Eisler, R. (2000). *Tomorrow's children*. Westview Press.

Eisler, R. (2002). *The power of partnership*. New World Library.

Eisler, R. (2007). *The real wealth of nations*. Westview Press.

Eisler, R. (2021). Caring for people and nature first: Four cornerstones for a successful progressive agenda. In P. Clayton, K. M. Archie, J. Sachs, and E. Steiner (Eds.), *The new possible: Visions of our world beyond crisis* (pp. 71–79). Cascade.

Eisler, R., and Fry, D. (2019). *Nurturing our humanity*. Oxford University Press.

Eisler, R., & Loye, D. (1985). The failure of liberalism: A reassessment of ideology from a new feminine-masculine perspective. *Political Psychology, 4*(2), 375–391.

Ell, F., Hill, M., & Grudnoff, L. (2012). Finding out more about teacher candidates' prior knowledge: implications for teacher educators. *Asia-Pacific Journal of Teacher Education, 40*(1), 55–65.

Erickson, D., Hayashi, S., Hosoe, Y., Suzuki, M., Ueno Y., & Maekawa, K. (2002). Perception of American English Sarcasm by Japanese Listeners. *Acoustical Society of Japan, 1*, 277–78.

Facione, P. (1990). *Critical thinking: A statement of expert consensus for purposes of educational assessment and instruction (the Delphi report)*. American Philosophical Association.

Faist, T. (2010). Diaspora and transnationalism: What kind of dance partners? In R. Bauböck & T. Faist (Eds.), *Diaspora and transnationalism: Concepts, theories, and methods* (pp. 9-34). Amsterdam University Press. https://library.oapen.org/bitstream/handle/20.500.12657/34853/350730.pdf

Fang, F. (2018). Review of English as a medium of instruction in Chinese universities today: Current trends and future directions. *English Today, 34*(1), 32–37. https://doi.org/10.1017/S0266078417000360

Faruk, S. (2013). English language teaching in Saudi Arabia: A world system perspective. *Scientific Bulletin of the Politehnica University of Timişoara Transactions on Modern Languages, 12*(1), 73–80.

Feez, S., & Joyce, H. D. S. (1998). *Text-based syllabus design*. National Centre for English Language Teaching and Research, Macquarie University.

Feng, A., & Adamson, B. (2018). Language policies and sociolinguistic domains in the context of minority groups in China. *Journal of Multilingual and Multicultural Development, 39*(2), 169–180. https://doi.org/10.1080/01434632.2017.1340478

Ferencz, I., Maiworm, F., & Mitic, M. (2014). Part II – Traits and daily operation of ETPs. In B. Wächter & F. Maiworm (Eds.), *English-taught programmes in European higher education: The state of play in 2014* (pp. 63–97). Lemmens. Retrieved from https://www.lemmens.de/dateien/medien/buecher-ebooks/aca/2014_english_taught.pdf

Ferris, D. (2011). *Treatment of error in second language student writing*. University of Michigan Press.

Fishman, J. A. (1967). Bilingualism with and without diglossia; Diglossia with and without bilingualism. *Journal of Social Issues, 23*, 29–38.

Fitzgerald, C. (2013). *A qualitative analysis of irony as humor in Japanese conversation* [Master's Thesis, Tohoku University].

Forman, E. A., and Cazden, C. B. (1985). Exploring Vygotskian perspectives in education: The cognitive value of peer interaction. In J. V. Wertsch (Ed.), *Culture, communication, and cognition: Vygotskian perspectives* (pp. 323–247). Cambridge University Press.

Fox, H. (1994). *Listening to the world: Cultural issues in academic writing*. National Council of Teachers of English.

Fredricks, J. A. (2014) *Eight myths of student disengagement: Creating classrooms of deep learning*. Corwin Publishing.

Freedman, M. (2020). *How to live forever: The enduring power of connecting the generations*. Public Affairs.

Fujii, K. (2020, August). 半期間の英語多読指導を通して見られた自由英作文の質的変化 (*Hankikan no eigo tadokushido wo toshite mirareta jiyueisakubun no shitsutekihenka*) [*Changes in the quality of essay writing after a half-year extensive reading course*] [Conference presentation]. Japan Extensive Reading Association Annual Conference, Tokyo.

Fujimoto, M. (2016). Management of L-café. In G. Murray and N. Fujishima (Eds.), *Social space for language learning: Stories from the L-Café* (pp. 31–39). Palgrave Macmillan.

Gallagher, F., & Colohan, G. (2017). T(w)o and fro: Using the L1 as a language teaching tool in the CLIL classroom. *The Language Learning Journal, 45*(4), 485–498. https://doi.org/10.1080/09571736.2014.947382

Galloway, N., Kriukow, J., & Numajiri, T. (2017). *Internationalization, higher education and the growing demand for English: An investigation into the English medium of instruction (EMI) movement in China and Japan*. British Council. Retrieved from https://www.teachingenglish.org.uk/sites/teacheng/files/H035%20ELTRA%20Internationalisation_HE_and%20the%20growing%20demand%20for%20English%20A4_FINAL_WEB.pdf

Gao, X. (2007). A tale of Blue Rain Cafe: A study on the online narrative construction about a community of English learners on the Chinese mainland. *System, 35*, 259–270.

García, O. (2007). Foreword. In S. Makoni & A. Pennycook (Eds.), *Disinventing and reconstituting languages* (pp. xi–xv). MultilingualMatters.

García, O. (2009). *Bilingual education in the 21st century: A global perspective*. Wiley-Blackwell.

García, O., & Li, W. (2013). *Translanguaging: Language, bilingualism and education*. Springer. https://doi.org/10.1057/9781137385765

García, O., & Wei, L. (2014). *Translanguaging*. Palgrave Macmillan. https://link.springer.com/book/10.1057/9781137385765

Gardiner, W. (2010). Mentoring two student teachers: Mentors' perceptions of peer placements. *Teaching Education, 21*(3), 233–246.

Gardner, S. (2020). Junior high English textbook interactional humor: Pragmatic possibilities. In J. Rucynski Jr. & C. Prichard (Eds.), *Bridging the humor barrier: Humor competency training in English language teaching* (pp. 107–133). Lexington Books.

Gergen, K. (2015). *An invitation to social construction* (3rd ed.). Sage.

Gibbons, P. (2006). *Bridging discourses in the ESL classroom: students, teachers and researchers*. Bloomsbury.

Gibbs, R. W. (2000). Irony in talk among friends. *Metaphor and Symbol, 15*(1-2), 5–27. http://dx.doi.org/10.1080/10926488.2000.9678862

Gibbs, R. W. (2007). Irony in talk among friends. In R. W. Gibbs & H.L. Colston (Eds.), *Irony in language and thought: A cognitive science reader* (pp. 339–360). Lawrence Erlbaum.

Gil, J. (2006). English in minority areas of China: Some findings and directions for further research. *International Education Journal, 7*(4), 455–465.

Gillespie, D., & Israetel, D. (2008). *Benefits of co-teaching in relation to student learning* [Conference Presentation]. 116th Annual Meeting of the American Psychological Association, Boston, MA.

Gorman, K., & Johnson, D. (2013). Quantitative analysis. In R. Bayley, R. Cameron, & C. Lucas (Eds.), *The Oxford handbook of sociolinguistics* (pp. 214–240). Oxford University Press.

Gray, G. (2020). Developing a practical critical thinking curriculum: A framework for structuring content in terms of student needs. *Critical Thinking in Language Learning, 7*(1), 30–66.

Gu, M. (2013). Individuality in L2 identity construction: The stories of two Chinese learners of English. In P. Benson & L. Cooker (Eds.), *The applied linguistic individual: Sociocultural approaches to identity, agency, and autonomy* (pp. 119–134). Equinox.

Guan, J. (2015, October). Theme-rheme theory and the textual coherence of college students' English writing. In *2015 International Conference on Economics, Social Science, Arts, Education and Management Engineering* (pp. 344–346). Atlantis Press.

Hafiz, F. M., & Tudor, I. (1989). Extensive reading and the development of language skills. *ELT Journal, 43*(1), 4–13.

Hafiz, F. M., & Tudor, I. (1990). Graded readers as an input medium in L2 learning. *System*, *18*(1), 31–42.

Hagler, A. (2014). A study of attitudes toward Western culture among Saudi university students. *Learning and Teaching in Higher Education: Gulf Perspectives*, *11*(1), 1–12.

Hahl, K. & Löfström, E. (2016). Conceptualizing interculturality in multicultural teacher education. *Journal of Multicultural Discourses*, *11*(3), 300-314.

Hahn, T. N. (2020). *Interbeing: The 14 mindfulness trainings of engaged Buddhism* (4th Ed.). Parallax Press.

Hallet, W. (1998). The Bilingual Tiangle: Überlegungen zu einer Didaktik des bilingualen Sachfachunterichts. *Praxis des neusprachlichen Unterrichts*, *45*(2), 115 – 125.

Halliday, M. A. K. (1975). Learning how to mean. In B. Schulman & N. Singleton (Eds.), *Foundations of language development* (pp. 239–265). Academic Press.

Halliday, M. A. K. (1984). Language as code and language as behavior: A systemic-functional interpretation of the nature and ontogenesis of dialogue. In R. P. Fawcett, S. M. Lamb, & A. Makkai (Eds.), *The semiotics of culture and language, vol. 1: language as social semiotic* (pp. 3–35). Frances Pinter.

Halliday, M. A. K. (1994). *An introduction to functional grammar*. Edward Arnold.

Halliday, M. A. K. & Hasan, R. (1976). *Cohesion in English*. Longman.

Halliday, M. A. K., & Martin, J. R. (1981). *Readings in systemic linguistics*. North Trafalgar Square Publishing.

Hammond, J. (2001). *Scaffolding: teaching and learning in language and literacy education*. Primary English Teaching Association.

Hattie, J. and Clarke, S. (2019). *Visible learning feedback*. Routledge.

Heffernan, N. (2015). Teaching critical thinking and academic writing skills to Japanese university EFL learners. In R. Al-Mahrooqi, V. S. Thakur, & A. Roscoe. (Eds.), *Methodologies for effective writing instruction in EFL and ESL classrooms* (pp. 131–147). IGI Global. https://doi.org/10.4018/978-1-4666-6619-1.ch009

Heick, T. (2015, May 24). Why Some Teachers Are Against Technology in Education. TeachThought. https://www.teachthought.com/pedagogy/why-some-teachers-are-against-technology-in-education/

Helm, F. (2018). *Emerging identities in virtual exchange*. Research-publishing.net.

Herder, S., & Clements, P. (2012). Extensive writing: A fluency-first approach to EFL writing. In T. Muller, S. Herder, J. Adamson, & P.S. Brown (Eds.), *Innovating EFL teaching in Asia* (pp. 232–244). Palgrave Macmillan.

Hirosawa, E. & Murphey, T. (In progress). Well becoming and language learning. In M. Sato (Ed.), *Wiley Encyclopedia of SLA 2023*. Wiley.

Hirose, K., & Harwood, C. (2019). Factors influencing English as a Foreign Language (EFL) writing instruction in Japan from a teacher education perspective. In L. Seloni, & S. Henderson (Eds.) *Second language instruction in global contexts: English language teacher preparation and development* (pp. 71–90). Multilingual Matters.

Hobbs, J. R. (1979). Coherence and coreference. *Cognitive Science*, *3*, 67-90.

Hodson, R. J. (2014). Teaching "humour competence." *Knowledge, skills, and competencies in foreign language education: Proceedings of CLaSIC 2014* (pp. 149–161). NUS Centre for Language Studies.

Hofstede, G. (2002). Dimensions do not exist: A reply to Brendan McSweeney. *Human Relations, 55*(11), 1355–1361. https://doi.org/10.1177/00187267025511004

Hofstede, G. (2011). Dimensionalizing cultures: The Hofstede Model in context. *Online Readings in Psychology and Culture, 2*(1). https://doi.org/10.9707/2307-0919.1014

Holmes, J. (2000). Politeness, power, and provocation: How humour functions in the workplace. *Discourse Studies, 2*(2), 159–185. https://doi.org/10.1177/1461445600002002002

Hooper, D. (2020). Modes of identification within a language learner-led community of practice. *Studies in Self-Access Learning Journal, 11*(4), 301–327.

Hooper, D., & Watkins, S. (2023). Collaborative reflection: Nurturing student leadership in self-access centres. *Autonomy, 83*, 8–11.

Hu, G. & Duan, Y. (2018). Questioning and responding in the classroom: A cross-disciplinary study of the effects of instructional mediums in academic subjects at a Chinese university. *International Journal of Bilingual Education and Bilingualism, 22*(3), 303–321. https://doi.org/10.1080/13670050.2018.1493084

Hu, G. & Lei, J. (2014). English-medium instruction in Chinese higher education: A case study. *Higher Education, 67*(5), 551–567.

Hu, G., Li, L., & Lei, J. (2014). English-medium instruction at a Chinese university: Rhetoric and reality. *Language Policy, 13*(1), 21–40.

Huang, H., & Curle, S. (2021). Higher education medium of instruction and career prospects: An exploration of current and graduated Chinese students' perceptions. *Journal of Education and Work, 34*(3), 331–343. https://doi.org/10.1080/13639080.2021.1922617

Hugh, M. (1979). "What time is it, Denise?": Asking known information questions in classroom discourse. *Theory into Practice, 18*(4), 285–294. https://doi.org/10.1080/00405847909542846

Hyland, K. (2011). Disciplinary specificity: Discourse, context and ESP. In D. Belcher, A. M. Johns, & B. Paltridge (Eds.), *New Directions in English for Specific Purposes Research* (pp. 6–24). University of Michigan Press.

Hyland, K., & Hyland, F. (Eds.). (2019). *Feedback in second language writing: Contexts and issues*. Cambridge University Press.

Hyon, S. (1996). Genre in three traditions: implications for ESL. *TESOL Quarterly, 30*(4), 693–722.

Inagaki, K., & Hatano, G. (1977). Amplification of cognitive motivation and its effects on epistemic observation. *American Educational Research Journal, 14*(4), 485–491. https://doi.org/10.3102/00028312014004485

Institute for Applied Language Studies, University of Edinburgh. (1995). *E.P.E.R. Edinburgh Project on Extensive Reading Placement Test Testpack A (Complete)*.

Ionin, T., Ko, H., & Wexler, K. (2004). Article semantics in L2 acquisition: The role of specificity. *Language Acquisition, 12*(1), 3–69. https://doi.org/10.1207/s15327817la1201_2

Israel, E., & Batalova, J. (2021, January 14). *International students in the United States*. Migration information source. https://www.migrationpolicy.org/article/international-students-united-states-2020

Jacob, W. J. (2015). Interdisciplinary trends in higher education. *Palgrave Communications, 1*. https://doi.org/10.1057/palcomms.2015.1

Jacobs, H., Zinkgraf, S., Wormuth, D., Hartfield, V., & Hughey, J. (1981). *Testing ESL composition: A practical approach*. Newbury House.

Janhunen, J. A. (2012). *Mongolian*. John Benjamins.

Jarvis, P. (1999). *The Teacher researcher: Developing Theory from Practice*. Jossey-Bass.

Jiang, L., Zhang, L.J. & May, S. (2016). Implementing English-medium instruction (EMI) in China: Teachers' practices and perceptions, and students' learning motivation and need. *International Journal of Bilingual Education and Bilingualism*, 22(2), 107–119. https://doi.org/10.1080/13670050.2016.1231166

Jiang, L., Zhang, L. J., & May, S. (2019). Implementing English-medium instruction (EMI) in China: Teachers' practices and perceptions, and students' learning motivation and needs. *International Journal of Bilingual Education and Bilingualism*, 22(2), 107–119. https://doi.org/10.1080/13670050.2016.1231166

Jin, Y., & Yang, H. (2018). Taking the road of language testing with Chinese characteristics: The thirty years' enlightenment of the CET-4 and CET-6 in China. *Foreign Language World*, 185(2), 29–39.

Jobert, M., & Sorlin, S. (Eds.) (2018). *The pragmatics of irony and banter*. John Benjamins Publishing Company.

Johns, A. M. (2002). Genre and ESL/EFL composition instruction. In B. Kroll (Ed.), *Exploring the dynamics of second language writing* (pp. 37–56). Cambridge University Press.

Johnson, D. W., & Johnson, R. T. (1979). Conflict in the classroom: Controversy and learning. *Review of Educational Research*, 49(1), 51–70. https://doi.org/10.3102/00346543049001051

Jones, B. (2017). Translanguaging in bilingual schools in Wales. *Journal of Language, Identity and Education*, 16(4), 199–215. https://doi.org/10.1080/15348458.2017.132 8782

Joyce, H. S., & Feez, S. (2012). *Text-based language and literacy education: Programming and methodology*. Phoenix Education.

Kanda University of International Studies Self-Access Learning Center. (2020). [Student survey] [Unpublished raw data]. SurveyMonkey.

Kanda University of International Studies Self-Access Learning Center Modules. (n.d.). https://thesalc.weebly.com/

Kao, S. (2012). Peer advising as a means to facilitate language learning. In J. Mynard & L. Carson (Eds.), *Advising in language learning: Dialogue, tools, and context* (pp. 87–104). Pearson.

Kaplan, R. (1966). Cultural thought patterns in inter-cultural education. *Language Learning*, 16, 1–20.

Kapogianni, E. (2011). Irony via 'surrealism': The humorous side of irony. *The pragmatics of humour across discourse domains*. John Benjamins Publishing Company. https://doi.org/10.1075/pbns.210

Karatsu, R. (2016). Fostering critical competence in CLIL classes through films: A case study at a Japanese university. *Association for Teaching English Through Multimedia Journal*, 21, 129-143.

Kato, S., & Mynard, J. (2016). *Reflective dialogue: Advising in language learning*. Routledge.

Kim, E. G. & Shin, A. (2014). Seeking an effective program to improve communication skills of non-English-speaking graduate Engineering students: The case of a Korean Engineering school. *IEEE Transactions on Professional Communication, 57*(1), 41–55.

Kim, J., & Lantolf, J. P. (2018). Developing conceptual understanding of sarcasm in L2 English through explicit instruction. *Language Teaching Research, 22*(2), 208–229. https://doi.org/10.1177/1362168816675521

Kim, S. & Lee, J-H. (2010). Private tutoring and demand for education in South Korea. *Economic Development and Cultural Change, 58*(2), 259–296.

Kivisto, P., & Faist, T. (2010). *Beyond a border: The causes and consequences of contemporary migration.* Pine Forge Press.

Klein, J. T. (2006). A platform for a shared discourse of interdisciplinary education. *Journal of Social Science Education, 5*(4), 10–18.

Komiyama, K. (2017). Ten-minute writing practice for Japanese high school students. In P. Clements, A. Krause, & H. Brown (Eds.), Transformation in language education (pp. 362–368). JALT.

Komiyama, K. (2018). 日本人高校生のライティング力の発達におけるエクステンシヴ・ライティングの効果に関する実証的研究 (*Nihonjinkōkōsei no writing ryoku no hattatsuniokeru extensive writing no kōkanikanikansuru jisshōtekikenkū*) [*An empirical study on the effects of extensive writing on the development of Japanese high school students' writing skills*] (Publication No. 34302-18) [Doctoral dissertation, Kyoto University of Foreign Studies]. Kyoto University of Foreign Studies Institutional Repository. http://id.nii.ac.jp/1289/00000339/

Kong, M., & Wei, R. (2019). EFL learners' attitudes toward English-medium instruction in China: The influence of sociobiographical variables. *Linguistics and Education, 52*, 44–51. https://doi.org/10.1016/j.linged.2019.03.005

Kongpetch, S. (2006). Using a genre-based approach to teach writing to Thai students: a case study. *Prospect: An Australian journal of TESOL, 21*(2), 3–33.

Kormos, J., Csizér, K., Menyhárt, A., & Török, D. (2008). "Great expectations": The motivational profile of Hungarian English language students. *Arts and Humanities in Higher Education, 7*(1), 65–82. https://doi.org/10.1177/1474022207084884

Kormos, J., & Kiddle, T. (2013). The role of socio-economic factors in motivation to learn English as a foreign language: The case of Chile. *System, 41*(2), 399–412. https://doi.org/10.1016/j.system.2013.03.006

Kramp, M. K. (2004). Exploring life experience through narrative inquiry. In K. deMarrais & S. D. Lapan (Eds.), *Foundations for research: Methods of inquiry in education and the social sciences* (pp. 103–121). Lawrence Erlbaum Associates.

Kramsch, C. (2001). *Context and culture in language teaching* (5th ed.). Oxford: Oxford University Press.

Krashen, S. (1989). We acquire vocabulary and spelling by reading: Additional evidence for the Input Hypothesis. *The Modern Language Journal, 73* (4), 440–464.

Kuhn, A. (November 26, 2016). The Place In China Where The Women Lead. *National Public Radio.* https://www.npr.org/sections/parallels/2016/11/26/501012446/the-place-in-china-where-the-women-lead

Kuiper, C., Smit, J., De Wachter, L., & Elen, J. (2017). Scaffolding tertiary students' writing in a genre-based writing intervention. *Journal of Writing Research*, 9(1), 27–59. https://doi.org/10.17239/jowr-2017.09.01.02

Kushida, B. (2020). Social learning spaces. In J. Mynard, M. Burke, D. Hooper, B. Kushida, P. Lyon, R. Sampson, & P. Taw (Eds.), *Dynamics of a social language learning community: Beliefs, membership, and identity* (pp. 108–124). Multilingual Matters.

Kusumi, T. (2015). はじめに (Hajimeni) [Introduction]. In T. Kusumi, & Y. Michita. (Eds.), ワードマップ: 批判的思考—２１世紀を生きぬくリテラシーの基盤 (Wādo mappu hihanteki shikō: 21seiki o ikinuku riterashīno kiban) [Word map critical thinking: Foundation of the literacy for living in the 21st century] (pp. i–vi). Shin-yo-sha.

Kusumoto, Y. (2018). Enhancing critical thinking through active learning. *Language Learning in Higher Education*, 8(1), 45–63. https://doi.org/10.1515/cercles-2018-0003

Kuwabara, H., McManus, K. M., & Watanabe, M. (2020). Peer mentoring and development of student agency. In P. Clements, A. Krause, & R. Gentry (Eds.), *Teacher efficacy, learner agency* (pp. 409–419). JALT.

Kvale, S. (2007). *Doing interviews*. SAGE Publications. https://dx.doi.org/10.4135/9781849208963

Kvale, S. & Brinkmann, S. (2009). *InterViews: Learning the craft of qualitative research interviewing* (2nd ed). Sage.

Kyriacou, C. (2001). Teacher stress: Directions for future research. *Educational Review*, 53(1), 27–35.

Kyriacou, C. (2011). Teacher stress: From prevalence to resilience. In J. Langan-Fox & C. L. Cooper (Eds.), *Handbook of stress in the occupations* (pp. 161–173). Edward Elgar.

Labov, W. (1963). The social motivation of a sound change. *Word*, 19(3), 273–309.

Labov, W. (1966). *The social stratification of English in New York City*. Center for Applied Linguistics.

Labov, W. (1972). *Sociolinguistic patterns*. University of Pennsylvania Press.

Labov, W. (1984). Field methods of the project on linguistic change and variation. In J. Baugh & J. Sherzer (Eds.), *Language Use* (pp. 28–53). Prentice Hall.

Lai, F. (1993). The effect of a summer reading course on reading and writing skills. *System*, 21(1), 87–100.

Lamb, M. (2013). 'Your mum and dad can't teach you!': Constraints on agency among rural learners of English in the developing world. *Journal of Multilingual and Multicultural Development*, 34(1), 14–29. https://doi.org/10.1080/01434632.2012.697460

Lantolf, J. P. (Ed.). (2000). *Sociocultural theory and second language learning*. Oxford University Press.

Larsen-Freeman, D. (2019). On language learner agency: A complex dynamic systems theory perspective. *The Modern Language Journal*, 103, 61-79. https://doi.org/10.1111/modl.12536

Lave, J., & Wenger, E. (1991). *Situated Learning: Legitimate Peripheral Participation*. Cambridge University Press.

Lawrence, M. S. (1972). *Writing as a thinking process*. University of Michigan Press.

Lea, M. R., & Street, B. V. (1998). Student writing in higher education: An academic literacies approach. *Studies in Higher Education*, 23(2), 157–172. http://doi.org/ http://dx.doi.org/10.1080/03075079812331380364

LeBane, M. C., Shilling, M., & Harris, A. (2016). Promoting independent English language learning within an Asian tertiary institution: The Lingnan experience. *Studies in Self-Access Learning, 7*(3), 322–330.

Lee, E., & Canagarajah, S. (2018). The connection between transcultural dispositions and translingual practices in academic writing. *Journal of Multicultural Discourses, 14*(1), 14–28. http://doi.org/10.1080/17447143.2018.1501375

Lee, M. & Gaard, M. B. (2015). Co-teaching the basic sciences, does it really influence student outcomes? *The FASEB Journal, 29*(S1). https://doi.org/10.1096/fasebj.29.1_supplement.687.2

Lee, S. Y., & Hsu, Y. Y. (2009). Determining the characteristics of extensive reading programs: The impact of extensive reading in EFL writing. *The International Journal of Foreign Language Teaching, 5*, 12–20.

Leggett, A. (1966). Notes on the writing of scientific English for Japanese physicists. *The Journal of the Physical Society of Japan (Butsuri), 21*(11), 790–805.

Lei, J., & Hu, G. (2014). Is English-medium instruction effective in improving Chinese undergraduate students' English competence? *International Review of Applied Linguistics in Language Teaching, 52*(2), 99–126. https://doi.org/10.1515/iral-2014-0005

Lems, K. (2013). Laughing all the way: Teaching English using puns. *English Teaching Forum, 51*(1), 26–33.

Lenning, O., Hill, D., Saunders, K., Solan, A., & Stokes, A. (2013). *Powerful learning communities: A guide to developing student, faculty, and professional learning communities to improve student success and organizational effectiveness.* Stylus Publishing.

Leone, P. (2014). Teletandem, video-recordings and usage-based tasks: Developing a socially situated scenario for learning. *International Journal of Learning, Teaching and Educational Research, 9*(1), 41–50.

Leone, P., & Telles, J. (2016). The Teletandem network. In R. O'Dowd & T. Lewis (Eds.), *Online intercultural exchange: Policy, pedagogy, practice* (pp. 243–248). Routledge.

Leonet, O., Cenoz, J., & Gorter, D. (2017). Challenging minority language isolation: Translanguaging in a trilingual school in the Basque Country. *Journal of Language, Identity and Education, 16*(4), 216–227. https://doi.org/10.1080/15348458.2017.1328281

Letterman, M. R., & Dugan, K. B. (2004). Team teaching a cross-disciplinary honors course: Preparation and development. *College Teaching, 52*(2), 76–79. https://www.jstor.org/stable/27559183

Lewis, T., & O'Dowd, R. (2016). Online intercultural exchange and foreign language learning: A systematic review. In O'Dowd, R. & Lewis, T. (Eds.), *Online Intercultural Exchange: Policy, Pedagogy, Practice.* (pp. 21–68). Routledge.

Lewis, T., & Walker, L. (2003). *Autonomous language learning in tandem.* Academy Electronic Publications.

Lewis, W. G. (2008). Current challenges in bilingual education in Wales. *AILA Review, 21*, 69–86. https://doi.org/10.1075/AILA.21.06LEW

Leydesdorff, L., Wagner, C. S., & Bornmann, L. (2014). The European Union, China, and the United States in the top-1% and top-10% layers of most-frequently cited publications: Competition and collaborations. *Journal of Informetrics, 8*(3), 606–617. https://doi.org/10.1016/j.joi.2014.05.002

Li, H., Martin, A. & Yeung, W., J. (2017). Academic risk and resilience for children and young people in Asia. *Educational Psychology, 37*(8), 921–929.

Li, W. (2011). Moment analysis and translanguaging space: Discursive construction of identities by multilingual Chinese youth in Britain. *Journal of Pragmatics, 43*(5), 1222–1235. https://doi.org/10.1016/j.pragma.2010.07.035

Lightbown, P., Halter, R., White, J., & Horst, M. (2002). Comprehension-based learning: The limits of do it yourself. *Canadian Modern Language Review, 58*(3), 427–464.

Lillis, T. M. (2001). *Student Writing: Access, Regulation, Desire.* Routledge.

Lillis, T. M., & Curry, M. J. (2006). Professional academic writing by multilingual scholars: Interactions with literacy brokers in the production of English-medium texts. *Written Communication, 23*(3), 3–35. http://doi.org/10.1177/0741088305283754

Lin, A. M. Y., & He, P. (2017). Translanguaging as dynamic activity flows in CLIL Classrooms. *Journal of Language, Identity and Education, 16*(4), 228-244.

Little, D. (1999). Learner autonomy is more than a western cultural construct. In S. Cotterall & D. Crabbe (Eds.), *Learner autonomy in language learning: Defining the field and effecting change* (pp. 11–18). Peter Lang.

Little, D. (2001). Learner autonomy and the challenge of tandem language learning via the Internet. In A. Chambers & G. Davies (Eds.), *ICT and language learning: A European Perspective* (pp. 29–38). Swets & Zeitlinger.

Little, D. (2007). Language learner autonomy: Some fundamental considerations revisited. *International Journal of Innovation in Language Learning and Teaching, 1*(1), 14–29.

Little, D., & Brammerts, H. (Eds.). (1996). A guide to language learning in tandem via the internet. *CLCS Occasional Paper, no. 46.* Trinity College Dublin, Center for Language and Communication Studies.

Little, D., Dam, L., & Legenhausen, L. (2017). *Language learner autonomy: Theory, practice and research.* Multilingual Matters.

Little, D., & Ushioda, E. (1998). Designing, implementing, and evaluating a project in tandem language learning via e-mail. *ReCALL, 10,* 95–101.

Lochtman, K. (2021). Does CLIL promote intercultural sensitivity? A case-study in Belgian CLIL and non-CLIL secondary schools. *Journal of Immersion and Content-Based Language Education, 9*(1), 31-57.

Lun, V., Fischer, R., & Ward, C. (2010). Exploring cultural differences in critical thinking: Is it about my thinking style or the language I speak? *Learning and Individual Differences, 20*(6), 604–616.

Macaro, E., Akincioglu, M., & Dearden, J. (2016). English-medium instruction in universities: A collaborative experiment in Turkey. *Studies in English Language Teaching, 4*(1), 51–76. https://doi.org/10.22158/selt.v4n1p51

Macaro, E., Akincioglu, M., & Han. S. (2019). English medium instruction in higher education: Teacher perspectives on professional development and certification. *International Journal of Applied Linguistics, 30*(1), 144–157. https://doi.org/10.1111/ijal.12272

Macaro, E., Curle, S., Pun, J., An, J., & Dearden, J. (2018). A systematic review of English medium instruction in Higher Education. *Language teaching, 51*(1), 36–76. https://doi.org/10.1017/S0261444817000350

MacIntyre, P., & Bohlke, D. (2014). *Reading explorer 2.* National Geographic.

MacPherson, S. (2003). TESOL for biolinguistic sustainability: The ecology of English as a lingua mundi. *TESL Canada Journal*, 20(2), 1–22. https://doi.org/10.18806/tesl.v20i2.945

Magno e Silva, W. (2018). Autonomous learning supportive base: Enhancing autonomy in a TEFL undergraduate program. In G. Murray & T. Lamb (Eds.), *Space, place, and autonomy in language learning* (pp. 219–232). Routledge.

Mahboob, A., & Elyas, T. (2014). English in the Kingdom of Saudi Arabia. *World Englishes*, 33(1), 128–142. https://doi.org/10.1111/weng.12073

Mann, C. (2005). *1491: New Revelations of the Americas before Columbus*. Vintage Books.

Marks, M. J., & DeWitt, S. L. (2020). *Teaching about diversity: Activities to start the conversation*. Information Age Publishing.

Martin, J. R. (2000). Design and practice: enacting functional linguistics. *Annual Review of Applied Linguistics*, 20, 116–126.

Martin, J. R., & Rose, D. (2008). *Genre relations: mapping culture*. Equinox.

Maruki, Y. (2020). CLIL and intercultural competence in teaching Japanese language and literature. *Journal of Language and Cultural Education*, 8, 53-63.

Matley, D. (2018). "This is NOT a#humblebrag, this is just a# brag": The pragmatics of self-praise, hashtags and politeness in Instagram posts. *Discourse, Context & Media*, 22, 30–38. https://doi.org/10.1016/j.dcm.2017.07.007

May, S. (2008). Bilingual/immersion education: What the research tells us. In N. H. Hornberger (Ed.), *Encyclopedia of language and education, volume 5: Bilingual education* (pp. 1483–1498). Springer.

McAllister, J., & Narcy-Combes, M. (2020). Reconsidering tandem learning through a translanguaging lens: A study of students' perceptions and practices. In C. Horgues & C. Tardieu (Eds.), *Redefining tandem language and culture learning in higher education* (pp. 31–47). Routledge.

McCarthy, P. M., Al-Harthy, A., Buck, R. H., Ahmed, K., Duran, N. D., Thomas, A. M., Kaddoura, N. W., & Graesser, A. C. (2021a). Introducing Auto-Peer: A computational tool designed to provide automated feedback. *Asian ESP Journal*, 17, 9–43.

McCarthy, P. M., Highland, K., & Ahmed, K. (2021b). Integrating technology for reading and writing in the ESL classroom. In Z. S. Genc & I. G. Kaçar (Eds.), *TESOL in the 21st century: Challenges and opportunities* (pp. 323–348). Peter Lang Publishing.

McCarthy, P. M., Thomas, A. M., Al-harthy, A., Duran, N. D., & Shpit, E. (2022). The discipline specificity analysis tool (DSAT). Research Grant Awarded by The American University of Sharjah. FRG22-C-S70.

McGuire, M., Weng, Z., & Macbeth, K. (2022). Humanizing an online ESOL composition course: A look at teacher presence, community-building, and student satisfaction during the COVID-19 pandemic. In J. LeLoup & P. Swanson (Eds.), *Effective online language teaching in a disruptive environment* (pp. 354-371). IGI Global. https://doi.org/10.4018/978-1-7998-7720-2

McKay, S. L., & Hu, G. (2012). English language education in East Asia: Some recent developments. *Journal of Multilingual and Multicultural Development*, 33, 345–362.

McKinley, J. (2013). Displaying critical thinking in EFL academic writing: A discussion of Japanese to English contrastive rhetoric. *RELC Journal*, 44(2), 195–208.

McKinley, J. (2015). Critical argument and writer identity: Social constructivism as a theoretical framework for EFL academic writing. *Critical Inquiry in Language Studies, 12*(3), 184–207.

McLean, S., & Rouault, G. (2017). The effectiveness and efficiency of extensive reading at developing reading rates. *System, 70*(1), 92–106.

McLoughlin, D. (2020). Interest development and self-regulation of motivation. In J. Mynard, M. Tamala, & W. Peeters (Eds.), *Supporting learners and educators in developing language learner autonomy* (pp. 63–76). Candlin & Mynard ePublishing.

McNeely, B. (2005). Using technology as a learning tool, not just the cool new thing. In D. G. Oblinger & J. L. Oblinger (Eds.), *Educating the net generation* (pp. 4.1–4.10). Educause Publications.

McNemar, Q. (1947). Note on the sampling error of the difference between correlated proportions or percentages. *Psychometrika, 12*(2), 153–157. https://doi.org/10.1007/bf02295996

McSweeney, B. (2002). Hofstede's model of national cultural differences and their consequences: A triumph of faith - a failure of analysis. *Human Relations, 55*(1), 89–118. https://doi.org/10.1177/0018726702551004

McVeigh, B. (2002). *Japanese higher education as myth*. M.E. Sharpe.

Méndez García, M. C. (2013). The intercultural turn brought about by the implementation of CLIL programmes in Spanish monolingual areas: a case study of Andalusian primary and secondary schools. *The Language Learning Journal, 41*(3), 268-283.

Méndez García, M. C. & Pavón Vázquez, V. (2012). Investigating the coexistence of the mother tongue and the foreign language through teacher collaboration in CLIL contexts: Perceptions and practice of the teachers involved in the plurilingual programme in Andalusia. *International Journal of Bilingual Education and Bilingualism, 15*, 1-20.

Mercer, S., MacIntyre, P., Gregersen, T., & Talbot, K. (2018). Positive language education: Combining positive education and language education. *Theory and practice of second language acquisition, 4*(2), 11–31.

Mercer, S., Talbot, K. R., & Wang, I. K. H. (2021). Fake or real engagement – Looks can be deceiving. In P. Hiver, A. H. Al-Hoorie & S. Mercer (Eds.), *Student engagement in the language classroom* (pp. 143–162). Multilingual Matters.

Mermelstein, A. (2015). Improving EFL learners' writing through enhanced extensive reading. *Reading in a Foreign Language, 27*(2), 182–198.

Miller, D., & Trump, J. (1973). *Secondary school curriculum improvement: Challenges, humanism, accountability*. Allyn & Bacon.

Ministry of Education, Culture, Sports, Science and Technology-Japan. (2018a). *Course of study for elementary and Junior high schools*.

Ministry of Education, Culture, Sports, Science and Technology-Japan. (2018b). 高等学校学習指導要領(*Kōtōgakkōgakushū shidō yōryō*) [*The course of study for senior high schools*]. Ministry of Education, Culture, Sports, Science and Technology. https://www.mext.go.jp/content/1407073_09_1_2.pdf

Ministry of Education, Culture, Sports, Science and Technology-Japan. (2020). *Measures* based on the four policy directions. https://www.mext.go.jp/en/policy/education/lawandplan/title01/detail01/sdetail01/1373805.htm

Ministry of Education of the People's Republic of China. (2001). 关于加强高等院校本科教学工作提高教学质量的若干意见 (Guānyú jiāqiáng gāoděng yuàn jiào běnkē jiàoxué gōngzuò tígāo jiàoxué zhìliàng de ruògān yìjiàn) [Guidelines for strengthening undergraduate education and improving the quality of undergraduate programs]. Retrieved from http://www.edu.cn/20030804/3088968.shtml

Miyahara, M. (2015). *Emerging self-identities and emotions in foreign language learning: A narrative oriented approach*. Multilingual Matters.

Miyake-Warkentin, K., Hooper, D., & Murphey, T. (2020). Student action logging creates teacher efficacy. In P. Clements, A. Krause, & R. Gentry (Eds.), *Teacher efficacy, learner agency* (pp. 341–349). Japan Association for Language Teaching. https://doi.org/10.37546/JALTPCP2019-40

Miyata, M. (2002). ここまで通じる日本人英語: 新しいライティングのすすめ (Koko ni tsuite nihongo eigo shinrai writing no susume) [Japanese English that can be understood so far]. Daishukan Shoten.

Moon, S. J., & Bai, S. Y. (2020). Components of digital literacy as predictors of youth civic engagement and the role of social media news attention: The case of Korea. *Journal of Children and Media*, 14(4), 458–474. https://www.tandfonline.com/doi/abs/10.1080/17482798.2020.1728700

Morita, L. (2017). Why Japan needs English. *Cogent Social Sciences*, 3(1). https://doi.org/10.1080/23311886.2017.1399783

Morita, N. (2002). *Negotiating participation in second language academic communities: A study of identity, agency, and transformation* [Unpublished doctoral dissertation, University of British Columbia]. https://open.library.ubc.ca/media/download/pdf/831/1.0078209/1

Moskovsky, C., & Alrabai, F. (2009). Intrinsic motivation in Saudi learners of English as a foreign language. *Open Applied Linguistics Journal*, 2(1), 1–10. https://doi.org/10.2174/1874913500902010001

Moskovsky, C., Assulaimani, T., Racheva, S., & Harkins, J. (2016). The L2 motivational self system and L2 achievement: A study of Saudi EFL learners. *The Modern Language Journal*, 100(3), 641–654. https://doi.org/10.1111/modl.12340

Motani, Y. (2002). Towards a more just educational policy for minorities in Japan: The case of Korean ethnic schools. *Comparative Education*, 38(2), 225–237. https://doi.org/10.1080/03050060220140593

Mozzon-McPherson, M., & Tassinari, M. G. (2020). From language teachers to language learning advisors. A journey map. *Philologia Hispalensis*, 34(1), 121–139.

Mueller, R. A. (2019). Episodic narrative interview: Capturing stories of experience with a methods fusion. *International Journal of Qualitative Methods*, 18, 1–11.

Muller, T. (2012). Critical discourse analysis in ESP course design: The case of medical English. *Professional and Academic English*, 40, 25–28.

Muller, T. (2014). Implementing and evaluating free writing in a Japanese EFL classroom. In T. Muller, J. Adamson, P. S. Brown, & S. Herder (Eds.), *Exploring EFL Fluency in Asia* (pp. 163–177). Palgrave Macmillan.

Muller, T. (2015). Critical discourse analysis in a medical English course: Examining learner agency through student written reflections. In P. Deters, X. (A.) Gao, E. R. Miller, & G. Vitanova (Eds.), *Theorizing and Analyzing Agency in Second Language Learning: Interdisciplinary Approaches* (pp. 232–251). Multilingual Matters.

Muller, T. (2018). *An Exploration of the Experiences of Japan-Based English Language Teachers Writing for Academic Publication* [Doctoral thesis, The Open University]. Open Research Online (ORO). http://oro.open.ac.uk/57835/

Muller, T., Adamson, J., Brown, P. S., & Herder, S. (Eds.) (2014). *Exploring EFL Fluency in Asia*. Palgrave Macmillan.

Muller, T., & de Boer, M. (2012). Classroom discourse analysis of student use of language scaffolding during tasks. In T. Muller, S. Herder, J. Adamson, & P. S. Brown (Eds.), *Innovating EFL Teaching in Asia* (pp. 145–161). Palgrave Macmillan.

Muller, T., Herder, S., Adamson, J., & Brown, P. S. (Eds.) (2012). *Innovating EFL Teaching in Asia*. Palgrave Macmillan.

Muller, T., & Skeates, C. (2022). Institutionality in Anglophone and Japan university job advertisements: A critical discourse analysis of representations of academic work. In Y. Porsché, R. Scholz, & J. N. Singh (Eds.), *Institutionality: Studies of Discursive and Material (Re-)ordering* (pp. 335–358). Palgrave Macmillan.

Murphey, T. (1998). Motivating students with near peer role models. In B. Visgatis (Ed.), *JALT 1997 Conference Proceedings* (pp. 201-206). JALT.

Murphey, T. (2014a). Singing well-becoming: Student musical therapy case studies. *Studies in Second Language Learning and Teaching*, 4(2), 205–235. https://doi.org/10.14746/ssllt.2014.4.2.4

Murphey T. (2014b). Scaffolding, participating, agencing friending and fluencing. In Muller, T., Adamson, J., Brown, P., & Herder, S. (Eds.), *Exploring EFL Fluency in Asia* (pp. 42–58). Palgrave Macmillan.

Murphey, T. (2016). Teaching to learn and well-become: Many mini-renaissances. In P. McIntyre, T. Gregerson, & S. Mercer (Eds.), *Positive Psychology in SLA* (pp. 324–343). Multilingual Matters.

Murphey, T. (2019). Peaceful social testing in times of increasing individualization & isolation. *Critical Inquiry in Language Studies*, 16(1), 1–18. https://doi.org/10.1080/15427587.2018.1564138

Murphey, T., (2021a). Ask your students for a change: Using student produced and selected materials (SPSMs) in dialogic pedagogy. *The Language Teacher*, 45(5), 9–16.

Murphey, T., (2021b). *Learning voices*. Candlin & Mynard.

Murphey, T., & Carpenter, C. (2008). The seeds of agency in language learning histories. In P. Kalaja, V. Menezes, and A.M.F. Barcelos (Eds.), *Narratives of Learning and Teaching EFL* (pp. 17–34). Palgrave Macmillan.

Murphey, T. & Edlin, C. (2020). The EcoEducational-BioPsychoSocial model in everyday education: A suggestion for researching holistic well-being as a contribution to healthier learner autonomy. *Relay Journal*, 3(1), 110–121.

Murphey, T., Falout, J., Elwood, J. & Hood, M. (2009). Inviting Student Voice. In R. Nunn and J. Adamson (Eds.), *Accepting alternative voices in EFL* (pp. 211–235). Asian EFL Journal Press.

Murphey, T., Falout, J., Fukuda, T., & Fukada, Y. (2014). Socio-dynamic motivating through idealizing classmates. *System*, *45*, 242–253. https://doi.org/10.1016/j.system.2014.06.004

Murphey, T., Fukada, Y., Fukuda, T., & Falout, J. (2022). Group dynamics. In T. Gregersen & S. Mercer (Eds.), *The Routledge handbook of the psychology of language learning and teaching* (pp. 285–299). Routledge.

Murphy, L. (2014). Autonomy, social interaction, and community: A distant language learning perspective. In G. Murray (Ed.), *Social dimensions of autonomy in language learning* (pp. 119–134). Palgrave Macmillan.

Murray, G. (2014). Exploring the social dimensions of autonomy in language learning. In G. Murray (Ed.), *Social dimensions of autonomy in language learning* (pp. 3–11). Springer.

Murray, G., & Fujishima, N. (2013). Social language learning spaces: Affordances in a community of learners. *Chinese Journal of Applied Linguistics*, *36(1)*, 141-157. https://doi.org/10.1515/cjal-2013-0009

Myers, M. D. (2013). *Qualitative Research in Business and Management* (2nd ed.). Sage.

Mynard, J. (2012). A suggested model for advising in language learning. In J. Mynard & L. Carson (Eds.), *Advising in language learning: Dialogue, tools and context* (pp. 26–41). Routledge.

Mynard, J., & McLoughlin, D. (2020). "Sometimes I just want to know more. I'm always trying.": The role of interest in sustaining motivation for self-directed learning. *Electronic Journal of Foreign Language Teaching*, *17(1)*.

Nagao, A. (2018). A genre-based approach to writing instruction in EFL classroom contexts. *English Language Teaching*, *11(5)*, 130–147.

Nagao, A. (2019). The SFL genre-based approach to writing in EFL contexts. *Asian-Pacific Journal of Second and Foreign Language Education*, *4(1)*, 1–18. https://doi.org/10.1186/s40862-019-0069-3

Nagao, A. (2020). Adopting an SFL approach to teaching L2 writing through the teaching learning cycle. English Language Teaching, 13(6), 144–161. https://doi.org/10.5539/elt.v13n6p144

Nakamura, Y. (2005). The samurai sword cuts both ways: A transnational analysis of Japanese and US media representations of Ichiro. *International Review for the Sociology of Sport*, *40(4)*, 467–480. https://doi.org/10.1177/1012690205065749

Nation, P., & Malarcher, C. (2007). *Reading for speed and fluency 2*. Compass Publishing Japan.

Neumann, H., & McDonough, K. (2015). Exploring student interaction during collaborative prewriting discussions and its relationship to L2 writing. *Journal of Second Language Writing*, *27*, 84–104.

New South Wales [NSW] Department of School Education. (1989). *A brief Introduction to Genre: Example of six factual genres and their genetic structures*. Metropolitan East Disadvantaged Schools Program. https://educationalsemiotics.files.wordpress.com/2012/11/introduction_to_genre.pdf

Newton, F. B., & Ender, S. C. (2000). *Students helping students: A Guide for peer educators on college campuses*. Jossey-Bass.

Norton, B. (2001). Non-participation, imagined communities, and the language classroom.

In M. Breen (Ed.), *Learner contributions to language learning: New directions in research* (pp. 156–171). Pearson Education.
Norton, B. (2015). Identity, investment, and faces of English internationally. *Chinese Journal of Applied Linguistics, 38*(4), 375–391. https://doi.org/10.1515/cjal-2015-0025
Norton, B. (2016). Identity and language learning: Back to the future. *TESOL Quarterly, 50*(2), 475–479. https://doi.org/10.1002/tesq.293
Norton, B., & Christie, F. (1999). Genre theory and ESL teaching: a systemic functional perspective. *TESOL Quarterly, 33*(4), 759–763. https://doi.org/10.2307/3587889
Nunan, D. (1990). Action research in the language classroom. In J. C. Richards and D. Nunan (Eds.), *Second language teacher education* (pp. 62–81). Cambridge University Press.
Nunan, D. (1992). *Research Methods in Language Teaching*. Cambridge University Press.
Nunan, D. (2003). The impact of English as a global language on educational policies and practices in the Asia-Pacific region. *TESOL Quarterly, 37*(4), 589–613.
O'Dowd, R. (2016). Emerging trends and new directions in telecollaborative learning. *CALICO Journal, 33*(3), 291–310.
O'Dowd, R. (2021). Virtual exchange: Moving forward into the next decade. *Computer Assisted Language Learning, 34*(3), 209–224.
O'Dowd, R., & Dooley, M. (2020). Intercultural communicative competence development through telecollaboration and virtual exchange. In J. Jackson (Ed.), *The Routledge handbook of language and intercultural communication* (pp. 361–375). Routledge.
Ohmori, A. (2014). Exploring the Potential of CLIL in English Language Teaching in Japanese Universities: An Innovation for the Development of Effective Teaching and Global Awareness. *The Journal of Rikkyo University Language Center Bulletin, 32*, 39-51.
Oi, K. (2005). Teaching argumentative writing to Japanese EFL students using the Toulmin Model. *JACET Bulletin, 41*, 123–140.
Oi, K. (2018). Developing critical thinking skills in EFL students' writing classes. *Bulletin of Seisen University, 65*, 1–22.
Okada, A. (2012). *Education and equal opportunity in Japan*. Berghahn Books.
Okamoto, S. (2007). An analysis of the usage of Japanese hiniku: Based on the communicative insincerity theory of irony. *Journal of Pragmatics, 39*(6), 1143–1169. https://doi.org/10.1016/j.pragma.2006.08.012
O'Leary, C. (2014). Developing autonomous language learners in HE: A social constructivist perspective. In G. Murray (Ed.), *Social dimensions of autonomy in language learning* (pp. 15–36). Springer.
Oliveira, L. C. (2015). A systemic-functional analysis of English language learners' writing. *DELTA: Documentação de Estudos em Lingüística Teórica e Aplicada, 31*(1), 207–237.
Ortega, L. (2017). New CALL-SLA research interfaces for the 21st century: Towards equitable multilingualism. *CALICO Journal, 34*(4), 285-316. https://doi.org/10.1558/cj.33855
Otheguy, R., García, O., & Reid, W. (2015). Clarifying translanguaging and deconstructing named languages: A perspective from linguistics. *Applied Linguistics Review, 6*(3), 281–307. https://doi.org/10.1515/applirev-2015-0014
Oxford, R. L. (2003). Toward a more systematic model of L2 learner autonomy. In D.

Palfreyman & R. Smith (Eds.), *Learner autonomy across Cultures—Language education perspectives* (pp. 75–91). Palgrave Macmillan.

Pabdoo. (n.d.). Personal identity wheel. Inclusive Teaching. *University of Michigan*. Retrieved March 24, 2023, from https://sites.lsa.umich.edu/inclusive-teaching/personal-identity-wheel/

Palfreyman, D. M. (2018). Learner autonomy and groups. In A. Chik, N. Aoki, & R. Smith (Eds.), *Autonomy in language learning and teaching* (pp. 51–72): Springer.

Pallant, J. (2013). *SPSS survival manual: A step by step guide to data analysis using IBM SPSS*. McGraw-Hill Education.

Papi, M., Bondarenko, A. V., Mansouri, S., Feng, L., & Jiang, C. (2019). Rethinking L2 motivation research: The 2 × 2 model of L2 self-guides. *Studies in Second Language Acquisition, 41*(2), 337–361. https://doi.org/10.1017/S0272263118000153

Park, J-K. (2009). 'English fever' in South Korea: Its history and symptoms. *English Today, 25*(1), 50–57.

Park, S. J., & Abelmann, N. (2004). Class and cosmopolitan striving: Mothers' management of English education in South Korea. *Anthropological Quarterly, 77*(4), 645–672.

Pavlenko, A. (2002). Narrative study: Whose story is it anyway? *TESOL Quarterly, 36*, 213–218.

Pavlenko, A. (2007). Autobiographic Narratives as Data in Applied Linguistics, *Applied Linguistics, 28*(2), 163–188.

Peeters, W., & Mynard, J. (2019). Peer collaboration and learner autonomy in online interaction spaces. *Relay Journal, 2*(2), 450–458.

Peled, L., & Reichart, R. (2017). Sarcasm SIGN: Interpreting sarcasm with sentiment based Twenge monolingual machine translation. *arXiv*. https://arxiv.org/pdf/1704.06836.

Peng, W., Adikari, A., Alahakoon, D., & Gero, J. (2019). Discovering the influence of sarcasm in social media responses. *Wiley Interdisciplinary Reviews: Data Mining and Knowledge Discovery, 9*(6), e1331. https://doi.org/10.1002/widm.1331

Penrose, A. M. (2002). Academic literacy perceptions and performance: Comparing first-generation and continuing-generation college students. *Research in the Teaching of English, 36*, 437–461.

Perret-Clarmont, A. N. (1980). *Social interaction and cognitive development in children*. Academic Press.

Pessoa, S., Mitchell, T. D., & Miller, R. T. (2018). Scaffolding the argument genre in a multilingual university history classroom: tracking the writing development of novice and experienced writers. *English for specific purposes, 50*, 81–96. https://doi.org/10.1016/j.esp.2017.12.002

Pham, V. P. H., & Bui, T. K. (2022). Genre-based approach to writing in EFL contexts. *Pham, VPH, & Bui, TKL (2021). Genre-based Approach to Writing in EFL Contexts. World Journal of English Language, 11*(2), 95-106.

Phillipson, R. (1992). *Linguistic imperialism*. Oxford University Press.

Piller, I., & Takahashi, K. (2006). A Passion for English: Desire and the language market. In A. Pavlenko (Ed.), *Bilingual minds: Emotional experience, expression, and representation* (pp. 59–83). Multilingual Matters.

Piriyasilpa, Y. (2010). Genre and discourse in online discussions: A study of online discussion postings in a Thai EFL writing course [Doctoral dissertation, Macquarie University]. Macquarie University Theses. https://doi.org/10.25949/19438484.v1

Platt, J., Walker-Knight, D., Lee, T., & Hewitt, R. (2001). *Shaping future teacher education practices through collaboration and coteaching* [Conference Presentation]. Annual Meeting of the American Association of Colleges for Teacher Education, New Orleans, LA.

Polkinghorne, D. E. (2007). Validity issues in narrative research. *Qualitative Inquiry, 13* (4), 471–486.

Pomerantz, A., & Bell, N. D. (2011). Humor as safe house in the foreign language classroom. *The Modern Language Journal, 95*, 148–161. https://doi.org/10.1111/j.1540-4781.2011.01274.x

Pomino, J., & Gil-Salom, D. (2016). Integrating e-tandem in higher education. *Procedia—Social and Behavioral Sciences, 228*, 668–673.

Prichard, C., & Rucynski, J. (2019). Second language learners' ability to detect satirical news and the effect of humor competency training. *TESOL Journal, 10*(1), e00366. https://doi.org/10.1002/tesj.366

Prichard, C., & Rucynski, J. (2020). Humor competency training for sarcasm and jocularity. In J. Rucynski Jr. & C. Prichard (Eds.), *Bridging the humor barrier: Humor competency training in English language teaching* (pp. 165–192). Lexington Books.

Prichard, C., & Rucynski, J. (2022). L2 learners' ability to recognize ironic online comments and the effect of instruction, *System, 105*. https://doi.org/10.1016/j.system.2022.102733

Prior, M. (2015). *Emotion and discourse in L2 narrative research*. Multilingual Matters.

Pun, J. K., & Thomas, N. (2020). English medium instruction: Teachers' challenges and coping strategies. *ELT Journal, 74*(3), 247–257. https://doi.org/10.1093/elt/ccaa024

Rahman, M., & Alhaisoni, E. (2013). Teaching English in Saudi Arabia: Prospects and challenges. *Academic Research International, 4*(1), 112–118.

Rear, D. (2017). Reframing the debate on Asian students and critical thinking: Implications for Western universities. *Journal of Contemporary Issues in Education, 12*(2), 18–33.

Reeve, J. (2016). Autonomy-supportive teaching: What it is, how to do it. In W. C. Liu, J. C. Wang, & R. M. Ryan (Eds.), *Building autonomous learners* (pp. 129-152). Springer.

Renninger, K. A., & Hidi, S. (2016). *The power of interest for motivation and engagement*. Routledge.

Reynders, G., Lantz, J., Ruder, S., Stanford, C., & Cole, R. (2020). Rubrics to assess critical thinking and information processing in undergraduate STEM courses. *International Journal of STEM Education, 7*(9), 1–15. https://doi.org/10.1186/s40594-020-00208-5

Richards, J., & Pun, J. (2022). Teacher strategies in implementing English medium instruction. *ELT Journal, 76*(2), 227–237. https://doi.org/10.1093/elt/ccab081

Richards, K. A. R., Hemphill, M. A., & Templin, T. J. (2018). Personal and contextual factors related to teachers' experience with stress and burnout. *Teachers and Teaching, 24*(7), 768–787.

Rose, D. (2013). Genre in the Sydney school. In J. P. Gee & M. Handford (Eds.), *The Routledge handbook of discourse analysis* (pp. 235–251). Routledge.

Rose, D. (2015). Genre, knowledge, and pedagogy in the Sydney School. In N. Artemeva & A. Freedman (Eds.), *Genre studies around the globe: beyond the three traditions* (pp. 299–338) Inkwell.

Rose, D., & Martin, J. R. (2012). *Learning to write, reading to learn: genre, knowledge, and pedagogy in the Sydney school*. Equinox.

Rose, H., McKinley, J., & Baffoe-Djan, J. (2019). *Data collection research methods in applied linguistics*. Bloomsbury Publishing.

Rothermich, K., & Pell, M. D. (2015). Introducing RISC: A new video inventory for testing social perception. *PloS one*, 10(7), e0133902. https://doi.org/10.1371/journal.pone.0133902

Rozas, B. (2009). Assessment and benchmarking: A new challenge for Content and Language Integrated Learning. In E. Davauz & M.C. Guerrini (Eds.), *CLIL across Educational Levels: Experiences from Primary, Secondary and Tertiary Contexts* (pp. 127-139). Richmond.

Rucynski, J., & Prichard, C. (Eds.) (2020). *Bridging the humor barrier: Humor competency training in English language teaching*. Lexington Books.

Rugen, B. (2013). Language learner, language teacher: Negotiating identity positions in conversational narratives. In G. Barkhuizen (Ed.), *Narrative research in applied linguistics* (pp. 199–217). Cambridge University Press.

Rusk, F., & Pörn, M. (2019). Delay in L2 interaction in video-mediated environments in the context of virtual tandem language learning. *Linguistics and education*, 50, 56–70.

Rustipa, K. (2010). Theme-rheme organization of learners' texts. *Dinamika Bahasa dan Budaya*, 4(2), 1-17.

Ryan, R. M., & Deci, E. L. (2017). *Self-determination theory: Basic psychological needs in motivation, development, and wellness*. Guilford Publications.

Ryan, S. (2009). Self and identity in L2 motivation in Japan: The ideal L2 self and Japanese learners of English. In Z. Dörnyei & E. Ushioda (Eds.), *Motivation, language identity and the L2 self* (pp. 120–143). Multilingual Matters.

Sahan, K., Galloway, N., & McKinley, J. (2022). 'English-only' English medium instruction: Mixed views in Thai and Vietnamese higher education. *Language Teaching Research*. https://doi.org/10.1177/13621688211072632

Sahan, K., & Rose, H. (2021). Translanguaging or code-switching? Re-examining the functions of language in EMI classrooms. In B. Di Sabato & B. Hughes (Eds.), *Multilingual perspectives from Europe and beyond on language policy and practice* (pp. 348–356). Routledge.

Sakai, H., Kudo, Y., Takagi, A., Kato, Y., Fukumoto, Y., & Tsukui, T. (2015). Interview survey on the English study of Japanese junior and senior high school students. *ARCLE*, 27–37. http://www.arcle.jp/research/books/data/html/data/pdf/vol9_3-3.pdf

Sakata, H., & Fukuda, S. (2018). Advising language learners in large classes to promote learner autonomy. In C. Ludwig & J. Mynard (Eds.), *Autonomy in language learning: Advising in action* (pp. 57–81). Candlin & Mynard ePublishing.

Saldaña, J. (2013). *The coding manual for qualitative researchers* (2nd ed.). Sage.

Sandholtz, J. H. (2000). Interdisciplinary team teaching as a form of professional development. *Teacher Education Quarterly*, 27(3), 39–54.

Sanger, C. S., & Gleason, N. W. (2020). *Diversity and inclusion in global higher education: Lessons from across Asia*. Palgrave Macmillan.

Santiago Sanchez, H., & Borg, S. (2015). Teacher research: Looking back and moving forward. In S. Borg & H. Santiago Sanchez (Eds.), *International Perspectives on Teacher Research* (pp. 185 –193). Palgrave Macmillan.

Sato, M. (2013). Beliefs about peer interaction and peer corrective feedback: Efficacy of classroom intervention. *Modern Language Journal, 97*(3), 611–633.

Sato, T. (2022). Assessing critical thinking through L2 argumentative essays: an investigation of relevant and salient criteria from raters' perspectives. *Language Testing in Asia, 12*(9), https://doi.org/10.1186/s40468-022-00159-4

Santos, A., Cenoz, J., & Gorter, D. (2018). Attitudes and anxieties of business and education students towards English: Some data from the Basque Country. *Language, Culture and Curriculum, 31*(1), 94–110. https://doi.org/10.1080/07908318.2017.135 0189

Saudi Ministry of Health. (2015). https://www.moh.gov.sa/en/Pages/default.aspx

Saudi Vision 2030. (2020). https://vision2030.gov.sa/en

Schleppegrell, M. J., Moore, J., Al-Adeimi, S., O'Hallaron, C., Palincsar, A., & Symons, C. (2014). Tackling a genre: situating SFL genre pedagogy in a new context. In L. de Oliveira & J. Iddings (Eds.), *Genre pedagogy across the curriculum* (pp. 26–39). Equinox.

Schmulian, A., & Coetzee, S. A. (2019). To team or not to team: An exploration of undergraduate students' perspectives of two teachers simultaneously in class. *Innovative Higher Education, 44*(4). 317–328.

Seidman, I. (2006). *Interviewing as qualitative research: A guide for researchers in education and the social sciences* (3rd ed.). Teachers College Press.

Seligman, M. E. (2011). *Flourish: A visionary new understanding of happiness and well-being*. Simon and Schuster.

Shao, L., & Rose, H. (2022). Teachers' experiences of English-medium instruction in higher education: A cross case investigation of China, Japan and the Netherlands. *Journal of Multilingual and Multicultural Development*, 1–16. https://doi.org/10.1080/01434632.2022.2073358

Shively, R. (2018). *Learning and using conversational humor in a second language during study abroad*. De Gruyter Mouton.

Shively, R. L., Acevedo, J., Cano, R., & Etxeberria-Ortego, I. (2022). Teaching humorous irony to L2 and heritage speakers of Spanish. *Language Teaching Research, 26*(2), 279–302.

Sinner, A. (2010). Negotiating spaces: The in-betweeness of becoming a teacher. *Asia-Pacific Journal of Teacher Education, 38*(1), 23–37.

Skarin, R. (2001). Gender, ethnicity, class, and social identity: A case study of two Japanese women in US universities. *Qualitative Research in Applied Linguistics: Japanese Learners and Contexts, 19*, 26–55.

Skeates, C. (2015). Turning teachers onto ESP: Searching for ESP in what we already do. *OnCUE Journal, 9*(2), 181–188. http://jaltcue.org/files/OnCUE/OCJ9.2/OCJ9.2_pp181-188_Skeates.pdf

Skeates, C. (2016). Student-created marketing case studies: Looking through the lens of Cheng (2011). *Proceedings of the 2nd International Symposium on Innovative Teaching and Research in ESP* (pp. 39–43). Research Station on Innovative Global Tertiary English Education (IGTEE), University of Electro-Communications.

Smith, J. A., Flowers, P., & Larkin, M. (2022). *Interpretative phenomenological analysis: Theory, method and research* (2nd ed.). Sage.

Smith, J. A., & Osborn, M. (2008). Interpretative phenomenological analysis. In J. Smith (Ed.), *Qualitative psychology: A practical guide to research methods* (pp. 53–80). Sage. https://doi.org/10.1002/9780470776278.ch10

Smorenburg, L., Rodd, J., & Chen, A. (2015). The effect of explicit training on the prosodic production of L2 sarcasm by Dutch learners of English. *Proceedings of the 18th International Congress of Phonetic Sciences (ICPhS 2015)*. https://www.internationalphoneticassociation.org/icphs-proceedings/ICPhS2015/Papers/ICPHS 0959.pdf

Song, J. J. (2011). English as an official language in South Korea: Global English or social malady? *Language problems & Language Planning, 35*, 35–55.

Soruç, A., & Griffiths, C. (2018). English as a medium of instruction: Students' strategies. *ELT Journal, 72*(1), 38–48. https://doi.org/10.1093/elt/ccx017

Stapleton, P. (2001). Assessing critical thinking in the writing of Japanese university students: Insights about assumptions and content familiarity. *Written Communication, 18*(4), 506–548.

Statistics Bureau of Inner Mongolia Autonomous Region. (2021). 内蒙古自治区第七次全国人口普查主要数据情况 (Nèiménggǔ zìzhìqū dì qī cì quánguó rénkǒu pǔchá zhǔyào shùjù qíngkuàng) [*Main Data of the Seventh National Population Census of Inner Mongolia Autonomous Region*]. http://tj.nmg.gov.cn/ztzl/dqcqgrkpc/202105/t20210526_15968 52.html

Subban, P. (2006). Differentiated instruction: A research basis. *International Education Journal, 7*(7), 935–947.

Sudhoff, J. (2010). CLIL and Intercultural Communicative Competence: Foundations and Approaches towards a Fusion. *The International CLIL Research Journal, 1*(3), 30-37.

Suk, N. (2017). The effects of extensive reading on reading comprehension, reading rate, and vocabulary acquisition. *Reading Research Quarterly, 52*(1), 73-89.

Swaantje, M. (2018). *Saudi women and their role in the labour market under Vision 2030* [BA thesis, Lund University].

Swiercz, P. M. (n.d.) *SWIF learning: A guide to student-written, instructor-facilitated case writing*. http://college.cengage.com/business/resource/casestudies/students/swif.pdf

Taguchi, T., Magid, M., & Papi, M. (2009). The L2 Motivational Self System among Japanese, Chinese and Iranian learners of English: A comparative study. In Z. Dörnyei & E. Ushioda (Eds.), *Motivation, language identity and the L2 self* (pp. 66–97). Multilingual Matters. https://doi.org/10.21832/9781847691293-005

Takase, A. (2007). Japanese high school students' motivation for extensive L2 reading. *Reading in a Foreign Language, 19*(1), 1–17.

Talandis, Jr., G. & Stout, M. (2015). Getting EFL students to speak: An action research approach. *ELT Journal, 69*(1), 11–25. https://doi.org/10.1093/elt/ccu037

Tang, C. (1997). On the power and status of nonnative ESL teachers. *TESOL Quarterly, 31*, 577–580.

Tange, H. (2010). Caught in the Tower of Babel: University lecturers' experiences with internationalisation. *Language and Intercultural Communication, 10*(2), 137–149.

Tardieu, C., & Horgues, C. (Eds.), (2020). *Redefining tandem language and culture learning in higher education*. Routledge.

Teimouri, Y. (2017). L2 selves, emotions, and motivated behaviors. *Studies in Second Language Acquisition, 39*(4), 681–709. https://doi.org/10.1017/S0272263116000243

Thomas, J. (1983). Cross-cultural pragmatic failure. *Applied Linguistics, 4*(2), 91–112.

Thorne, S. L., & Black, R. W. (2011). Identity and interaction in Internet-mediated contexts. In C. Higgins (Ed.), *Identity formation in globalizing contexts* (pp. 257–277). Mouton de Gruyter.

Tomasello, M. (2009). *Why we cooperate*. MIT Press.

Tomlinson, C. A., & McTighe, J. (2006). *Integrating differentiated instruction & understanding by design: Connecting content and kids*. Association for Supervision and Curriculum Development.

Toth, J., & Paulsrud, B. (2017). Agency and affordance in translanguaging for learning: Case studies from English-medium instruction in Swedish schools. In B. Paulsrud, J. Rosen, B., Straszer, & A. Wedin (Eds.), *New Perspectives on Translanguaging and Education*. (pp.189–207). Multilingual Matters.

Toulmin, S. (1958). *The uses of argument*. Cambridge University Press.

Tsang, S. J. (2019). News Credibility and Media Literacy in the Digital Age. In S. J. Tsang (Ed.), *Handbook of research on media literacy research and applications across disciplines* (pp. 135–155). IGI Global. https://doi.org/10.4018/978-1-5225-9261-7.ch009

Tsang, W. (1996). Comparing the effects of reading and writing on writing performance. *Applied Linguistics, 17*(2), 210–233.

Tsybulski, D. (2019). The team teaching experiences of pre-service science teachers implementing PBL in elementary school. *Journal Of Education for Teaching, 45*(3), 244–261. https://doi.org/10.1080/09589236.2019.1599500

Tuckwell, K. J. (1997). *Canadian Marketing in Action*. Pearson Education Canada.

Tudini, V., & Liddicoat, A. J. (2017). Computer-mediated communication and conversation analysis. In S. L. Thorne & S. May (Eds.), *Language, education and technology. Encyclopedia of language and education* (3rd ed.). (pp. 415–426). Springer.

Ushioda, E. (2000). Tandem language learning via e-mail: From motivation to autonomy. *ReCALL, 12*, 121–128.

Ushioda, E. (2011). Why autonomy? Insights from motivation theory and research. *Innovation in Language Learning and Teaching, 5*(2), 221–232.

Ushioda, E. (2017). The impact of global English on motivation to learn other languages: Toward an ideal multilingual self. *Modern Language Journal, 101*(3), 469–482. https://doi.org/10.1111/modl.12413

Ushioda, E., & Dörnyei, Z. (2012). Motivation. In S. Gass & A. Mackey (Eds.), *The Routledge handbook of second language acquisition* (pp. 396–409). Routledge.

Üstünda-Algin, P., Karaaslan, H. & Murphey, T. (2022). *Universal Caring and Sharing Advising (UCASA)*. Manuscript submitted for publication in *The Research Institute for Learner Autonomy Education (RILAE journal - KUIS)*.

Vaughn, M. (2020). What is student agency and why is it needed now more than ever? *Theory Into Practice, 59*(2), 109-118. https://doi.org/10.1080/00405841.2019.1702393

Vaughn, S., Schumm, J., & Arguelles, M. (1997). The ABCDEs of co-teaching. *Teaching*

Exceptional Children, 30(2), 4–10.
Vygotsky, L. S. (1935). *Mental development of children during education*. Uchpedgiz.
Vygotsky, L. S. (1978). Interaction between learning and development. In M. Cole, V. John-Steiner, S. Scribner, & E Souberman (Eds.) *Mind and Society: The Development of Higher Psychological Processes* (pp. 79–91). Harvard University Press.
Vygotsky, L. S. (1980). *Mind in society: Development of Higher Psychological Processes* (M. Cole, V. John-Steiner, S. Scribner, & E. Souberman, Eds.). Harvard University Press. (Original work published 1935)
Wakisaka, M. (2013). How tandem learning changes attitude towards learning English: A case study of a Japanese learner. In M. Hobbs & K. Dofs (Eds.), *ILAC selections: Autonomy in a networked world* (pp. 70-71). Independent Learning Association.
Wang, H., Ko, E., Woodside, A., & Yu, J. (2021). SNS marketing activities as a sustainable competitive advantage and traditional market equity. *Journal of Business Research, 130*, 378–383. https://doi.org/10.1016/j.jbusres.2020.06.005
Wang, S., & Seepho, S. (2017). Facilitating Chinese EFL learners' critical thinking skills: The contributions of teaching strategies. *SAGE Open, 7*(3). https://doi.org/10.1177/2158244017734024
Wassler, P., Liang, W., & Kam, H. (2019). Identity and destination branding among residents: How does brand self-congruity influence brand attitude and ambassadorial behavior? *International Journal of Tourism Research, 21*(4), 437–446.
Watanabe, M., & Ohba, H. (2018). 教室内英語多読が日本人高校生の作文力に与える効果 (Kyōshitsu-nai eigo tadoku ga nihonjin kōkōsei no sakubun-ryoku ni ataeru kōka) [The effects of extensive reading in the EFL classroom on English writing ability among Japanese high school students]. 日本教科教育学会誌, *41*(1), 73–84. https://doi.org/10.18993/jcrdajp.41.1_73
Watkins, S. (2015). Enhanced awareness and its translation into action: A case study of one learner's self-directed language learning experience. *Language Learning in Higher Education, 5*(2), 441–464.
Watkins, S. (2019). Learners' perceptions of benefits in a self-directed teletandem course: An approach to encourage EFL learners to use English outside the classroom. *The Asia EFL Journal Quarterly, 20*(2), 3–28.
Watkins, S. (2021). Becoming autonomous and autonomy-supportive of others: Student community leaders' reflective learning experiences in a leadership training course. *JASAL Journal, 2*(1), 4–25.
Watkins, S. (2022). Creating social learning opportunities outside the classroom: How interest-based learning communities support learners' basic psychological needs. In J. Mynard & S. Shelton-Strong (Eds.), *Autonomy support beyond the language learning classroom: A self-determination theory perspective* (pp. 109–129). Multilingual Matters.
Watkins, S., & Hooper, D. (2023). *From student to community leader: A guide for autonomy-supportive leadership development*. Candlin & Mynard ePublishing. https://doi.org/10.47908/25
Watson, G., & Glaser, E.M. (1991). *Watson-Glaser critical thinking appraisal manual*. Psychological Corporation.
Watson Todd, R. (2003). EAP or TEAP? *Journal of English for Academic Purposes, 2*(2), 147–

156. https://doi.org/10.1016/S1475-1585(03)00014-6
Wei, L. (2018). Translanguaging as a practical theory of language. *Applied Linguistics, 39*(1), 9–30. https://doi.org/10.1093/applin/amx039
Weng, Z., McGuire, M., & Roose, M. T. (2020). Applying culturally responsive pedagogy to engage with cultural differences in an ESL composition course. In J. K. Shin & P. Vinogradova (Eds.), *Contemporary foundations for teaching English as an additional language: Pedagogical approaches and classroom applications* (pp. 113-117). Routledge. https://doi.org/10.4324/9780429398612
Wenger, E. (1998). *Community of practice: Learning, meaning, and identity*. Cambridge University Press.
Wenger, E., McDermott, R., & Snyder, W. M. (2002). *Cultivating communities of practice: A guide to managing knowledge*. Harvard Business School Press.
Wenger-Trayner, E., Fenton-O'Creevy, M., Hutchinson, S., Kubiak, C., & Wenger-Trayner, B. (Eds.). (2014). *Learning in landscapes of practice*. Routledge.
Wenzlaff, T., Berak, L., Wieseman, K., Monroe-Baillargeon, A., Bacharach, N., & Bradfield-Kreider, P. (2002). Walking our talk as educators: Teaming as a best practice. In E. Guyton & J. Ranier (Eds.), *Research on meeting and using standards in the preparation of teachers* (pp. 11–24). Kendall-Hunt.
Wilson, K. (2016). Critical reading, critical thinking: Delicate scaffolding in English for Academic Purposes (EAP). *Thinking Skills and Creativity, 22,* 256–265.
Woo, C., Cho, B-K., Kim, Y-C., Lee, Y., Kim, T., Kim, D-I., Kim, J-Y., Jang, S., & Kim, K-K. (2004). 사교육의 효과, 수요 및 그 영향요인에 관한 연구 (*Sakyoyukei Hyokwa, Suyo Mit Keu Yeonghangyoineo Kwanhan Yeonku*) [*Study on the effect, demand, and determinants of private education*]. Korea Development Institute.
Woodin, J. (2020). From a cultural to an intercultural approach: Tandem learning and the intercultural speaker. In C. Horgues & C. Tardieu (Eds.), *Redefining tandem language and culture learning in higher education* (pp. 31–47). Routledge.
Wu, B. (2009). An investigation to language uses in Mongolian learners' third language acquisition. *English Language Teaching, 2*(1), 68–74. https://doi.org/10.5539/elt.v2n1p68
Wulf, D. (2010). A humor competence curriculum. *TESOL Quarterly, 44*(1), 155–169. https://doi.org/10.5054/tq.2010.21
Xu, X., Rose, H., McKinley, J., & Zhou, S. (2021). The incentivisation of English medium instruction in Chinese universities: Policy misfires and misalignments. *Applied Linguistics Review*. https://doi.org/10.1515/applirev-2021-0181
Yamamoto, K. (2019). Transitional self in study abroad: An analysis of a Japanese female student's positioning in narratives. *Learner Development Journal, 3,* 151–169.
Yamano, Y. (2013). Utilizing the CLIL approach in a Japanese primary school: A comparative study of CLIL and EFL lessons. *The Asian EFL Journal, 15*(4), 70-92.
Yang, H. (2014). Toward a model of strategies and summary writing performance. *Language Assessment Quarterly, 11*(4), 403–431. https://doi.org/10.1080/15434303.2014.957381
Yang, S., & Yi, Y., (2017). Negotiating multiple identities through eTandem learning experiences. *CALICO Journal, 34*(1), 97–114.

Yashima, T. (2013). Individuality, imagination, and community in a globalizing world: An Asian EFL perspective. In Benson, P. and Cooker, L. (Eds.), *The applied linguistic individual: Sociocultural approaches to autonomy, agency, and identity.* (pp. 46–58.). Equinox.

Yasuda, S. (2015). Exploring changes in FL writers' meaning-making choices in summary writing: a systemic functional approach. *Journal of second language writing, 27,* 105–121. https://doi.org/10.1016/j.jslw.2014.09.008

Yi, Y., & Adamson, B. (2017). Trilingual education in the Inner Mongolia Autonomous Region: Challenges and threats for Mongolian identity. In C. Reid & J. Major (Eds.), *Global Teaching* (pp. 145–163). Palgrave Macmillan. https://doi.org/10.1057/978-1-137-52526-0_8

Yin, R. K. (5th ed.) (2014). *Case Study Research: Design and Methods.* Sage.

Young, R., & Bayley, R. (1996). VARBRUL analysis for second language acquisition research. In R. Bayley & D. Preston (Eds.), *Second language acquisition and linguistic variation* (pp. 253–306). John Benjamins Publishing Company. https://doi.org/10.1075/sibil.10.11you

Ytsma, J. (2001). Towards a typology of trilingual primary education. *International Journal of Bilingual Education and Bilingualism, 4*(1), 11–22. https://doi.org/10.1080/13670050108667715

Yu, S., Wang, Y., Jiang, L., & Wang, B. (2021). Coping with EMI (English as a medium of instruction): Mainland China students' strategies at a university in Macau. *Innovations in Education and Teaching International, 58*(4), 462–472. https://doi.org/10.1080/14703297.2020.1784248

Yuan, R., Li, M., Peng, J., & Qiu, X. (2022). English-medium instruction (EMI) teachers as 'curriculum makers' in Chinese higher education: A textual analysis. *Journal of Multilingual and Multicultural Development,* 1–16. https://doi.org/10.1080/01434632.2022.2061268

Zainuddin, M., Yasin, I. M., Arif, I., & Abdul Hamid, A. B. (2018). *Alternative cross-cultural theories: Why still Hofstede?* (SSRN Scholarly Paper No. 3309633). https://papers.ssrn.com/abstract=3309633

Zhang, J. (2012). A cross-cultural study of generic structure and linguistic patterns in MA thesis acknowledgements. *The Asian ESP Journal, 8*(1), 141-165. https://www.asian-esp-journal.com/wp-content/uploads/2013/11/Volume-8-1.pdf

Zhang, M., & Pladevall-Ballester, E. (2021). Students' attitudes and perceptions towards three EMI courses in mainland China. *Language Culture and Curriculum, 35*(2), 200–216. https://doi.org/10.1080/07908318.2021.1979576

Zhang, R., & Chan, B. H. S. (2021). Pedagogical translanguaging in a trilingual context: the case of two EFL classrooms in a Xinjiang university. *International Journal of Bilingual Education and Bilingualism, 25*(8), 2805–2816. https://doi.org/10.1080/13670050.2021.1978383

Zhang, Y. (2016). History and Future of the National College Entrance Exam (NCEE) in China. In Y. Zhang, *National College Entrance Exam in China: Perspectives on Education Quality and Equity* (pp. 1–15). Springer. https://doi.org/10.1007/978-981-10-0510-7

Zhou, Y., Jindal-Snape, D., Topping, K., & Todman, J. (2008). Theoretical models of culture shock and adaptation in international students in higher education, *Studies in Higher Education, 33*(1), 63–75.

Zhu, H., & Li, W. (2016). Transnational experience, aspiration and family language policy. *Journal of Multilingual and Multicultural Development, 37*(7), 655–666. https://doi.org/10.1080/01434632.2015.1127928

www.ingramcontent.com/pod-product-compliance
Lightning Source LLC
Chambersburg PA
CBHW050852160426
43194CB00011B/2126